Doc
Holliday

John Henry Holliday, D.D.S., on the occasion of his March 1, 1872, graduation from the Pennsylvania College of Dental Surgery. He was unaware that soon fate would send him west and destiny would turn him into a legend. Photo by O. B. DeMorat, 2 Sth Eighth Street, Philadelphia. Courtesy of R. G. McCubbin.

Doc Holliday

A Family Portrait

By
Karen Holliday Tanner

Foreword by
Robert K. DeArment

University of Oklahoma Press
Norman

This book is published with the generous assistance of Edith Gaylord Harper.

Tanner, Karen Holliday, 1940–
    Doc Holliday : a family portrait / by Karen Holliday Tanner ; foreword by Robert K. DeArment.
        p.   cm.
    Includes bibliographical references and index.
    ISBN 978-0-8061-3320-1 (paper)
    1. Holliday, John Henry, 1851–1887. 2. Outlaws—West (U.S.)—Biography. 3. Gamblers—West (U.S.)—Biography. 4. Holliday family. 5. West (U.S.)—Biography.   I. Title.
F594.H74T36   1998
364.15'23'092—dc21
[B]   97-52734
                                                              CIP

The paper in this book meets the guidelines for permanance and durability of the Committee on Production Guidelines for Book Longevity of the Council on Library Resources, Inc. ∞

        9   10   11   12   13

To Mary Holliday Olson
(1913–95)

Contents

Contents

Illustrations

ix

Illustrations

Maps

Unless otherwise indicated, all maps are by
  Karen Holliday Tanner.

Charts

All charts are by Karen Holliday Tanner.

Foreword

By Robert K. DeArment

John Henry Holliday, known in the West as "Doc," is a mythic character in the history of the American West. Through popular literature and motion picture and television portrayal, the enigmatic figure of the tubercular dentist with the genteel southern manners and deadly gunfighting reputation has become firmly etched upon the public consciousness. The name "Doc Holliday" is instantly recognized in every American household and in many foreign homes as well.

Holliday's legend was largely created by two widely read writers of semifictional works, Walter Noble Burns, whose *Tombstone: An Iliad of the Southwest* was published in 1927, and Stuart N. Lake, whose *Wyatt Earp: Frontier Marshal* appeared four years later. The legend was embellished and further circulated by a host of hack contributors to newspapers and popular magazines. Burnished by Hollywood scriptwriters and projected larger than life size onto the motion picture screen, the legend reached an even more extensive audience. It has fascinated readers and theater patrons for well over half a century.

The faculty of moviemakers to reshape popular perception by deliberate or careless distortion of historical fact cannot be overemphasized. A small example will illustrate: W. B. "Bat" Masterson, who knew the tubercular dentist well, described him as a physical "weakling who could not have whipped a healthy fifteen-year-old boy in a go-as-you-please fist fight," but Hollywood has chosen large, robust actors such as Walter Huston, Victor Mature, Kirk Douglas, Jason Robards, and Cesar Romero to portray the cadaverous consumptive on the screen.

Over the last forty years a few serious researchers and writers have attempted to relate Holliday's true story, most notably John Myers Myers (*Doc Holliday*, 1955); Pat Jahns (*The Frontier World of Doc Holliday, Faro Dealer from Dallas to Deadwood*, 1957); Albert S. Pendleton, Jr., and Susan McKey Thomas (*In Search of the Hollidays*, 1973); Sylvia D. Lynch (*Aristocracy's Outlaw: The Doc Holliday Story*, 1994); and Ben T. Traywick (*John Henry: The "Doc" Holliday Story*, 1996).

Although some of these researchers and writers managed to uncover previously unknown information about Holliday's life, none was able to shed any real light on the man's true character, for reasons explained by Karen Holliday Tanner in her preface to this new biography. The facts of Holliday's early history (his heritage, family influences, education, and upbringing)— the factors that shape the character of a man—have been virtually unknown for more than a century. This historical void was filled by inventions of writers who covered a paucity of information with a wealth of imaginative speculation.

The life of John Henry Holliday in Georgia has never been accurately depicted, says Tanner, because of refusal on the part of Holliday family members to cooperate with researchers. Doc's notoriety, first developed in the yellow periodicals of his own day and embellished by later writers, dismayed his proud Georgia kin, who "circled the wagons" and rebuffed inquiring writers.

"Enough time has now passed," writes Tanner, a cousin of the noted gunfighter, "so that there is no one left who feels either shame or guilt over the life of John Henry Holliday." She has had access to family bibles, letters, unpublished manuscripts, genealogical records, and other documents closely guarded for many years by members of the Holliday family and unavailable to outsiders. With these materials, augmented by information from other primary sources, she has established a factually accurate foundation upon which her engrossing account of the early life of John Henry Holliday is based. From the perspective of the family, Holliday for the first time emerges as a real man, a tragic figure whose life was shaped by a birth defect, civil war, family death and disruption, and, finally, contraction of terminal illness.

In relating the story of John Henry and the Hollidays of Georgia, the author brings fresh insight into the history and culture of the antebellum South, the cataclysm of the War between the States, and the catastrophe of the Reconstruction period. Fully a third of the book deals with Holliday's life in the South before he contracted tuberculosis, went west in an effort to regain his health, and found his place in frontier legend.

To recount Holliday's career in the West, the author for the most part has eschewed the abundant secondary sources, finding most of them seriously flawed, and instead has consulted primary material: archival collections, contemporary newspapers, and court and government records. Her research has been meticulous. She has followed Holliday's erratic trail from Dallas, where he first settled and took up the precarious career of professional frontier gambler, to Fort Griffin, Denver, Cheyenne, Deadwood, Dodge City, Las Vegas, Tombstone, Leadville, and other hell-roaring boomtowns.

Understandably, Tanner's empathy for her biographical subject tends to extend to Doc Holliday's friends and close associates, principally Wyatt Earp and his brothers, but she manages to maintain objectivity while recounting the turbulent events that took place in Tombstone, Arizona, in the early 1880s—a story in which Holliday played a major role. These events were fraught with considerable controversy at the time and are still hotly debated by western history scholars today. The author avoids becoming an advocate of the Earp faction as she deftly negotiates the dangerous minefield of the Earps versus the Clantons controversy. She presents the facts as she finds them in her study of the period and relates a very complicated story without getting bogged down in its ambiguities or caught up in its contentiousness.

Scholars and general readers alike should welcome *Doc Holliday: A Family Portrait* as a significant addition to our knowledge of one of the most fascinating figures of the American western frontier. The book will undoubtedly take a place among the foremost works in the western gunfighter genre.

Acknowledgments

No work like this can be written unassisted, and my thanks go to those who have offered me their time, efforts, support, cooperation, and friendship. My husband, Professor John D. Tanner, Jr., has worked at my side and deserves equal credit.

Glenn G. Boyer encouraged me to write this biography and generously provided unrestricted access to the archives of documentation accumulated during his half-century of Earpiana research. Robert K. DeArment, historian of the western frontier and biographer of Bat Masterson, read the manuscript and offered many valuable suggestions, as did Ben T. Traywick, author and collector of Tombstone history, who freely shared copies of documents from his collection, many of which no longer survive in the original. Professor Charles Hanlen gave invaluable assistance by critiquing the manuscript and by graciously sharing his unpublished study of Father Edward T. Downey. Richard W. Heald greatly enhanced the accuracy of this book by reading the manuscript, which profited much from his insightful suggestions. Jane Candia Coleman's stream of astute advice enabled me to keep in perspective the myriad of opinions in the controversial arena of the saga of Doc Holliday and Wyatt Earp.

My thanks also go to the members of my family who endured hours of inquisition and strained their memories to answer my endless questions: my mother, Mary Holliday Olson, Aunt Elise Holliday McCormick, Uncle Robert Lee Holliday, Uncle Lewis Hooper Holliday, Uncle John Prindiville Holliday, Cousin Morgan De-Lancey Magee, Cousin Carolyn Holliday Manley, Cousin Constance Knowles McKellar, and Cousin Regina Rapier. Also helpful were George Kirby, my husband's cousin, and his wife, Joyce, who plays the organ for the Presbyterian Church in Griffin where John Henry was baptized in 1852. I also thank Blair Carl Mielke of Dallas, Texas, cousin of Doc Holliday, for his research assistance.

Additional help was received from Emma Walling, a researcher and author with unlimited energy and intense interest; Craig Fouts, collector of western manuscripts and photographs; Dr. Robert M. George, lecturer in anatomy, Florida International University; Susan McKey Thomas, Valdosta, Georgia; Linda Acord, Irving, Texas; Michael Kalen Smith, archivist, Texas/Dallas History and Archives Division, City of Dallas Public Library; Clifton Caldwell, The Lynch Line, Albany, Texas; Frances Wheeler, county and district clerk, Shackelford County, Texas; Lester W. Galbreath, Fort Griffin State Historical Park, Shackelford County, Texas; Charis Johnson, deputy clerk, Stephens County, Breckenridge, Texas; Kelli L. Pickard, director, Red River Historical Museum of Sherman, Texas; H. V.

Acknowledgments

O'Brien, publisher, Eastland–Callahan County Newspapers, Eastland, Texas; Jerry and Robert Eckhart, Cisco, Texas; Ty Cashion, assistant professor of history, East Texas State University; Lois Ann McCollum and Willa Soncarty, archivists, Frontier Historical Society, Glenwood Springs, Colorado; Mary Billings-McVicar, Leadville, Colorado; Carolyn J. Cary, Fayette County Historical Society, Fayetteville, Georgia; Charles B. Greifenstein, reference librarian, College of Physicians of Philadelphia; Peter J. Blodgett, curator of Western Manuscripts, Huntington Library, San Marino, California; W. B. W. Hickearody, Rodeo, New Mexico; Hugh McKinney, media technologist, Palomar College, San Marcos, California; Al Regensberg, senior archivist, State of New Mexico Records Center and Archives, Santa Fe; Richard Rudisill, curator of photographic history, and Arthur L. Olivas, photographic archivist, Museum of New Mexico, Santa Fe.

I would like to thank the staffs of the Atlanta History Center; Colorado Historical Society; Denver Public Library; Lake County Public Library, Leadville, Colorado; New Mexico Highlands University, Donnelly Library; San Miguel County Court, Las Vegas, New Mexico; Arizona Historical Society; and University of Arizona. Lee Silva, Seal Beach, California, and Chuck Hornung, Odessa, Texas, also helped.

Finally, a special thanks to the talented Robert "Shoofly" Shufelt and to Robert G. McCubbin for his generosity.

Preface

"Tales were told that he had murdered men in different parts of the country; that he had robbed and committed all manner of crimes, and yet when persons were asked how they knew it they could only admit it was hearsay, and that nothing of the kind could really be traced up to Doc's account" (Virgil Earp, *Arizona Daily Star* [Tucson], May 30, 1882). As Virgil Earp accurately noted, little was known of the true character and activities of the notorious lead-throwing dentist "Doc" Holliday.

The mystery that surrounded John Henry Holliday for over one hundred years still prevails. His reputation has gained legendary proportions in the history of the American Southwest and has been the subject of numerous fictionalized biographies. These efforts have suffered from lack of knowledge, overactive imaginations, or deliberate fabrications. Holliday's biographers have not agreed as to his age or birthplace, the names of his family members, his alma mater, when, where, or why he went west, the women he loved, or the men he killed. No two writers have concurred on the itinerary of his western travels. Few facts have been presented and fewer questions have been resolved. A century has passed, yet the enigma remains.

Only two authors attempted to seek out family sources. The first, Pat Jahns in *The Frontier World of Doc Holliday* (1957), produced some fine research in a book that has great value as a directory to source material. Although her contacts with John Henry Holliday's mother's family, the McKeys, produced some valuable information regarding his youth, an obvious void existed that could only be filled by input from the Hollidays. In an early attempt at psychohistory, Jahns made some errors of fact that seriously detract from her efforts to reveal the inner workings of the mind of Doc Holliday. Susan McKey Thomas (a maternal relative of John Henry Holliday) and Albert S. Pendleton, Jr., in *In Search of the Hollidays: The Story of Doc Holliday and His Holliday and McKey Families* (1973), revealed important material concerning Holliday's formative years, but relied excessively upon the research of other writers in detailing his career in the West.

Criticism of earlier efforts to portray the life of John Henry Holliday accurately must be tempered because the writers lacked contributions from the Holliday family. This reticence on the part of the Hollidays requires an explanation.

Family members felt an inordinate amount of sympathy when John Henry was born with a familial defect. In that era babies with imperfections were discussed in hushed tones and shielded from the public and from possible ridicule. His mother's overprotection resulted in an abnormal bonding that turned John Henry into a shy, retiring child. When the ravages of the long and violent war tore apart his family, it greatly affected this sensitive young man. The Hollidays shared John Henry's grief when his childhood ended abruptly with the death of his mother when he was only fifteen. The immediate introduction to a young stepmother left him bitter and estranged from his father. John Henry was encouraged to attend dental school, largely to provide an escape from his unhappy surroundings. His college experience gave him his independence from his father as well as much-needed self-confidence. After earning his degree, he lived in his uncle's home in Atlanta. He enjoyed a fine life there for almost two years until his life was again shattered when his tuberculosis was diagnosed. In order to recuperate in a drier, healthier climate, John Henry was sent to the frequently crude and often violent West. This marked the end of his life as a southern sophisticate. He was about to undergo an amazing transformation. Within a few short years, he would become a man whose character was not recognizable to his aristocratic family. Fortunately, his relatives were spared the lurid details of his new life on the frontier.

When the family learned of John Henry's participation in the gunfight in Tombstone, it is probable that he himself masterminded the effort to ensure that they also learned that he had acted under the badge of authority and that he had been exonerated of any crime. Pacified, they refused to believe the stories that were occasionally published. Imagine the family's shame in 1927 when Walter Noble Burns published his *Tombstone: An Iliad of the Southwest* and stated unequivocally that Doctor Holliday was "the fighting ace of the Earp faction and considered by connoisseurs in deadliness the coldest-blooded killer in Tombstone" (p. 47). The socially prominent and always proper Hollidays found it convenient to avoid all discussion of John Henry, who had died forty years earlier. His father and mother were both dead; Uncle John and his cousin Robert had also passed away. A few cousins remained, along with Mary Fulton Holliday, Robert's widow. Some family members even denied that John Henry Holliday had ever existed. Mrs. Robert Holliday told a grandson that Doc Holliday was nothing more than a fictitious character. It was shame, possibly even some guilt, that caused the self-imposed silence of the Hollidays.

Enough time has now passed so that there is no one left who feels either shame or guilt over the life of John Henry Holliday. The biographical facts are finally being presented so that they may serve as the foundation for future work. The pieces of the puzzle of Doc Holliday's life can now be fitted together in order to understand the complexities of this tragic man.

In spite of the family cover-up, the memories of John Henry's youth were well preserved. Sophie Walton, who was born a slave in Georgia, was taken in by the Holliday family in 1864. She served as a seamstress and nanny for the young children and quickly became a playmate for the older ones. She knew John Henry well and taught him many important lessons. Seventy years later, while serving her fourth generation of Hollidays, Sophie was the last survivor of those who had watched John Henry board the Western and Atlantic bound for Dallas. Her recollections in the early 1930s fascinated Carl B. Olson, a young Swedish immigrant who was the fiancé of one of the Holliday children. Sophie bragged of her most famous student, the notorious John Henry Holliday. She died in 1933, just prior to Olson's marriage to the younger of the two Mary Hollidays. Fortunately, he preserved those recollections.

Mary Holliday Olson was the namesake of her father's mother. After her marriage, Mary took her husband to New York to meet her grandmother, Mary Fulton Holliday. The widow of Robert A. Holliday, D.D.S., was a progressive woman living among authors, actors, and artists at New York's Algonquin Hotel, a haven for the free-thinking society, where she developed many friendships, most notably with Rudolph Valentino and Eugene O'Neill. Mrs. Holliday joined an artists' and writers' guild and devoted herself to the arts. She enjoyed taking her granddaughter and grandson-in-law on a tour of the former speakeasies. A strong friendship developed between grandmother and grandson-in-law. Both were well educated, spoke several languages, and had a keen interest in the arts. Mrs. Holliday had studied art in Paris and Rome. Carl Olson had studied at the prestigious Art Institute in Chicago.

Over the next eight years, their friendship flourished. Both fancied themselves as writers. When Olson wrote a fictional account of an episode in the career of Doc Holliday, he showed the story to his wife's grandmother, who had written a novel and several shorter items. She was impressed with his ingenuity and eventually gave him her memoirs, along with the mementos of John Henry that had been so treasured by her husband. She granted Olson permission to use these recollections in a book on the life of Doc Holliday, but extracted from him one promise: no book would be published that might embarrass any member of the Holliday family. Following Mary Holliday's death in 1942, Olson began to organize all of the Holliday materials—his own writings, the writings of Mary Fulton Holliday, and the notes he had written after his talks with Sophie Walton. He knew he could not write his book during the lifetime of his widowed mother-in-law, Mrs. Lewis W. Holliday. Fate intervened, and Carl Olson died in 1969 at the age of sixty-one, almost twenty years before his mother-in-law. In 1988 Mary Holliday Olson gave me my father's "Doc box" along with the request that I complete his work. I am the great-granddaughter of Robert A. Holliday, D.D.S., and Mary Fulton Holliday—and a cousin of Doc Holliday. This is his story.

Doc
Holliday

THE HOLLIDAY FAMILY

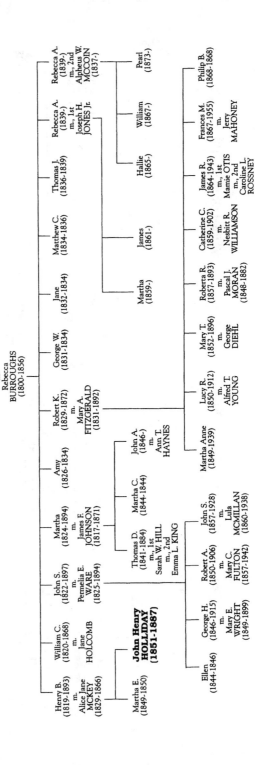

HOLLIDAY-FITZGERALD-MITCHELL CONNECTION

HOLLIDAY-WARE-LONG CONNECTION

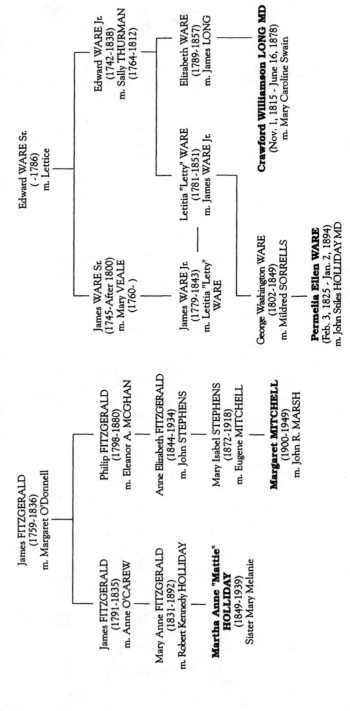

James FITZGERALD
(1759-1836)
m. Margaret O'Donnell

Philip FITZGERALD
(1798-1880)
m. Eleanor A. MCGHAN

Anne Elizabeth FITZGERALD
(1844-1934)
m. John STEPHENS

Mary Isabel STEPHENS
(1872-1918)
m. Eugene MITCHELL

Margaret MITCHELL
(1900-1949)
m. John R. MARSH

James FITZGERALD
(1791-1835)
m. Anne O'CAREW

Mary Anne FITZGERALD
(1831-1892)
m. Robert Kennedy HOLLIDAY

Martha Anne "Mattie" HOLLIDAY
(1849-1939)
Sister Mary Melanie

Edward WARE Sr.
(-1786)
m. Lettice

Edward WARE Jr.
(1742-1838)
m. Sally THURMAN
(1764-1812)

Elizabeth WARE
(1789-1857)
m. James LONG

James WARE Sr.
(1745-After 1800)
m. Mary VEALE
(1760-)

James WARE Jr.
(1779-1843)
m. Letitia "Letty" WARE

Letitia "Letty" WARE
(1781-1851)
m. James WARE Jr.

George Washington WARE
(1802-1849)
m. Mildred SORRELLS

Crawford Williamson LONG MD
(Nov. 1, 1815 - June 16, 1878)
m. Mary Caroline Swain

Permelia Ellen WARE
(Feb. 3, 1825 - Jan. 2, 1894)
m. John Stiles HOLLIDAY MD

1

Farewell

In September 1873 John Henry Holliday, D.D.S., of Atlanta, Georgia, boarded the Western and Atlantic train. He was bound for Dallas, Texas, where, it was hoped, the dry climate would cure his consumption and eventually allow him to return.[1] All the family members who had played an important role in his life were gathered at the depot to see him off, with the notable exception of the most important of all, his mother, who had died seven years earlier.

Young John Henry had endured much in his twenty-two years. His physical handicap caused by a birth defect had required years of therapy. Alice Holliday had assumed the role of therapist for her son, overseeing his rehabilitation while attempting to protect him from the cruelties of society. The family credited her with instilling in him his gentle qualities— his respect for women, love of animals, fine manners, and strong faith. In contrast, it was generally known that Maj. Henry Burroughs Holliday, John Henry's father, had taught his son the prerequisites of manhood—the ability to shoot, ride, fish, and hunt. While the major was away fighting for his ideals, for southern rights, and for the Confederacy, ten-year-old John Henry was left with the manly responsibilities of taking care of the home and animals and protecting his mother. During the war, John Henry and his mother never experienced personal confrontation, though they were surrounded by death and injury, disease, and crime, which caused an overwhelming sense of anger and bitterness throughout the South.

Alice's untimely death came the year after the end of the war. John Henry's devastating loss was magnified when his period of mourning was interrupted by the shameful remarriage of his father a mere three months after his mother's funeral. The farewell party at the depot did not include Rachel, Major Holliday's young wife, who was only eight years older than her stepson. The tension between father and son was evident to the entire family. Henry, after awkwardly embracing his son, must have realized that he might never again set eyes on his only son, who suffered from the same debilitating disease that had killed his first wife, Alice.

John Henry said good-bye to his cousin Robert, who was also his best friend. The two boys had shared a lot through the years. Robert had introduced John Henry to many of the young ladies of Atlanta. The two handsome young bachelors had been very much in demand on the social scene. Both had matured a great deal after having been forced to endure the horrors of war, and they planned to share a dental practice when Robert completed dental school and John Henry recovered and returned home.

Robert's parents, John and Permelia Holliday, were also among the well-wishers. They had assumed the role of surrogate parents for their nephew when the major married Rachel. John Henry had spent a year and a half as part of his uncle and aunt's household when he came to Atlanta to begin his career in dentistry. Aunt Permelia had made sure that he met everyone who mattered in the local society. Uncle John was equally generous to his brother's only son. He presented him with a gold and diamond stickpin as a going-away present.[2] The diamond was from Dr. Holliday's private collection. In the years to come, this stickpin served as John Henry's link to his aristocratic past and the home he would never see again.

Also at the depot was Sophie Walton, who had come to the Holliday family eight years ago, a frightened little black girl with nowhere to go. The former slave became the family mainstay—servant, seamstress, nanny, source of strength, and, as John Henry knew, an expert at manipulating cards.

John Henry waved his last good-byes. He was wearing his new diamond stickpin as he boarded the train. Perhaps at that moment some of the family's thoughts drifted back to the day of his birth in August 1851. They could not have realized that John Henry Holliday, D.D.S., age twenty-two, would soon become a legend.

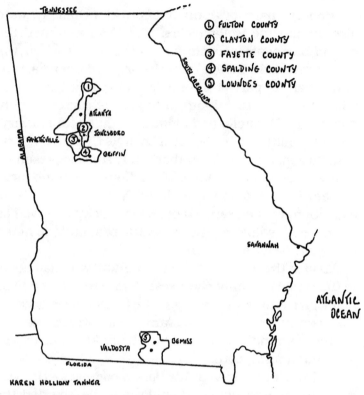

TENNESSEE

① FULTON COUNTY
② CLAYTON COUNTY
③ FAYETTE COUNTY
④ SPALDING COUNTY
⑤ LOWNDES COUNTY

SOUTH CAROLINA

ALABAMA

① ATLANTA
② JONESBORO
③ FAYETTEVILLE
④ GRIFFIN

SAVANNAH

ATLANTIC OCEAN

⑤ BEMISS
VALDOSTA

FLORIDA

KAREN HOLLIDAY TANNER

Georgia counties, cities, and towns of the Holliday family in the 1850s, 1860s, and 1870s

2

Birth of a New Holliday

It was hot and humid in the middle of August 1851 when Alice Jane Holliday asked her husband, Henry, to go fetch his brother, Fayetteville physician John Stiles Holliday, M.D. Alice knew that her new baby would be arriving within a day and, like most women, probably had little faith in the local midwives because of the high infant mortality rate of the times. Only fourteen months before, Henry and his wife had lost their first child, Martha Eleanora, in infancy (she was born on December 3, 1849, and died on June 12, 1850), possibly due to diphtheria, which was appearing in epidemic proportions in many areas of the South.[1]

Alice's brother-in-law, Dr. John S. Holliday, had graduated from the highly regarded Georgia Medical College only seven years previously and was already considered one of the finest surgeons in the area. Even so, he had not able to save the life of his little niece. Yet Henry and Alice were both confident in his abilities

Henry Burroughs Holliday, ca. 1852. Collection of Karen Holliday Tanner

and felt it was important to have the best professional assistance in the delivery of this coming child. Their home on Tinsley Street in Griffin, Georgia, was about twenty miles from Fayetteville, where the doctor resided.

Permelia Ellen Ware Holliday, ca. 1852. Collection of Karen Holliday Tanner

Dr. Holliday would also bring his wife, Permelia. Alice and Permelia were not only sisters-in-law but, in spite of their widely differing personalities, close friends as well. Permelia would be a welcome sight. She was nice looking and fun-loving, but also an intelligent and capable woman. It was said that she took after the women of her prominent family, the Wares of Georgia, who were warm-hearted, generous, outgoing, and impulsive, Episcopalian by birth and rearing. The staid Presbyterians of Fayetteville said that Permelia, who dressed well and enjoyed the pleasures of life, was worldly and outspoken. Today's society would definitely consider her a progressive, modern woman who was born ahead of her time. Alice, in contrast to her sister-

11

in-law, was a benevolent, soft-spoken woman with an artistic bent whose main interest was tending to her home and her husband. She gave much of her time and effort to the First Presbyterian Church of Griffin.

Perhaps the two women hoped that Alice's new baby would be a boy so that he could be a playmate for John and Permelia's year-old son Robert Alexander, who had been named after his grandfather, Robert Holliday. The four-year age difference between Robert and his older brother, George, prevented them from being good playmates. Alice's new baby, if a boy, was to have been named Henry Burroughs Holliday, Jr., but the events of the next twenty-four hours would result in his being named John Henry Holliday.

The entire family was waiting to celebrate this birth as they did all births in the family. The baptism would be followed by a joyous gathering with family and friends and lots of food and drink. The branches of the Holliday family were closely knit, and they spent much time together. The men had family business partnerships and invested in real estate together. The deeds in Fayette and surrounding counties verify the Hollidays' proclivity for joint buying and selling of property. The family played an integral part in their social lives. Fortunately, most of their homes were large, so they had plenty of room to gather for holidays, birthdays, anniversaries, weddings, and births.

Alice and Henry Holliday's unborn child would become a part of this large family, whose members were not only socially prominent and politically influential, but successful in their chosen professions. Henry, who had been inclined to the military, had developed quite a disciplined personality. Alice's gentleness proved to have a softening effect on his somewhat rigid outlook. Following his marriage, Henry decided to adopt his father's approach to success. He began to invest in commercial real estate, purchasing three lots in West Griffin, and joined the professional ranks, becoming a druggist. Henry was therefore able to be near his wife as they awaited this birth, rather than being posted to some distant military installation. Also anxiously awaiting the news were Alice's parents, William and Jane McKey. Since the death of little Martha the year before, this would be their only grandchild. Alice remained close to her family after her marriage. While the McKeys' farm was off the Old McDonough Road on the Towaliga River nine miles northeast of Griffin, their other residence in town was much nearer to Alice and Henry's home.

On August 14, 1851, Dr. Holliday, accompanied by his brother and Permelia, arrived in time to deliver Alice and Henry's new baby, a son.[2] It was immediately evident that his new nephew had a serious birth defect: a cleft palate and partially cleft lip (commonly called a harelip), a trait that was to recur several times in future Holliday generations.[3] This made it impossible for the baby to perform the normal sucking action. Dr. Holliday cleared the air passages and later taught Alice the proper way to feed her new son with the aid of an eyedropper and a small teaspoon. If not fed properly and carefully, the newborn could quickly choke to death. Pneumonia was another hazard for cleft-palate infants due to possible introduction of fluids into the lungs during ingestion. When the baby gained some weight he would be able to drink from a shot glass. (It is ironic that John Henry started off his life sustained by a shot glass since excessive use of a shot glass may have hastened his death many years later.) Dr. Holliday

John Stiles Holliday, M.D., ca. 1860. Collection of Morgan DeLancey Magee

was also able to reassure his brother and sister-in-law that surgery could be performed to correct the malformation when their son was approximately a month old. Though the surgery still would not enable the baby to suckle, it would ensure that he would be able to eat and breathe normally as he grew older. The child would have minimal obvious scarring because the lip was involved only to a minor extent.

Henry prevailed upon his brother to promise to do the surgery himself as soon as was prudent. At this time, Henry and Alice had no trouble deciding that their new son should be named after his Uncle John, who had saved their newborn's life. The infant was

14

named John Henry Holliday, namesake of both his uncle and his father.

In the weeks to come, Alice was diligent in the care of young John Henry. With the use of the implements recommended by her brother-in-law, she was able to provide the infant with the nourishment that enabled him to thrive. Feeding him took approximately an hour and a half. The effort required would tire the newborn, who would fall asleep before the feeding ended. Because of this, he was not receiving an adequate amount to eat at any one time. He would cry out with hunger within an hour or two of having been fed.[4] Alice must have been consumed with exhaustion. It required patience to get up and repeat the feeding routine with the shotglass and eyedropper. Weariness did not prevent her from spending all the time necessary to ensure that her son gained enough strength for his operation. An intense bonding began between mother and child because of all this special care. The two were never apart. Alice's determination must have rubbed off on little John Henry as they overcame the odds together and he slowly gained weight and strength.

When Dr. Holliday returned to Fayetteville, he informed the family of the arrival of John Henry. Robert and Rebecca Holliday must have been especially pleased to hear that they had another grandson. The birth of a Holliday grandchild was a rare occurrence. Because they had lost five of their eleven children, they must have feared that a similar tragedy could occur at the home of their oldest son.

While the rest of the family celebrated the arrival of little John Henry, Dr. Holliday sought advice concerning the future surgery on his nephew's cleft palate. Permelia contacted her father's cousin, Dr. Crawford

Williamson Long, who was then living in Atlanta. He was a graduate of Franklin College (now the University of Georgia) and had received his medical degree from the University of Pennsylvania in 1839. In 1842 Dr. Long was the first physician to use ether as an anesthetic, in the removal of two small tumors from the neck of a young student, James M. Venable, in Franklin, Georgia. Dr. Holliday, along with other physicians of the area, had great respect for Dr. Long's knowledge of how and when to administer ether for various types of surgeries and childbirths. The two surgeons consulted, and Dr. Long accompanied Dr. Holliday to Griffin to examine John Henry. Following the examination, the two doctors agreed to combine their skills when the time came to operate on the infant.

When John Henry was eight weeks old and had gained enough weight and strength, Dr. Holliday and Dr. Long operated on his mouth and lip. Permelia was present to provide moral support. There is no doubt that the members of the Ladies Guild of the First Presbyterian Church of Griffin provided spiritual support. After several hours of surgery, Drs. Holliday and Long completed the successful operation. Often two operations were needed on cleft palates, but in this case one was sufficient. John Henry came through the surgery splendidly and was left with a lip that would heal to reveal only slight scarring. He also had a misshapen palate that, with proper therapy, would cause only a minor speech impediment. This speech defect would become negligible with diligent exercises a few years later. Fortunately, his Georgia drawl helped to camouflage the imperfect speech in years to come.

John Henry was a healthy, beautiful baby with blue eyes and wavy blond hair. With considerable thankful-

Crawford Williamson
Long, M.D., the
"Father of Ether."
Collection of Karen
Holliday Tanner

ness, the Holliday, McKey, and Ware families gathered
at the First Presbyterian Church in Griffin to celebrate
his belated christening on Sunday, March 21, 1852.
This was the same church in which his mother had
been baptized only one and one-half years earlier, on
September 1, 1850.[5] Though born into a Methodist
family, Alice had never joined a church prior to 1850.
At the age of twenty-three, ostensibly to please her
husband, she became a Presbyterian.

Six weeks prior to John Henry's baptism, his father
was commissioned as the first clerk of the Superior
Court for Spalding County on February 5, 1852. Spalding County had been created three months earlier, in
December 1851. The area formerly had been part of

John Henry Holliday and his mother, Alice Jane McKey Holliday,
1852. Craig Fouts Photo Collection

Fayette, Henry, and Pike Counties. Though this new position made considerable demands on Henry Holliday's time, it was politically, financially, and socially very gratifying. The family had everything needed to be happy. Alice remained very devoted to her husband and little son. The baby still required much of her attention, but it was worthwhile as she saw him improve. His crooked little smile was delightful. He was a sweet child who must have been adored by all who saw him.

Alice and Permelia spent as much time as they could together, and their sons became very close. The lively, impish Robert was a good change of pace for quiet little John Henry, who was very sheltered by his mother. The children spent most of their time playing outdoors. Frequently their mothers would make a picnic lunch and take them to nearby Cabin Creek in Griffin, where they would eat in the shade of the large trees. The boys would run around in the sunshine and play with the dogs while their mothers chatted and did their needlework. Though the children were very active, both women demanded good behavior and proper manners.

In 1852 the sisters-in-law hired a photographer to preserve the likenesses of the two little cousins, who could pass for twins if it were not for their age difference. Robert was two years old and John Henry one year old at the time of the picture. They looked more like brothers than did Robert and his own brother, George. Their features were remarkably similar. Both had blue eyes and were developing the high cheekbones and broad chins typical of the Holliday men. The main difference was Robert's hair, which was a darker blond than John Henry's. After the daguerreotype was

Left, Robert Alexander Holliday; right, John Henry Holliday; tinted daguerreotype, 1852. Collection of Karen Holliday Tanner

developed, the image was encased in an eighteen-karat gold pendant and was presented to the boys' grand-mother, Rebecca Burroughs Holliday, on the occasion of her fifty-second birthday, on November 11, 1852.[6] Rebecca proudly wore this pendant on a black velvet ribbon until her death two years later.[7]

3

Early Childhood

The year 1852 brought the death of one of John Henry's great-grandmothers, Amy Stiles Burroughs.[1] He was too young to understand the significance of the passing of another generation, but Amy's death had a profound effect on the Holliday family. Amy was the widow of Revolutionary War veteran Henry Burroughs, who had died in 1829. The terms of the will of her late husband stated that upon her death Isaac, a devoted old favorite slave, would be given his freedom.[2] The other two slaves, Lila and Wilson, and the remainder of her possessions were to be given to various family members. The sword and pistols that Henry Burroughs had used in service during the Revolutionary War were passed on to his grandson and namesake, Henry Burroughs Holliday.[3] In future years both John Henry and his cousin Robert would get their first pistol lessons with these old guns that had belonged to their great-grandfather Burroughs.[4] The Holliday men were no different than most well-bred southern gentlemen of the era. The ability to handle a weapon with both skill and ease was a necessary part of a young man's education. It was considered important not only for defense of self and family but for sporting purposes as well.

Seven months after the death of Amy Burroughs, Alice's mother died at the age of forty-nine on January 26, 1853.[5] In less than three years Alice had suffered two great losses, the death of her first child in 1850 and now the death of her mother. Jane Cloud McKey was buried in Indian Creek Church Cemetery near Griffin. Alice's grief must have made her cling even more tightly to her shy little son.

As a toddler, John Henry was more serious than most. He was forced to spend many of his waking hours in speech therapy. His uncle and Dr. Long had done a fine job on the cleft-palate surgery, which allowed this boy with the intense blue eyes to have a normal childhood. Alice Holliday was determined that a speech impediment would not affect the sweet personality of her son, insisting that no one comment on his inability to speak properly and shielding him from unthinking strangers. She created a picture book full of stimulating and interesting items whose names included all the sounds that are difficult for a cleft-palate child to pronounce.[6] Pictures had great appeal for the curious little boy, who could not yet read. As mother and son went through the book together, Alice carefully pronounced the name of each picture. She showed John Henry where to place his tongue in order to produce the correct sounds. Every consonant sound formed with the tongue pressing against a portion of the palate was difficult for young John Henry. Alice brought out the picture book to have her "reading" sessions with her son as often as his patience allowed. They would go over and over the scrapbook. Repetition was the key to success, and Alice was always trying innovative ways to avoid boredom while teaching her son. He must have loved all the attention, as well as the praise that he received when he tried his best to do well. Alice's determination was contagious, and John Henry doggedly worked at his speech therapy. Although he was an excellent student, progress was slow.

With therapy of such quality and intensity, cleft-palate patients with his degree of impediment usually were able to speak without a noticeable defect by the age of four or five. Alice was always on the lookout for new pictures that would help in the lessons and have an educational value in other areas as well. The lessons not only paved the way for improved speech, but instilled a desire to learn to read.

Alice was not without help in her tutoring. The ladies of the First Presbyterian Church of Griffin took turns going to the Holliday home to assist in the speech therapy.[7] It was time-consuming, but the ladies were quite willing as the Holliday family was both well known and extremely well liked in Spalding County. Now that Henry was clerk of the Superior Court, he was in constant demand to participate in numerous civic affairs and on many committees in addition to his full work schedule. Though Henry always maintained his strong, sober Presbyterian beliefs, Alice was the more active member of the church, having more time to devote to church activities such as quilting bees and box suppers. She kept an open door for the members of the community and most certainly was appreciative of all the help that she received from the members of the guild. In return, she gave piano lessons at the church for any of the children who wished to learn. This also provided her with the opportunity to maintain the skills that she had learned as a child. All the McKey girls had learned to play on an old pianoforte.[8] Alice was a talented pianist and made sure that her son's education included music.

Though John Henry was responding well to the speech lessons, at age two he could utter only a few words that were understandable. Those words that were the most difficult for him contained the sounds *s*, *sh*, *c*, *ch*, hard and soft *g*, and *k*, which were completely omitted from his speech. Some cleft-palate patients would substitute sounds, but John Henry just left them out all together. At times when he spoke it sounded like grunts and groans. Because of his shyness, he did best when tutored by his mother or a relative. John and Permelia and their sons, George and Robert, came as often as possible to help.

Usually during these visits the men would occupy themselves with talk of business. The Holliday men were actively investing in real estate in Griffin and Fayetteville. In early 1853 Henry was in preliminary negotiations to buy a farm northwest of Griffin, while the elder Robert Holliday had recently acquired more farmland in Fayette County. Dr. Holliday had purchased property adjacent to his Fayetteville town residence.

While the men were engrossed in their business discussions, the speech therapy sessions were often cut short because the children were anxious to play. John Henry and Robert remained close, and they both looked up to Robert's brother, George, who now had his own pony and was becoming quite adept at riding. In addition, he was already learning to handle a pistol. By the time they were grown, the boys would be equally skilled in the handling of pistols, rifles, and shotguns. In October 1853 Henry made an important decision. He sold the family home on Tinsley Street and purchased a 147-acre farm two and one-half miles northwest of Griffin. Located along the east side of the railroad, it enabled Henry to combine farming with commercial real estate. A year later Henry sold 136 of the acres where the new home was located and purchased the 278 acres just south of the family home. In the tradition of his father, Henry was balancing a future involving agriculture, commerce, and real estate.[9]

In 1857 Robert Kennedy Holliday, another of John Henry's uncles, and his wife, Mary Anne, and their four daughters (Martha Anne "Mattie," Lucy Rebecca, Mary Theresa, and baby Roberta Rosalie) moved to Jonesboro, a fast-growing community approximately seven miles from Fayetteville. It was a fine location for Uncle Robert's mercantile business to thrive, and he purchased three acres on the east side of the tracks of the Macon and Western Railroad line. Sometimes Henry and his family would travel by horse and buggy up the Whitehall Wagon Road from Griffin to gather at Uncle Robert and Aunt Mary Anne's for a festive outing. The cousins always had a grand time playing together, swimming, and wading in the creeks that flowed into the Flint River. Customarily included in the gatherings were Aunt Mary Anne's Uncle Philip and Aunt Eleanor Fitzgerald.[10] Philip was a hearty old Irishman who would regale everyone with stories of his homeland.[11] After emigrating to America, this Irish-Catholic family had kept many of the traditions of the old country. The family enjoyed Uncle Philip's tales, which became more raucous as the decanter in Robert's study emptied when the afternoon wore on.

The children would spend the day playing while their parents socialized. The three girls were quite demure and contented themselves by playing with their dolls and mimicking the actions of their mothers. All of the cousins were aware of Alice's strict admonition not to mention John Henry's speech impediment, which therefore did not inhibit him when he was with his family.

The Holliday family always shared love and loyalty with their slaves and often brought the favored ones to family gatherings. Slaves were commonly with a family for generations and were sometimes reunited with their own families when their masters died. Often the slaves would be inherited by the next generation. John Henry's grandmother had acquired a slave, Chainey, when her father died. Years later she also was bequeathed Wilson, Chainey's brother, when there was another death in the family.[12] Chainey and Wilson were loved by the entire family and helped to raise four generations of Burroughs/Hollidays.[13] These two slaves were ever-present at these family get-togethers and were held responsible for the behavior of all the children. They would organize games and prepare candy for the taffy pulls, which always delighted the children. Chainey and Wilson made sure that, in spite of all their merrymaking, the children were well behaved and polite. Manners and respect for their elders were ingrained in the youngsters at the earliest age possible. Little Mattie developed a particular fondness for young John Henry with his blond hair and blue eyes and his quiet personality. She helped to look after her cousin, who was two years her junior.[14] A strong bond of friendship grew between the two that was to last for the rest of John Henry's life.

In 1855 Dr. John Stiles Holliday and Permelia began construction of their new home in Fayetteville on property he had purchased in 1846, adjacent to their existing house on West Lanier Avenue near the town's public square. Dr. Holliday designed and built a refined Greek Revival–style house. He supervised the construction and personally selected the timber, secured the finest materials and workmanship, and insisted that everything be done to perfection. The house featured central halls with unusually large flanking rooms and extremely high ceilings. Window lights surrounded both the rear and front doors and a long verandah extended across the entire front of the house.[15] Permelia must have been anxious to move into their larger home. More room would be needed to comfortably house any future sons or daughters along with George and Robert, who were rapidly growing up.

Aunt Martha and her husband, Col. James Franklin Johnson, also played prominent roles in this large family. Martha Holliday was the third-born child of Robert and Rebecca Holliday and the first sister of Henry Burroughs and John Stiles Holliday. She was the first of her brothers and sisters to marry and the first to give Robert and Rebecca a grandchild. James and Martha Johnson were known throughout Georgia. He was not only an attorney, planter, and merchant, but represented Fayette (and later Clayton) County in the State Senate. Martha was instrumental in convincing her husband to introduce a bill to create Clayton County. She must have considered Fayetteville somewhat unrefined because, it is said, she hoped that when they moved to Jonesboro as part of a new county

Dr. John Stiles Holliday's home on West Lanier Avenue, Fayette-ville, Georgia. Used with permission of the Fayette County (Georgia) Historical Society

it would create a desire on the part of the aristocrats of Fayetteville to follow their example. The home that they purchased on Main Street, just north of the business district in Jonesboro, was the only antebellum house in town to have the two-story classical columns popularly associated with southern romantic history. The home had been built in 1840, and the Johnsons enlarged and remodeled it after the move. The remodeling was inspired by the work that had been done a few years earlier on the plantation belonging to Dr. and Mrs. Crawford Long. Dr. Long, part of the extended family, remained close to all the Hollidays after the key role he had played in John Henry's cleft-palate surgery.

It was not uncommon to see the men of the Holliday family socializing with the political leaders of Georgia at the Johnson home. The men would ride, shoot, hunt, and discuss the general unrest of the nation. The Republican Party was growing in the North, and that party's opposition to the extension of slavery was always a topic that provoked heated debate. The name of John Charles Fremont, the Republican presidential nominee in 1856, began to creep into the conversations along with the word *secession*. Most were uneasy as to what the future would bring. The women were not welcome in these discussions, so they confined their political talk with their husbands to the privacy of their own homes. The women maintained light-hearted demeanors, chatted, and did needlework as they supervised the slaves in caring for the children and preparing the food to be served. After the heated political discussions, the men would often mount their horses and go riding or hunting to work off the tension evoked by the conversations.

The young Holliday boys were probably quite anxious to grow older so that they could join the men. It was a sign of acceptance into manhood when a boy was first allowed into Uncle James's smoke-filled study. Of all the cousins at that time, the only boy allowed to join the men was Thomas, the eldest son of Aunt Martha and Uncle James.[16] The Holliday men also went on outings on horseback, sometimes for the better part of the day. The sounds of their guns and the barking of the dogs could be heard from afar.

John Henry acquired new cousins with each passing year. His family also experienced more tragedy. On August 12, 1856, only two days before his fifth birthday, John Henry's other grandmother died. The next

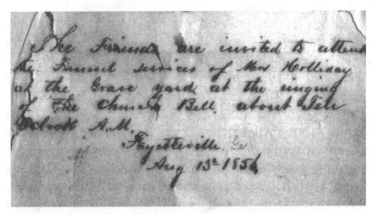

Funeral announcement of Rebecca Burroughs Holliday, John Henry Holliday's grandmother, Fayetteville, Georgia, August 13, 1856. Collection of Karen Holliday Tanner

morning at ten o'clock the family again gathered at the Fayetteville City Cemetery, where they buried fifty-six-year-old Rebecca Burroughs Holliday next to her mother, Amy Stiles Burroughs. Chainey and Wilson, having reached an advanced age themselves, mourned along with all the Hollidays near the graves of mother and daughter, their two former mistresses who had died only four years apart. The two slaves would now devote most of their time to making their present master, the elder Robert Holliday, comfortable in his period of mourning.

Henry and Alice made the trip to Fayetteville often so that John Henry could spend time with his grandfather, the newly widowed Robert Holliday, as well as Uncle John, Aunt Permelia, George, and young Robert. As always, this was wonderful fun for John Henry and Robert. John and Permelia's new home had been completed in 1856 but was on loan to the Fayetteville

Seminary for use as faculty headquarters and a student dormitory. Dr. Holliday served as a trustee of the school, which was originally slated to be named Fayetteville Female Seminary. By the time it actually opened, it was the Fayetteville Academy.[17] The new school was built on land that had been owned by Uncle James Johnson before the school trustees purchased it from him for one hundred and fifty dollars. They, in turn, sold it to the academy for a mere five dollars. Located two blocks south of the courthouse, the school opened in 1857 as a coeducational institution. It gained considerable renown when the trustees, including Dr. Holliday, contracted with the highly regarded Morgan Harbin Looney and his brother George Cleveland Looney on January 16, 1857. The quality of the academy was important to the citizens because there was no public school until 1872 in Fayette County. The Looney brothers fulfilled everyone's expectations as the academy became well known over the entire state of Georgia. Dr. Holliday enrolled his sons, George and Robert, in the academy. Young John Henry received most of his early education at home in Griffin under the tutelage of his mother. Griffin's first school had been organized in 1840 and was chartered in 1841 as the Griffin Male and Female Academy.[18] It was private; there was no public school in Griffin at that time. John Henry did not begin his formal schooling at the academy until his speech therapy concluded. Alice Holliday had done such a fine job with his early education that he was well ahead of his classmates academically though he was less advanced socially, probably because he was self-conscious about his speech impediment.

The black drape of mourning was often seen on the door of the Holliday household. In November 1856

John Henry lost another grandparent, William Land McKey, only three and one-half years after his wife, Jane, had died. William McKey passed away in Griffin and was laid to rest next to his wife at nearby Indian Creek Cemetery. The court appointed Henry Burroughs Holliday to be guardian of four of his wife's young siblings who had not yet reached legal age.[19] Soon after the funeral, the house was readied for the arrival of John Henry's Uncle Thomas, age fourteen, and the three young aunts, Margaret Ann and Melissa Ella, both teenagers, and Eunice Helena, who was ten years old, just five years older than John Henry. Accompanying the three girls was the pianoforte, bequeathed to them by their father. The arrival of the four McKey children and the piano marked the end of the quiet life for young John Henry.[20] This only child suddenly became the youngest of a large household. His young aunts and uncle were very good to him, though he must have yearned for the old quiet times when he had his mother all to himself. Three years later another child was brought into the household, compounding and crowding the situation even more. Henry Holliday agreed to become the legal guardian of a homeless young orphan, Elisha Pritchard.[21]

Five months after the death of Grandfather McKey, Alice's older sister, Martha, died on April 25, 1857.[22] Alice had become the matriarch of this large family, though she was only four days past her twenty-eighth birthday. Because of increasing family responsibilities, she began to give her son some much-needed freedom. Often John Henry was allowed to visit his Uncle John and Aunt Permelia in their new home, which they had reclaimed from the academy and had only recently occupied. He loved visiting Fayetteville and playing with his cousin Robert, who now had a new little brother, John Stiles Holliday, Jr. Aunt Permelia had given birth to her third son in February 1857.

Dr. Holliday was experiencing some disillusionment with the medical profession because of the lack of acceptance of many of the new methods and discoveries in the field of medicine and pharmacology. In the 1850s the standards for the practice of medicine were very lax. Anyone who wanted to practice medicine was allowed to do so. Licensing standards disappeared, and the prestige of the practice of medicine was also disappearing. County practitioners performed the functions of physician, pharmacist, and dentist. Dr. Holliday spent strenuous hours treating the patients who were able to pay for their medical care as well as fulfilling his moral obligation by seeing those needy patients with no funds for health care. He was forced to neglect research because of the time required to maintain his practice.

Dr. Holliday also spent a lot of time with Dr. Crawford Long philosophizing about the antiquated attitudes of educators toward the science of healing. The two doctors were not only related through marriage but had remained friends following Dr. Long's move to Athens, Georgia. Both were quite proud of the surgery they had done on John Henry. The boy's scarring was minimal, and his speech defect was waning. Due to social pressure in the 1840s, Dr. Long had been forced to limit his use of ether in surgery. There had been an element of society that felt that the ability to make someone sleep in order to avoid pain during surgery bordered on witchcraft or was at best mind-tampering. It was considered immoral as well as socially unacceptable. Now, in the late 1850s, the use of ether was beginning to gain acceptance in Europe, and Dr. Long was once again openly using it on patients with regularity. It took years for the use of ether to be completely accepted in the United States. Many years later, when its value was fully understood and appreciated, the country hailed Dr. Long as the "Father of Ether."[23]

Still a practicing physician in 1856, Dr. Holliday had purchased a 300-acre farm just south of Fayetteville's city limits. In 1857 he formed a partnership with his brother-in-law, George Washington Ware. Previously, they had acquired 450 acres in Fayette County. Now they established a mercantile firm, Holliday and Ware, on Cambleton Street in Fayetteville, which soon became one of the county's most successful businesses. By 1858 the names Holliday and Ware were two of the most important in Fayette County.

The year 1860 saw Dr. Holliday devoting much more time to commerce and agriculture and less time to his practice of medicine. The business philosophy that he and his brothers had learned from their father was proving to be quite lucrative. The income from the investments in real estate was nicely balanced with the retail partnerships that had been established. The family enjoyed their farm south of Fayetteville, though they still maintained the town home on West Lanier Avenue. Dr. Holliday's town home served as the central point for many of the business and political conversations that Grandfather Robert Holliday had with his sons and son-in-laws. When Henry came up from Griffin to join them, he usually brought John Henry along to see his grandfather, uncle, and cousins.

Permelia spent most of her time at the farm with the baby, John Stiles Holliday, Jr. She missed her frequent visits with Alice, who was being kept very busy at home in Griffin with her newly enlarged family. John Henry and his cousin Robert enjoyed the freedom of the country. John Henry especially loved it because his home in Griffin had become such a busy place since the arrival of his young aunts and uncle. He and Robert rode Dr. Holliday's horses, fished, and practiced their skills with pistols and shotguns. Their fathers had taught them well. The diminishing squirrel and rabbit population testified to their abilities.

The decade of the 1850s had brought prosperity to the Holliday family, but in 1860 the black cloud of political unrest continued to grow as discussions of secession became more and more prevalent.

4

The War Years

On Friday, May 18, 1860, Abraham Lincoln was nominated as the Republican Party's presidential candidate on the convention's third ballot. Lincoln moved swiftly to disassociate himself from the radical abolitionists in his party and insisted that he would be rigidly constitutional in dealing with slavery. Still, southern sentiment was largely shaped by the Republican negative attitude toward the Supreme Court's Dred Scott decision. In southern minds, Lincoln's subsequent election on November 6 portended the demise of the traditional southern culture. South Carolina quickly responded to Lincoln's election by passing a bill calling for the convening of a secession convention on November 9. On December 20 came the electrifying news that South Carolina had adopted an Ordinance of Secession.

In January of 1861 Milledgeville, the state capital in central Georgia, filled with delegates for Georgia's secession convention. When the Ordinance of Secession was offered on January 19, Col. James Franklin Johnson, John Henry Holliday's uncle, numbered among the 208 aye voters. Only 89 delegates voted against secession. Thus, Georgia followed in the footsteps of South Carolina, Mississippi, Florida, and Alabama in seceding from the Union. The Hollidays were not generally in favor of breaking up the Union, but when Georgia seceded they supported their state and completely dedicated themselves to the southern cause.

The war commenced on April 12, 1861, when the South Carolinians opened fire on Fort Sumter. Georgia quickly marshaled its support for the Confederacy. In Fayetteville the Baptist Church donated its bell to be melted into bullets. Permelia Holliday led a small group of women to the shop of a Jewish merchant named Hidhammer in Atlanta to buy the finest silk available for a flag. The ladies met in the Hollidays' home and under the direction of Mrs. Carolyn Huie (wife of Col. John Huie) pieced together the flag to be carried by Fayetteville's first volunteer company, the Fayetteville Rifle Grays (Company I of the Tenth Georgia Regiment), commanded by Capt. Young L. Wooten. The flag bearer of the company was Pvt. J. M. Dorsey.[1] John Manson Dorsey was the seventeen-year-old son of Solomon Dawson Dorsey, whose family resided in the house adjacent to Dr. Holliday's home. Fortunately, he was among those who survived the war experience.

On September 2, 1861, Henry Holliday accepted a presidential appointment from Jefferson Davis to serve in the Georgia Volunteer Infantry as assistant quartermaster of the Twenty-seventh Regiment.[2] His service did not begin until December 1, when he assumed his position at Camp Pickens in Manassas, Virginia.[3] Twenty-four days later, on Christmas Day of 1861, he was promoted to quartermaster with the field rank of major.[4]

Dr. John S. Holliday enlisted in the Fayette Dragoons, Company E, Second Georgia Cavalry Regiment (State Guards), commanded by Capt. John J. Whitaker. Though he had semiretired from the practice of medicine, Dr. Holliday served as a surgeon for the duration of the conflict. On May 31, 1861, another of John Henry's uncles, Robert Kennedy Holliday, accepted a presidential commission in the Confederate Army as a quartermaster with the rank of captain in the Seventh Regiment of Georgia Volunteer Infantry, Army of Northern Virginia.[5] Robert saw immediate action when the Seventh Georgia, under Col. Lucius Gartrell, reached Manassas Junction, Virginia, on July 21. They held the far left extension of Gen. Thomas J. "Stonewall" Jackson's line and suffered tremendous casualties at the Battle of First Manassas (also known as First Bull Run). Doing his part for the war effort, John Henry's uncle James Johnson was a member of the Clayton County Relief Committee organized to secure provisions for the Confederate Army. Uncle James and Aunt Martha's beautiful home in Jonesboro served as a warehouse for the storage of the provisions that James procured. The house was also used as a field hospital during the Battle of Jonesboro.[6]

The response of the Holliday family to the coming of the war prompted Jarred I. Whitaker, a native of Fayette County and editor of the *Atlanta Intelligencer*, to write: "No county in Georgia can boast of more patriotic men in proportion to numbers [referring to Fayette County]. They are all ready for the fight, and when other companies shall go out to battle from the county we should not be surprised to see Uncle Bob

Holliday [John Henry's grandfather] in the ranks, if his friends would permit him to go. He is of a fighting stock and no mistake, as his boys have long since proven."[7]

Throughout Georgia, young men were taking up arms to defend their beloved South. In Griffin, three more of John Henry's uncles—James, William, and Thomas McKey—also enlisted in Georgia infantry regiments. Ultimately, six of John Henry's uncles saw action.

His cousin George, the eldest son of Uncle John and Aunt Permelia, was attending the Georgia Military Institute in Marietta as the war began. George occasionally returned home, and both Robert and John Henry saw how impressive he looked in his cadet uniform. Most young boys were envious of the older cadets and wished that they were old enough to join them. The two young boys probably fantasized about their potential bravery. Eventually, George saw action in this bloodiest of American wars, a duty definitely not to be envied.

When the war started, both John Henry and Robert, as young as they were, could handle a weapon. Henry had enjoyed letting the boys fire the old Revolutionary War pistols that he had inherited from Grandfather Burroughs. Henry, who had twice previously experienced war, had seen to it that the boys were proficient with revolvers and rifles as well as shotguns. Though John Henry and Robert were only ten and eleven years old when their fathers enlisted, they were quite capable of defending their homes. John Henry had become the "man of the house" at the outset of the war. When his father and older brother George left home, Robert likewise shared that distinction. Their weapons were kept ready for use at all times.

Maj. Henry Holliday's Twenty-seventh Georgia Infantry fought in the Peninsula battles in Virginia. Shortly after the Battle of Malvern Hill, Henry was forced to tender the resignation of his commission for reasons of chronic diarrhea and general disability.[8] His official discharge was dated August 24, 1862.[9] John Henry's uncle, Capt. William H. McKey, fighting with the Thirteenth Georgia, also participated in the Battle of Malvern Hill, where he was wounded. Fortunately, the wounds that he suffered were not fatal.[10] Major Holliday must have been disappointed when his health forced him to leave his regiment and return to Georgia. Of course, Alice and John Henry must have been extremely thankful to have him home and safe. There was more reason for thanks when, four weeks later, word reached them of the Battle of Antietam in Maryland on September 17. Of the ten field officers in Colquitt's Brigade who had gone into action, four were killed, five were wounded, and the tenth was stunned by a shell. Major Holliday would have been one of those officers!

Less than three months after his father's discharge, John Henry's grandfather Robert, the patriarch of the Holliday family, died in Fayetteville on November 16, 1862. The following morning, most of the family were able to gather at the Fayetteville City Cemetery as Robert was buried beside his wife, Rebecca. John Henry, only eleven years old, was old enough to realize the meaning of death, having already lost so many of his Holliday and McKey family members. He must have felt great concern for the men in the family who were still off defending the Confederacy.

In August 1863 Henry Holliday made a far-sighted decision that would have a major impact upon the life of John Henry. Though Vicksburg had fallen and Gen. Robert E. Lee had been repulsed at Gettysburg, the war was still very distant from northern Georgia. Despite this, Henry determined to move his wife, twelve-year-old son, and wife's family south to Lowndes County, Georgia, which was even further removed from the smoldering action of the war. The final real estate purchase that Henry Holliday made in Griffin was on August 5, 1863. Two weeks later he sold three rental homes to Patrick Wiley and two thousand acres to Samuel B. McWilliams. In October he sold more commercial property to Patrick Wiley. Then, on April 14, 1864, he sold seventeen acres in the northeast part of Griffin to T. G. Manley.[11] In a period of six months Henry raised $23,700 from these sales of real estate in the coin of the realm—Confederate dollars.

On February 9, 1864, Henry Burroughs Holliday bought 2,450 acres in Lowndes County from the estate of James D. Shanks for $31,500, again using Confederate dollars.[12] In April 1864 he moved his household, including his wife, son, and Alice's three sisters, Margaret, Melissa, and Eunice, and settled near Bemiss, about seven miles north of Valdosta.[13] The following year, on January 4, he purchased an additional 980 acres from the Shanks estate for $3,150.[14]

While his father had deemed the move wise, the decision to leave Griffin was not popular with John Henry. He was uprooted not only from his home, but from his classmates at the academy, the Holliday family, and his cousin Robert. Bemiss, 190 miles from Griffin, must have seemed like a different world to the twelve-year-old boy. Already quiet, John Henry became more withdrawn and somewhat sullen, though news of the war was always interesting.

Gen. Ulysses S. Grant's breaking of the siege of Chattanooga in late November 1863 opened the door for Gen. William T. Sherman's Army of the Tennessee to begin the move toward Atlanta the following May. During the interim, Uncle Robert Kennedy Holliday secured a leave and briefly returned to Jonesboro in February 1864. Captain Holliday then took his two oldest daughters, Martha Anne and Lucy Rebecca, to Savannah, where they were enrolled in Saint Vincent's Academy.[15]

John Henry later learned that on May 1, 1864, at the Marietta campus of the Georgia Military Institute studies were virtually abandoned as the cadets anticipated being placed on active duty. Schoolbooks were set aside, and guns, haversacks, and canteens were taken up. The Cadet Battalion, under the command of Maj. Frank W. Capers, the institute's superintendent, was divided into two companies. Cousin George was about to go on active duty—with the rank of private in Company B, commanded by Capt. Victor E. Manget, professor of French.

On May 10, 1864, George Holliday's Cadet Battalion entered the Confederate service. Their first duty was as provost guard around the city of Marietta. They also performed a variety of duties related to their position at the rear of Gen. Joseph E. Johnston's Confederate Army. On May 14 the Cadet Battalion was sent 64 miles north to Resaca, Georgia, situated on the Western and Atlantic Railroad line. Sherman had ordered a flanking maneuver around Dalton, Georgia, 16 miles north of Resaca, and Gen. James B. McPherson's Union force of 24,500 men had pushed through to within a mile of Resaca. There the cadets received their first exposure to Union fire.[16] When General Johnston learned that the bluecoats had crossed the Oostanaula River downstream, he ordered his Confederate force to withdraw from Resaca during the night of May 15. It was imperative that he maintain his hold on the Western and Atlantic, his railroad lifeline. George Holliday later fought in the trenches around Atlanta, at the Oconee bridge between Milledgeville and Dublin, and in the rear guard that covered the evacuation of Savannah on December 20. He continued on active duty until the war's end.

By mid-August 1864 the fighting had been going on near Atlanta for a number of weeks and Sherman, frustrated, determined to break the strength of the city's defenders by seizing the Macon railroad at Jonesboro, twenty miles below Atlanta. He intended to cut the city off from the southern railroads bringing supplies to the army of Gen. John Bell Hood, who had superseded Johnston. On the night of August 18 Union cavalry leader Judson Kilpatrick raided Jonesboro, set fire to the depot, and destroyed a few miles of track. Within five days Confederate trains loaded with supplies were again reaching Atlanta. Sherman realized that cavalry raids could not properly disable a railroad and ordered a three-pronged assault against the line. On August 27 he sent Gen. Oliver Howard to advance on Jonesboro from the west. Four days later Hood took the offensive and commanded Gen. William Hardee to attack the Federals at first light on August 31. The Confederate offensive was unsuccessful. The Federals held Jonesboro as well as the Macon and Western Railroad. General Hood, knowing that he was cut off from supplies with the fall of the railroad, evacuated Atlanta on the evening of September 1. Sherman was poised to launch his "March to the Sea."

On August 30, the day before the Battle of Jonesboro, Mary Anne Holliday took her four remaining children, Mary, Roberta, Catherine, and Jim Bob, fled the family home, and sought refuge at the home of her uncle, Philip Fitzgerald, four miles outside of the town. They remained there for two weeks, during which time the Fitzgerald farm was occupied by Federal troops.[17] Fortunately, the family was unharmed. When Mary Anne returned to Jonesboro, she found only the framework of the house standing and all of their possessions gone. The siding had been removed to construct breastworks for the troops. Mary Anne decided to flee northern Georgia with the children and seek the protection of her brother-in-law, Henry Holliday, in Bemiss. She could only pray for the safety of her two older daughters, Mattie and Lucy, still in school in Savannah. Her fears would have been much greater had she known that Savannah was the point where General Sherman intended to reach the sea.

It took the family two weeks, traveling by train in a boxcar, to reach Gordon, forty miles south of Macon. Sherman's army was moving south by way of Jonesboro and McDonough and fighting was taking place. Mary Anne and the children had to wait two additional weeks at Gordon before she could locate another train that would take the family further south to the depot at Valdosta. When they finally arrived, Henry and Alice were relieved that their sister-in-law and her five children were safe. Of course, they readily took Mary Anne and the children into their household.[18] The arrival of these Holliday cousins brought some familiarity to John Henry, who had been in Lowndes less than six months. In December Savannah was besieged by Sherman's forces. Uncle Robert and Aunt Mary

Anne's two older daughters, Mattie and Lucy, left St. Vincent's Academy. Alone, they fled the city and managed to get to their Uncle Henry's house, where they were reunited with their mother, sisters, and brother.[19] The family was able to relax, knowing that all their children were safe.

After her arrival in south Georgia, Mary Anne received word that on September 15, 1864, her husband, Robert, had been assigned as assistant brigade quartermaster to Gen. George Anderson's brigade, Gen. Charles Field's division of Gen. James Longstreet's corps. He had served with the same regiment throughout the war in the Army of Northern Virginia, from First Manassas through the engagements at Seven Days, Second Manassas, Antietam, Fredericksburg, Chancellorsville, Chattanooga, Knoxville, Spottsylvania, and Cold Harbor. In September he was serving on the Richmond-Petersburg front.

Back in northern Georgia, the devastation caused by General Sherman's bluebellies affected not only the Confederate soldiers and their families: all residents felt the tremendous impact of the scourge. Homes were destroyed, farms were ruined, stores were ransacked, and property was pillaged. The war did not discriminate—blacks also felt a profound impact. Many of the slaves found themselves with nowhere to go because their owners were suffering devastation and were no longer able to care for them. Only the most fortunate slave families were able to stay together. Most struggled to find food and shelter or someone to care for them. Little Sophie Walton was one such child.

Sophie was born a slave in January 1856 on a farm owned by the Walton family. Fathered by Mr. Walton,

Sophie had a higher status than the other slave children on the farm. She assisted her mother with the care of the Walton's white children. As a child of only three or four, Sophie had slept on a palette on the floor of the nursery, with the responsibility of using her foot to rock the cradle of the new Walton baby, whom everyone recognized to be her half-sister.[20] Through the open window, she could hear the singing coming from the slave quarters, where her mother and the others would be gathered around a campfire popping corn on a shovel over the fire, and heard the laughter of the children as they jumped to get the popped corn when it flew through the air.[21] She stayed inside and devotedly kept the cradle rocking.

During the next few years Sophie was taught by her mother to sew and assisted in mending the Walton family clothing. Late in 1864, with the scourge of the war upon them, Mr. Walton could no longer afford to care for all of the slaves. He knew that with the Federals now in control of the region the blacks were free to leave, but most had no place to go. Mr. Walton assisted some of them in finding homes nearby where they would be given room and board and perhaps meager wages. Sophie was fortunate that he was a friend of Dr. and Mrs. John S. Holliday. Mr. Walton arranged for this little girl to go live at the Holliday house on West Lanier Avenue in Fayetteville. She was given room and board and a very small stipend. Her responsibilities included serving as nanny to the Holliday children even though she was still a child herself. Permelia knew that little Sophie was frightened and lonely so she instructed Martha Fuller, the cook, to take the child under her wing.[22]

Within six months of Sophie's arrival at the Holli-days' home, news came that General Lee had surren-dered the Army of Northern Virginia on April 9, 1865. Though no one celebrated, there was a sense of relief along with the sorrow. The physical danger was finally over. It was the end of an era for all southerners. When Robert Kennedy Holliday returned to Jonesboro on May 24, 1865, he needed to make living arrangements so his family could return. At the war's conclusion, he had been in the mountains of Tennessee, seeking food for his brigade.[23] His journey back from a northern internment camp, mostly on foot, had been long and miserable. Not only had he lost his home and posses-sions, but he had lost his health. Four years earlier he had left Jonesboro a strong man. A frail man with a broken spirit returned. Dr. John Holliday was also home now, as was his son George, who, at his young age, had seen more fighting than most of the men in the family. Permelia's family was once again home and intact. James and Martha Johnson and their family miraculously survived in Jonesboro. Their house was one of the few still standing.

Soon the news reached Lowndes County that all of the Holliday men had returned safely. Alice also received word that her brothers were all safe. They learned from Dr. Holliday that more than twenty-five percent of the men from Fayetteville who fought never returned. Similar statistics were repeated throughout the state and throughout the South. John Henry was fortunate that his family was one of the few that had survived the war without loss of life, although the presence of the Federal troops that occupied Georgia was a bitter reminder of the humility and totality of defeat. He surely felt the same intense frustration that

Capt. Robert Kennedy Holliday, C.S.A. Collection of Carolyn Holliday Manley

was experienced by all southern men, young and old alike, and could not yet realize that the war's aftermath and Republican Reconstruction would bring still more crises.

5

Reconstruction

The war had been the most significant event in the life of young John Henry Holliday as well as the lives of tens of thousands of other young people in the South. The aftermath of the war was equally challenging, as the Holliday family, their neighbors, and the rest of Georgia's residents came to grips with the postwar occupation. Confiscation of property was still threatened, and Confederate money was now worthless. Henry Holliday had successfully avoided the worst of Sherman's pillaging with the timely move to the southern part of the state during the war. His farm near Bemiss, originally purchased with $34,650 in Confederate money, represented sixteen years of hard work. This farm, together with the remaining real estate investments in Griffin, had declined in value to a mere $1,700.[1] Lowndes County suffered from a commercial drought, as did the rest of Georgia. Supplies needed for trade, medicine, and agriculture were unavailable. Both Macon to the north and Savannah to the east were controlled by the Federals. The nearest seaport to the south was Jacksonville, Florida, which was also occupied by the Yankees. Only the barest necessities were available.

Dr. Holliday fared better than most of his neighbors. Most of Fayette County's soldiers who survived the war returned to find their homes and much of their personal property missing or destroyed. Their slaves had been freed and the farm stock was gone. John Stiles Holliday's home and family were intact. Permelia and the three boys were safe and their former slaves remained devoted. While the men struggled to restore their farms and businesses, Permelia and the servants worked hard at trying to recreate some semblance of their antebellum lives. The war had resulted in the destruction of most of their comforts. Commerce throughout the state was at a standstill. The women became very resourceful in making use of the little that remained from the past. Damask curtains were transformed into lovely frocks, and palmetto leaves were woven into wide-brimmed bonnets adorned with flowers fashioned from colorful feathers. Persimmon seeds were utilized as buttons, while thorns were carved into hairpins. They brewed roasted rye and wheat to compensate for the scarcity of coffee and tea. Without complaining, these women wasted nothing and were able to provide a degree of comfort so that their men could devote their energies to the necessary rebuilding. By 1870 Dr. Holliday's real property had regained its 1860 value—$4,500.[2]

Robert Kennedy Holliday, who had accumulated over three thousand dollars in real estate prior to 1860 and had owned a successful mercantile establishment in Jonesboro, returned to total devastation. Not only had he lost his home, but his business no longer existed. His wife and children returned from his brother's home in Bemiss. Unfortunately, he was never able to regain his wealth and stature in the community. At the time of his death in 1872, he was working as a baggage clerk for the railroad and his estate was valued at little more than five hundred dollars.[3]

In Bemiss, John Henry's father devoted the majority of his time after the war to agriculture. The family also established itself among its new neighbors. On December 3, 1864, the Presbyterians in the area formed the First Presbyterian Church of Valdosta. The Hollidays were among the first members of this new church, less than ten miles south of the farm.[4] Alice Jane had been able to maintain her musical skills as she was still in possession of her younger sisters' pianoforte. She supplemented their income and made new friends when she began to offer piano lessons to Valdosta's young ladies.[5]

Soon after the Holliday family's arrival in Bemiss, Alice Jane became ill. During the next two years, her health steadily declined. This illness, presumed to be tuberculosis, finally took her life on September 16, 1866.[6] Prior to her death, Alice Jane abandoned the Presbyterian Church, which she had joined in Griffin sixteen years earlier. On her deathbed, she returned to the Methodist beliefs that she had learned as a child. She objected to the Presbyterian stress on the doctrine of predestined salvation and did not want John Henry to grow up thinking that she accepted it. She saw to it that her beliefs were put in writing so that he would know specifically what she did believe.[7] Following his mother's death, John Henry Holliday promptly became a Methodist.[8]

Dr. Holliday took time off from his commercial enterprises to travel south to Bemiss after receiving the news of his sister-in-law's death. He paid his respects to his brother and offered greatly needed solace to his nephew. Uncle John's visit provided comfort to John Henry and gave him an opportunity to hear the news of his cousins, especially Robert, firsthand. The two cousins had not seen each other for over two and one-half years. Uncle John assured his nephew that he was welcome to come for a visit in the not-too-distant future. Dr. Holliday also stressed the importance of doing well in school in order to lay the groundwork for more advanced education in the future.

Three months after Alice's death, while John Henry was still mourning his mother, Henry B. Holliday married Rachel Martin, the daughter of neighbors Stephen and Sarah Fouchtore Martin. Rachel, born on March 5, 1843, was only eight and one-half years older than John Henry, her new stepson.[9] They were again uprooted when Henry moved the family from Bemiss into the town of Valdosta. Though he continued to own the farm and to market trees and cuttings from his nursery, he moved the family into a home belonging to Rachel's father at 405 East Savannah Avenue.[10]

The 1864 move with his family to Lowndes County had separated John Henry from his Holliday relatives and friends. The loneliness occasioned by the move and the devastation of the war naturally were very unsettling for this sensitive boy. The death of his mother combined with the rapid remarriage of his father to a much younger woman added to the loneliness and caused more emotional withdrawal.[11] He devoted most of his time to his studies, with little time for recreation.

John Henry attended the Valdosta Institute, founded by Samuel McWhir Varnedoe. After having purchased Mason's Hall in 1865, Varnedoe subsequently added two wings and founded the institute, with himself and his two daughters, Matilda and Sallie Lou, as instructors.[12] Thanks to the strong academic foundation provided by his mother, John Henry readily met the stringent demands of Varnedoe's Valdosta Institute. There he received a classical secondary education including grammar, rhetoric, mathematics, history, and languages, principally Latin, considerable French, and some Greek.

Letters John Henry received from his Holliday relatives in the northern part of Georgia indicated that they, too, were experiencing some major adjustments to the postwar period. After returning from the war, his cousin George, with Dr. Holliday's financial support, had moved to Atlanta and had founded a grocery partnership with R. W. Tidwell on Whitehall Street. On March 8, 1867, Dr. Holliday sold his town home in Fayetteville to his mother-in-law, Mildred Ware, and joined his son in Atlanta.[13]

John and Permelia moved the family to Atlanta in order to participate in the rejuvenation of this important southern community, still a railroad crossroads. Dr. Holliday acquired a large piece of property at 66 Forrest Avenue, between Collins and Calhoun Streets, north of Atlanta's business community.[14] He began the construction of a large home. Though he continued to practice medicine, his main interests switched to business. He assisted his son in operating Tidwell and Holliday, family grocers. For a while the company also employed Dr. Holliday's son Robert, as well as the doctor's brother, Robert Kennedy Holliday. In 1868

George Henry Holliday following his return from the war, Atlanta, Georgia, December 1865. Collection of Constance K. McKellar

Atlanta replaced Milledgeville as the state capital, which further increased the economic potential of the city.

Sophie Walton, the young mulatto servant, accompanied Dr. Holliday's family when they moved to Atlanta. She spent a lot of her time entertaining the Holliday sons, George, Robert, and John, Jr., while Mrs. Holliday was busy with her other activities. Sophie was very quick and proved to be lots of fun for the three brothers. She was an expert cardplayer and promptly taught the boys several of the old slave gambling games. A card game called "Skinning" was Sophie's favorite. The original rules of the game were adapted from faro. It was played with three players and a dealer.

The players would each be dealt or "skinned" a card from the deck and then would place bets that their card would be the last to pair up as successive cards were dealt. A player who could rapidly compute the changing odds as cards were skinned and discarded to the "deadwood" pile had an advantage.[15] Sophie's lack of formal education did not seem to handicap her. Though she could neither read nor write, she was quick with numbers and had no problem competing with the boys. As young children, the boys always used buttons from Sophie's sewing box for placing their bets. As the boys got older, Sophie was able to supplement her small wages by winning a share of their spending money. The method of skinning the cards from the deck made it possible for a skillful player to determine the outcome of the game. Though some would have looked upon this as cheating, the Holliday boys quickly learned from Sophie how to "skin" the cards in such a way as to influence the outcome without the other players realizing what they were doing. They devoted much effort to developing this skill so that they could trick their cousins and friends.

Another card game that Sophie taught them was "Up and Down the River," which was a version of the dice game "Put and Take." With cards, the game required that each person be dealt five face-up cards. Then five more cards were dealt, one up at a time. If players paired, they had to put into the pot the number of buttons (later the amount of money) represented by the number on the face of the card paired. Then the same procedure was followed by five more up-cards, but this time the players took from the pot instead of putting in when they had two cards that were paired.[16] The entertainment provided by Sophie gave the boys some lighthearted moments during an era that was dominated by despair.

As Dr. Holliday began to regain his economic success in the late 1860s, he sought a means to preserve what he was rebuilding. With his prior experience with Confederate money—and a fear of Reconstruction policies that called for land confiscation—Dr. Holliday decided to maintain a portion of his wealth in diamonds. He initially acquired a dozen or so fine diamonds from Brazil, ranging in size from one carat to two and one-half carats. They tended to look larger than diamonds of comparable size do today because they were of the Old-Mine and old European cuts of the time as opposed to the American brilliant cut, which began to dominate after the turn of the century. He knew that the diamonds would serve not only as a source of wealth, but as a source of pleasure as well. Dr. Holliday had some of them fashioned into stickpins to be worn by several of the Holliday males, never considering that more than a few of these diamonds would eventually be used as collateral during high-stakes gambling games.[17]

In the late 1860s, John Henry was involved in a shooting affray at a white swimming hole on the Withlacoochee River where a number of blacks had gathered. John Henry's uncle, Thomas McKey, was the only witness when his nephew fired over the heads of the black swimmers in order to scare them off.[18] This incident was repeatedly exaggerated in the retelling until it was described by some as a massacre, instead of the relatively minor event that it was.[19] Following the incident, John Henry was sent to visit his uncle, Robert Kennedy Holliday. This trip also enabled him to spend some time with his cousin Robert and Uncle John and Aunt Permelia.[20]

During this visit, Dr. Holliday convinced his nephew of the importance of continued education. Young John Henry thought a career in medicine would be a good choice but was dissuaded by his uncle. By this time, the doctor was thoroughly disillusioned with his field and told his nephew how dentistry had surpassed medicine as a respectable profession. Licensing standards for doctors had just about disappeared, forcing educated physicians to compete with charlatans in their day-to-day practice. Additionally, he noted, dentistry had long since accepted the use of anesthesia while doctors who offered the use of ether were still viewed with skepticism. The dental community's rapid acceptance of nitrous oxide as an anesthetic after Gardner Q. Colton's demonstration of painless extractions in Hartford, Connecticut, in 1863 suggested to Dr. Holliday that dentistry was the more progressive profession. John Henry had great respect for his uncle's opinion and immediately reacted with interest when his uncle suggested attending dental school.[21] As they discussed the merits of various schools, Dr. Holliday conveyed the views of Dr. Crawford Long: the University of Pennsylvania in Philadelphia, Dr. Long's alma mater, was a progressive school with a fine reputation and the nearby Pennsylvania College of Dental Surgery also had a fine reputation.[22] Dr. Holliday suggested that a school in the North might be a better choice for the time being because of the ongoing political unrest in the South. Although Dr. Holliday wanted to support the rebuilding of the South, he believed that the northern schools were better equipped to provide a good education. John Henry decided to return to Valdosta to discuss the possibility of a career in dentistry with his father.

Although he had decided on a professional career, John Henry remained a product of Reconstruction—embittered by war and deprivation. Soon after returning, he and several of his friends made plans to blow up the Lowndes County Court House, then housing the Freedmen's Bureau, the hated arm of the Reconstruction policy. This agency was responsible for overseeing the rights of the freed slaves, an idea that defied traditional white southern philosophy. A number of Valdosta's prominent citizens discouraged the conspirators by announcing that they were going to be in the courthouse on the designated night to hear a political speaker. The kegs of powder that had been secretly placed beneath the courthouse were then quietly removed.[23]

After this incident, John Henry's father readily agreed that it was time for his son to train for a profession. The suggestion of a school that was some distance away was a welcome idea. John Henry and his father decided that the Pennsylvania College of Dental Surgery in Philadelphia was a fine choice. They immediately wrote to the school for information on entrance requirements as well as an application. In 1870 John Henry Holliday paid the five dollar matriculation fee and the one hundred dollar tuition and enrolled in the Pennsylvania College of Dental Surgery for the fifteenth annual session.

In September of that year John Henry traveled to Philadelphia and commenced his dental education. Following the required course of instruction, he began five months of classroom lectures on Monday, October 3. At nine o'clock each morning he attended a two-hour lecture and demonstration, followed by a second two-hour lecture and demonstration beginning at one o'clock each afternoon. His course work included chemistry taught by T. L. Buckingham, D.D.S.; mechanical dentistry and metallurgy under E. Wildman, M.D., D.D.S.; dental pathology and therapeutics under Professor G. T. Barker, D.D.S.; dental histology and operative dentistry under James Truman, D.D.S.; physiology and microscopic anatomy under professor James Tyson, M.D.; and anatomy and surgery under J. Ewing Mears, M.D. On Saturdays, John Henry participated in clinical operations in the college's two-thousand-square-foot operating room, assisted by demonstrators. During his first year's course of instruction he operated on approximately thirty-nine patients, filling about thirty-two teeth, extracting an additional thirty-eight teeth, and performing about a dozen other operations such as fitting bridge work.[24] One of his patients was a six-year-old girl who had been brought to the school because of its reputation for providing fine dental care at no cost. John Henry created a crown of pure swaged gold and attached it to the child's diseased molar with red copper cement. The so-called six-year molars decayed in over twenty-five percent of children within the first year of surfacing.[25] John Henry did an excellent job: the crown remained intact until the little girl died at the age of 102 in 1967.[26]

In the first week of March 1871 he returned to Valdosta and, as required by his school, studied dentistry under preceptor Dr. Lucian Frederick Frink, for the next eight months. Dr. Frink, a twenty-four-year-old native of Georgia, was a friend of Maj. Henry Holliday. Both men were officers in the Valdosta Chapter of Royal Arch Masons when Frink offered to accept the responsibility to serve as preceptor for John Henry.[27] He had also served as preceptor for P. H. Braswell.[28]

John Henry Holliday's graduation announcement from the Pennsylvania College of Dental Surgery, March 1, 1872. Collection of Karen Holliday Tanner

Practicing dentistry under Dr. Frink's tutelage, John Henry periodically extracted and filled teeth for Frink's patients. Though the student dentist did not normally receive fees himself, John Henry did on occasion get paid, as is evidenced by the case in October 1871 when he provided dental services for Miss Corinthia Morgan and received payment in the amount of $21.00.[29]

In October 1871 John Henry again traveled to Philadelphia to resume his studies on November 6. After attending lectures for an additional twenty-two weeks, he prepared a thesis entitled "Diseases of the Teeth," required for graduation. Additionally, he was required to treat a patient in need of all the usual dental operations and to present that patient before his professor of operative dentistry, Dr. Elihu R. Pettit. He also had to prepare an artificial denture for a patient and present that patient before his professor of mechanical dentistry, Dr. Charles E. Edwards. After preparing a specimen case to be deposited in the college collection and passing an examination by the faculty, he was recommended for graduation to the Board of Trustees. John Henry fulfilled all requirements and graduated from the Pennsylvania College of Dental Surgery on Friday, March 1, 1872, with the degree of Doctor of Dental Surgery.[30]

Following his graduation, the newly titled dentist left Philadelphia and headed south. His quick departure was indicative of his eagerness to leave the North and return to familiar southern surroundings. He would soon participate in the reemergence of Atlanta. Uncle John and Aunt Permelia invited him to become a part of the Holliday household at 66 Forrest Avenue while he established himself in his new career.[31]

6

Atlanta Dentist

John Henry Holliday, D.D.S., was greeted by his cousin Robert at the Richmond Air-line Railroad depot in Atlanta. Throughout the years of separation, they had remained best of friends; now they would be able to make up for lost time, revive old memories, and make future plans.

John Henry and Robert were a handsome pair of eligible bachelors who easily could have passed for brothers. Both were blond with blue eyes, had fair complexions, and shared a sprinkling of the Holliday family freckles. John Henry was close to six feet tall and weighed a little shy of one hundred and sixty pounds. Robert was slightly over six feet in height and weighed just a bit more. The tall, slender cousins, with their good looks and amiable personalities, possessed the charm and manners that were considered important to any gentleman of the South. Robert was the more outgoing of the two, with a lighthearted demeanor and whimsical sense of humor. John Henry, in contrast,

Robert Alexander Holliday, D.D.S., Atlanta, Georgia, 1882. Collection of John P. Holliday

tended to be more serious and mature. During his stay in Philadelphia he had developed a cosmopolitan outlook while sharply honing his droll, quick wit. Both cousins possessed a keen intellect.

The second floor ballroom of the Forrest Street home of John Stiles Holliday, M.D., and his wife, Permelia, the location of many lavish social and political functions, was the site of a large party to introduce their recently graduated nephew to the city's society.

The belles of Atlanta quickly determined that this newly arrived Holliday was just as important to the success of any social event as was his cousin Robert. When not amid the laughter of the young ladies, the Holliday cousins could generally be found riding the doctor's handsome geldings in the countryside nearby or target practicing with their 1851 Colt revolvers, a gift from Dr. Holliday.[1] The doctor had purchased four matching revolvers and had given one to each of his three sons—George, Robert, and John, Jr.—and one to his nephew, John Henry. The war, followed by the years of Reconstruction, had made him mindful of the necessity for his family, including the women, to maintain proficiency with guns. Years afterward Mrs. Robert Alexander Holliday explained:

> Through the years of war when every man left his family, and not one white man to protect them, the blacks protected their white folks, as they called them, with their lives. They were fully aware that their masters trusted them. The women felt perfectly safe, and knew the respect the negroes held for them. But when the Reconstruction days came, every woman and girl was taught to shoot and to use a gun. No girl in Georgia ventured out without being armed. No girl was safe in that state. I know not what conditions existed in other states. Of course, in the city, they could have protection, but not so in the country and smaller places. The Carpet-Baggers—so called—had taught the Blacks revenge, poisoning their minds. The Blacks were not to blame. The Carpet-Baggers made them what they were.[2]

Robert Alexander Holliday's Colt revolver, Model 1851, Navy. One of the four Colt Navy revolvers given by Dr. John S. Holliday to his three sons and his nephew, John Henry Holliday. Collection of Karen Holliday Tanner

The corrupt government of Radical Republican governor Rufus B. Bullock had concluded with his resignation six months prior to John Henry's return to Atlanta. Dr. Holliday had witnessed three separate Federal military governments in Georgia since the war as well as intermittent Carpetbagger excesses and was insistent that his family be capable of protecting themselves.

When John Henry moved into his uncle's house following his graduation, Sophie still played cards with the boys, now young men. The stakes remained low because of Sophie's meager earnings. She only won about half the time, but the intense rivalry remained. Although she laughingly won John Henry's loose change for a while, his intense competitive spirit coupled with his remarkable memory and mathematical ability soon prevailed. Before long John Henry was as skilled at "Skinning" and "Put and Take" as his cousins and Sophie. They would sit at the large round oak table in

Sophie Walton, Atlanta, Georgia, 1895. Collection of Karen Holliday Tanner

the Holliday kitchen and play for hours, often well into the night. He quickly learned the importance of keeping track of the deadwood (discard pile) and developed the ability to know which cards remained unplayed and could rapidly compute the odds for each.[3] This provided the foundation for his future success at faro, which proved to be easy for him because the casekeeper always displayed what cards had been played. As a faro player, John Henry would be able to devote his thoughts mainly to computing odds. As a faro dealer, he would be able to implement the various dealing "skills" taught to him by Sophie. She had prepared her students well for the gentlemen's sporting games of their futures.

Of course, the Holliday cousins did not spend all their time at leisure activities. On Sundays John Henry regularly attended the First Methodist Episcopal Church (formerly called Wesley Chapel) on the east side of Peachtree Street near the junction of Broad Street with his aunt and uncle, his cousin George, and George's new wife, Mary. His cousins Robert and John, Jr., had both rebelled against the family wishes and attended St. Luke's Episcopal Church at Forsyth and Walton Streets in Atlanta.

Most importantly, John Henry needed to start his profession. Also living within the Holliday household at that time was Samuel Hape, D.D.S. Though not a practicing dentist, Dr. Hape owned the Southern Dental Depot, which manufactured and supplied Hape Gold Foil for dentists. During the Civil War he had run the northern blockade and was the sole source of dental supplies for the Confederacy. His twenty-eight-year-old brother, Albert, was also a dentist and had previously practiced dentistry with Dr. Arthur C. Ford in the Bank Block on Alhambra Street. Dr. Albert Hape was moving his practice to Thomson, Georgia, so he knew that his former partner, Dr. Ford, was in need of a new associate.[4] He arranged for an interview, and within a few months of his arrival in the city John H. Holliday, D.D.S., had secured a position with the dental practice of the prestigious Dr. Ford.

Dr. Arthur C. Ford was born on October 11, 1832, at Cape Good Hope. After completing his education in London, he emigrated to New York and studied dentistry there with Dr. Benjamin Lord. At the age of twenty-five he moved to Augusta, Georgia, and then to Louisville, Georgia, where he served with the Louisville Guard of the Twentieth Georgia Regiment. Dr. Ford was

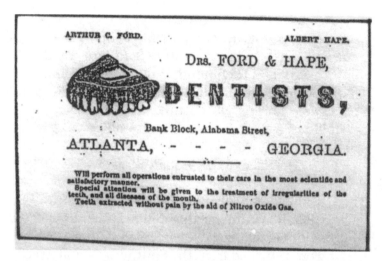

ARTHUR C. FORD.   ALBERT HAPE.

Drs. FORD & HAPE,

DENTISTS,

Bank Block, Alabama Street,

ATLANTA, - - - - GEORGIA.

Will perform all operations entrusted to their care in the most scientific and satisfactory manner.
Special attention will be given to the treatment of irregularities of the teeth, and all diseases of the mouth.
Teeth extracted without pain by the aid of Nitrous Oxide Gas.

Advertisement for Drs. Ford and Hape, *Atlanta Constitution.*
Collection of Karen Holliday Tanner

wounded at the battle of Sharpsburg, temporarily loosing the use of his right hand.[5] He then moved to Atlanta with his wife, Emily, and established his practice in partnership with Dr. Albert Hape.

In 1872 the Georgia Legislature enacted the Dental Practice Act and established the state's first Board of Dental Examiners, largely at the insistence of the Georgia State Dental Society. In 1872 Dr. Ford's practice was located at the corner of Alabama and Whitehall Streets, near the Western and Atlantic Railroad depot, about fourteen blocks from the Holliday home. He had served as recording secretary of the society in 1869–70 and was then serving as chairman of the society's legislative committee. Dr. Ford was seeking an associate to cover for him during his travels. On Friday, July 26, 1872, he published the following notice in the *Atlanta Constitution*:

CARD

I HEREBY inform my patients that I leave to attend the Sessions of the Southern Dental Association in Richmond, Virginia this evening, and will be absent until about the middle of August, during which time Dr. Jno. [*sic*] H. Holliday will fill my place in my office.

　Arthur C. Ford DDS,

　　Office 26 Whitehall Street.[6]

It was a considerable feather in John Henry's cap that he was able to commence his dental career associated with one of Georgia's most esteemed dentists.

Dr. Ford returned from the Southern Dental Association's convention on August 14.[7] However, as chairman of the Dental Society's legislative committee, he was frequently called out of Atlanta. His patients were often in need of young Dr. Holliday's services. Dr. Ford was subsequently elected president of the Georgia State Dental Association in 1874, but continued to practice, eventually specializing in pedodontics.[8]

The summer of 1872 went by quickly for John Henry. When he was not at the dental practice, he sometimes helped out at Tidwell and Holliday. In addition, the young women of Atlanta saw to it that he had an active social life. Shortly after he celebrated his twenty-first birthday in August, his father, Maj. Henry Holliday, paid the necessary ten-dollar fee on September 10, 1872, and transferred the piece of property located on the southwest corner of Solomon Street and State Alley in Griffin from "John Henry Holliday by Guardian" to John Henry Holliday as required by law now that his son was no longer a minor.[9] This property, a portion of the legacy left by John Henry's mother,

Alice, had been transferred to Major Holliday in 1868 by her brother, Thomas Sylvester McKey, as executor, to be held in guardianship until young John Henry came of age. John Henry was now a property owner and fast becoming an active member of the Atlanta community.

John Henry never returned to his birthplace, Griffin, to practice dentistry. On January 14, 1873, he sold the two-story brick building located on the southwest corner of Solomon and State Alley that was transferred to him in September of 1872 to N. G. Philips of Spalding County for eighteen hundred dollars.[10]

While John Henry was pursuing his profession in Philadelphia, young Robert Holliday had decided that he did not need to further his education in order to be a successful part of Atlanta's business community. The common belief in north Georgia at that time was that what mattered was whether a man could raise good cotton, handle both a gun and a horse well, treat women gently and other men squarely, and carry his liquor like a gentlemen. After having started his secondary schooling at the Fayetteville Academy, Robert had completed it at a private school in Atlanta. When he made the decision that he had adequate formal education, he took a position as a clerk at Tidwell and Holliday after his graduation. This greatly disappointed Dr. Holliday, who felt that a true gentlemen also required the niceties of a classical education with an emphasis on one of the professions.[11] When John Henry arrived in Atlanta with his degree in dental surgery in hand, Robert observed the respect and admiration that his cousin received. He must have envied his younger cousin, who had become a professional man as well as a landowner. Dr. John S.

John Henry Holliday's inheritance, Improved Lot No. 10 of the Baptist Church Lot Survey, southwest corner of Solomon Street and State Alley, Griffin, Georgia. Collection of Karen Holliday Tanner

Holliday was pleased when his son had a change of heart regarding furthering his education. He told Robert that if he wanted to attend dental school he would financially assist the two new dentists in setting up a practice together.[12]

The young men, obviously excited at this prospect, immediately started making their plans. Robert applied for admission and was accepted to the Pennsylvania College of Dental Surgery for the term beginning in October 1873. John Henry readily agreed to serve as preceptor for his cousin.[13] Robert started his dental training by accompanying John Henry to the office and learning terminology, the use of the equipment, and some basic science, which allowed him to fulfill the apprenticeship requirement for the degree prior to beginning his first term of instruction at the college. With Robert beginning his dental career and John Henry gaining a reputation among Atlanta's dental community, the future looked bright for the Holliday cousins. Yet the fates that so frequently plagued John Henry were about to strike again.

On Christmas Eve, 1872, John Henry's uncle, Robert Kennedy Holliday, died in Jonesboro in Clayton County.[14] Forty-three years old and a baggage master for the Macon and Western Railroad, he had not been able to recover either his fortune or his health following the war. The day after Christmas the Holliday family traveled south to Fayetteville to attend the funeral. Robert was buried in the Fitzgerald family plot in Fayetteville Cemetery, about twenty yards from his parents, Robert and Rebecca, brothers William, George, Matthew, and Thomas, and sisters Amy and Jane.[15]

Soon after this sad Christmas season, John Henry began losing weight. The loss was barely perceptible at first, and he attributed it to his active schedule. Six months later, in the summer of 1873, he developed a nagging cough that forced him to take some time off from his dentistry. When the cough did not subside, he sought his uncle's assistance in diagnosing a possible

Matriculants.

NAME.	STATE.	PRECEPTOR.
Emilio Alvarez	Central America	
Caspar E. Assy	Pennsylvania	Dr. A. M. Assy.
Caspar E. Babcock	New York	Dr. H. J. Smith.
John M. Dentz	Pennsylvania	Dr. Geo. S. Searight.
Thomas W. Buckingham	Pennsylvania	Dr. T. L. Buckingham.
Charles F. Bonsall	Pennsylvania	Dr. Wm. H. Trueman.
William S. Breaker	South Carolina	Dr. S. R. Screven.
George A. Coe	New York	Dr. Horace A. Coe.
Alfredo Carnot	Cuba	Dr. G. W. Raffo.
Frank F. Cook	Massachusetts	Dr. A. A. Howland.
Frank D. Clum	New York	Dr. T. G. Lewis.
Sherman W. Chipman	Connecticut	Dr. A. D. Fuller.
Samuel A. Cook	Pennsylvania	Dr. Geo. T. Barker.
Thomas B. Downes	Missouri	
Hartwell A. Dalrymple	Massachusetts	Dr. S. B. Pike.
Thomas S. Daniel	Georgia	Dr. J. W. Daniel.
J. H. Douglass	Pennsylvania	Dr. U. A. Thompson.
Harry Y. Eastlack	Pennsylvania	Dr. I. S. Foss.
Addison S. Elliott	Pennsylvania	Dr. L. C. Longwell.
Jacob F. Fryer	Pennsylvania	Dr. J. A. Andre.
Liberato J. Flores	Cuba	Dr. J. Bustillo.
Willard L. Ferris	Connecticut	Dr. C. W. Strang.
Domingo Ferrer	Cuba	Dr. J. Arce.
F. Alfredo Goulé	Cuba	Dr. Geo. L. Rauch.
Jose R. Gonzales	Cuba	Dr. D. G. Harrington.
Bradley Hull, M. D.	Ohio	Dr. Lewis Buffett.
Ambrose W. Huckel	Pennsylvania	Dr. Wm. P. Henry.
F. Ellis Hancocks	Pennsylvania	Dr. T. L. Buckingham.
Robert A. Holliday	Georgia	Dr. J. H. Holliday.
Reuben B. Holder	Maine	Dr. F. J. Babcock.
Albert P. Johnstons	South Carolina	Drs. Thomson and Jones.
Hugh J. Linn	Pennsylvania	Dr. A. D. Abell.
Manuel Lopez	Cuba	Dr. Laury.
James A. McAllister	N. B., Canada	Dr. J. C. Hatheway.
Augusto Méram	Switzerland	Dr. C. A. Alden.
Arthur D. Murphy	Russia	Dr. S. H. Linn.
James E. Murphy	England	Dr. D. B. Murphy.
Maxwell S. Meriweather	Tennessee	Dr. H. E. Brach.
Fred. Meyer	Germany	Dr. M. Meyer.
Elmer Nelson	New York	Dr. Frank B. Darby.
Thomas A. Ortiz	Cuba	Dr. U. L. Howard.
Jose Oranguren	Cuba	Francisco de Chaguaceda.
Jose Ma. Perez	Cuba	Joseph Corvison.
Danlo D. Ramberger	Pennsylvania	Dr. James Truman.
William P. Richards	Illinois	Dr. J. M. & W. M. Trusdell.

Robert A. Holliday's matriculation announcement from the Pennsylvania College of Dental Surgery, listing his cousin, Dr. John Henry Holliday, as preceptor. Collection of Karen Holliday Tanner

ailment. Though Dr. Holliday was no longer practicing, he maintained a keen interest in medicine and kept his skills current by reading the medical journals that were once again being published after a hiatus during and after the war. Therefore, he was able to keep abreast of new techniques and views held by doctors throughout the country in the diagnosis and treatment of both common and uncommon ailments.

Using a stethoscope and bronchoscope, Uncle John diagnosed what he and John Henry both feared, pulmonary tuberculosis, which presumably had been the cause of the death of his mother, Alice. After considerable discussion with his nephew, Dr. Holliday prescribed a climate of warm, dry air combined with a nutritious diet, a moderate amount of wine, and prolonged rest during convalescence.[16] There was a growing belief among well-informed physicians that this regimen of rest, diet, and fresh air offered definite therapeutic and prevention possibilities and that tuberculosis should no longer be viewed simply as "an act of God" with no prospect for remission or cure. The diagnosis was by no means a death warrant. The Holliday family both hoped for and anticipated a full recovery.[17]

A family conference was called. It was decided that Robert would continue with his plans to attend dental college and a replacement preceptor would be found. The prescription for a drier climate necessitated that John Henry Holliday take up residence in the West. Charles Nordhoff, a traveler-publicist and one-time managing editor of the *New York Evening Post*, had recently published his classic *California: For Health, Pleasure and Residence*. Nordhoff described southern California as a haven for consumptives. He related the story of a neighbor, struggling for life at Aiken in South

Carolina, who having only recently arrived in southern California "ate heartily and slept well, enjoyed his life, and coughed hardly at all."[18] Dr. John S. Holliday had purchased a copy of Nordhoff's popular work on November 12, 1872, and recommended southern California as a suitable site for John Henry's convalescence.[19] John Henry's father, who was much better traveled than Dr. Holliday, argued that many regions west of the Mississippi offered climates similar to that of southern California and were more readily accessible from Georgia. After much discussion, a consensus was reached. John Henry would depart for Dallas, Texas, as soon as possible. He would convalesce there while Robert completed dental school.[20]

John Henry discussed his problem with both Dr. Arthur Ford and Dr. Samuel Hape. Dr. Hape consulted his files at the Southern Dental Depot and located the address of Dr. John A. Seegar, formerly of Georgia and now a practicing dentist in Dallas. They had maintained contact over the years as Seegar had routinely purchased dental supplies from Hape. John Henry wrote to Dr. Seegar and included both a letter of introduction from Dr. Hape and a letter of recommendation from Dr. Ford. Dr. Seegar must have been impressed with his educational background as well as the stature of the two dentists who testified to his qualifications. He promptly responded and offered John Henry a position as partner in his dental practice in Dallas.[21]

Henry purchased a portmanteau as a going-away gift for his son's use on the journey west. John Henry packed most of the clothing and personal belongings that he wanted to take. The remainder of his possessions were stowed away at Dr. Holliday's home to await his return.[22]

It was hot and humid on the September morning of 1873 when the family gathered at the Western and Atlantic Depot to bid John Henry farewell. Henry Holliday had stayed in Atlanta in order to see his son off on his trip. Father and son awkwardly embraced, and John Henry certainly promised to keep in touch. He shook hands with his cousin Robert and hugged Aunt Permelia and Uncle John, who gave him a small package containing a diamond stickpin. John Henry could never have anticipated such a generous gift. He also had a big hug for Sophie, who had tears in her eyes. She hoped that he would be able to find some companions with whom he could spend his time and have the same kind of fun as they had had around the old Holliday kitchen table.[23]

With a final good-bye, John Henry turned and boarded the 8:30 A.M. train, beginning his trip west. He was on his way to Texas.

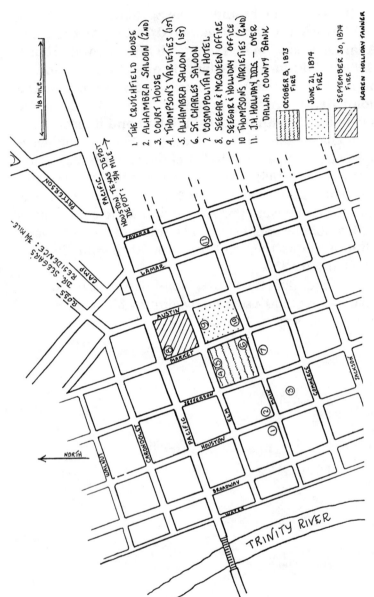

1. THE CRUTCHFIELD HOUSE
2. ALHAMBRA SALOON (2ND)
3. COURT HOUSE
4. THOMPSON'S VARIETIES (1ST)
5. ALHAMBRA SALOON (1ST)
6. ST. CHARLES SALOON
7. COSMOPOLITAN HOTEL
8. SEEGAR & MCQUEEN OFFICE
9. SEEGAR & HOLLIDAY OFFICE
10. THOMPSON'S VARIETIES (2ND)
11. J.H. HOLLIDAY, DDS — OVER DALLAS COUNTY BANK

OCTOBER 8, 1873 FIRE

JUNE 21, 1874 FIRE

SEPTEMBER 30, 1874 FIRE

KAREN HOLLIDAY TANNER

Downtown area, Dallas, Texas, ca. 1873–74

7

Gone to Texas

The Houston and Texas Central pulled into the depot in Dallas in the third week of September 1873 with John H. Holliday aboard. The long, tiresome journey had finally come to an end.

Chattanooga, Memphis, New Orleans, Houston—those were only a few of the many towns through which he had traveled. The first leg of his trip had been the 138-mile stretch from Atlanta to Chattanooga aboard the Western and Atlantic Railroad. The eight-hour train ride by day was enjoyable for John Henry since he had never before traveled through this area. The second day was spent traveling from Chattanooga to Memphis. By this time, any initial excitement must have fallen victim to fatigue as he passed through 325 miles of rural Tennessee countryside. In Memphis the New Orleans–bound passengers transferred to the Mississippi and Tennessee Railroad heading to Jackson, Mississippi. Upon arrival in Jackson, the Louisiana-bound travelers transferred to the New Orleans, Great

Northern and Jackson Railroad. By the time John Henry arrived in New Orleans, he had been gone from home for almost a week. There he boarded another train for a journey of about ninety miles across the peninsula to Morgan City, at the head of Berwick's Bay on the western side of the Louisiana peninsula.

In 1873 there were two ways of traveling from Morgan City to Houston. The Morgan Line steamer made the trek across the bay to Galveston, charging the exorbitant fare of eighteen dollars.[1] John Henry did not know if his earnings in Dallas would cover all of his expenses. Therefore, in order to conserve his funds, he most certainly chose the less costly way, the stage-coach from Morgan City to Beaumont, Texas. From Beaumont, the Texas and New Orleans Railroad took him to Houston, where he purchased a ticket on the Houston and Texas Central Railroad for the final leg of the trip to Dallas.

Newcomers to the city observed the growth that was occurring. Not much more than a year had passed since the railroad first arrived on July 16, 1872, causing the city to undergo a tremendous increase in size. In that brief span of time, the population had soared from twelve hundred to over seven thousand people. More than seven hundred new buildings had been constructed, and new businesses were appearing all over town. Retail stores were having trouble keeping up with the rapid growth, and new arrivals found that an abundance of saloons and gaming parlors had been rapidly built to accommodate the huge influx of people. Faro was commonplace, as were poker, monte, keno, and dice games. The faro dealers, called bankers, were most anxious to teach the game to any newcomer who wandered into a saloon searching for a way to spend his spare time as well as his money.

By prior arrangement, John Henry was met at the train depot by Dr. John A. Seegar, his new partner. Dr. Seegar, who had been practicing in Dallas since March 1869, was having trouble serving the rapidly expanding populace, as his was one of only four dental offices in the city.[2] J. H. Holliday, D.D.S., arrived just in time to be included in the 1873 edition of Lawson and Edmondson's *Dallas City Directory*.[3] John Seegar was fortunate to have this young associate with such fine credentials and excellent references. John Henry's sophistication, southern manners, gentleness, and good looks, combined with his modern methods of dentistry, must have favorably impressed the patients of Seegar and Holliday.

John Henry met the rest of his new extended family at the Seegar family home on Boll Street just south of Ross Avenue. He learned that Dr. Seegar, now forty-one years old, had brought his teenaged bride, Martha, to Dallas from Georgia before the war. Martha had since given birth to five children. The eldest was their daughter Lenora, who was twelve years old. The three boys ranged from Eugene, eleven years old, down to Bunyon, who was four. Several months prior to John Henry's arrival, Martha Seegar had given birth to a baby daughter.[4] The arrival of their new house guest not only brought some welcome relief to the overworked Dr. Seegar but also brought firsthand news of Reconstruction in their home state of Georgia.

John Henry wasted no time in acquainting himself with their office at 56 Elm Street, which, along with Main Street, was one of Dallas's two main thoroughfares.

Located over Dr. A. M. Cochrane's Drug Store on Elm between Market and Austin Streets, the office was one mile from the Seegar home.[5] The gilt sign on the front had been repainted by sign painter Pink Thomas and now bore two names, Seegar and Holliday. With only a handshake, the two men commenced their partnership.

Determined to introduce John Henry to Dallas, and Dallas to John Henry, Dr. Seegar expressed his desire that the partners display their talents at the Annual Fair of the North Texas Agricultural, Mechanical, and Blood Stock Association at the Dallas County fairgrounds, scheduled to begin the following week. When John Henry unpacked some of the exhibits he had previously prepared for his professors at dental school in Philadelphia, Dr. Seegar was impressed with the skill of his young partner. They decided to use these as their entries. On Tuesday, September 30, the two dentists entered their exhibits. On Friday, October 3, they returned to the Dallas fairgrounds in time to hear the announcer call out the awards. Drs. Seegar and Holliday swept the dental awards, winning three premium prizes of a plate and five dollars for each of their displays: the best set of teeth in gold, the best in vulcanized rubber, and the best set of artificial teeth and dental ware. The two dentists celebrated as their new partnership got off to a fine start.[6] Obviously, this elated John Henry, after having been forced to leave a very promising dental career in Atlanta. Perhaps these prizes foretold the possibility of success in Dallas.[7]

As John Henry settled into his new household, it is likely that the Seegars encouraged him to join them on Sundays at the Baptist Church to which they belonged. John Henry, however, declined their invitation and, mindful of his mother's last wishes, joined the congregation of the Reverend R. W. Thompson's Methodist-Episcopal Church, on the corner of Lamar and Commerce Streets. He also soon became "a prominent member of a temperance organization till [he] deviated from the path of rectitude."[8]

John Henry was barely settled into his new surroundings when, on Wednesday morning, October 8, shouts indicated that fire had broken out near the dental office. The Kentucky Store, at the corner of Main and Market Streets, just one block away from Cochrane's Drug Store, was ablaze, and the fire was threatening the entire neighborhood. Pushed by a southeast wind, the conflagration was especially threatening because most of the buildings in the area were wood-framed structures. Dallas's Hook and Ladder Company quickly arrived on the scene but was unable to contain the inferno. By five o'clock in the afternoon the entire block bounded by Main, Market, Elm, and Jefferson Streets had been destroyed. Nothing was left standing, save several chimneys. Fortunately for Drs. Seegar and Holliday, Cochrane's Drug Store was several buildings east of the fire's limits and survived. Unfortunately, at least in the judgment of Dallas's sporting crowd, Johnny Thompson's Varieties and the Alhambra Saloon, also located on Elm Street, were destroyed.[9]

The city's rapid expansion of the past year and a half stopped by the end of the year. The national Panic of 1873, instigated by the overconstruction of railroads, brought about one of the country's greatest recessions. It slowed immigration to many railroad cities, including Dallas. Further extension of the Texas and Pacific Railroad out of Dallas was halted, fueling the recession and causing the population growth to proceed at a snail's pace. The next seven years showed an influx of only three thousand additional people. On the positive side, on Tuesday, December 2, 1873, Texans went to the polls and participated in the first election since the conclusion of the war that was not influenced by Radical Reconstruction policies.[10]

The combination of his consumptive condition and the city's new recession made it increasingly difficult for John Henry to maintain a successful dental practice. Therefore, he had a lot of leisure time, which he used in expanding his circle of friends and acquaintances outside the Seegar family. The hectic existence in this family with five children was similar to the atmosphere that had pervaded his home in Bemiss, Georgia, after the arrival of his young aunts and uncle. He found he needed a private life apart from the Seegars.

It did not take long for the young dentist to discover the St. Charles Saloon on Main Street, with its popular gaming tables. He also became a regular at the Alhambra Saloon, which had moved to an excellent location on the corner of Main and Houston Streets opposite the Crutchfield House, one of the city's finest hotels. The Alhambra had been rebuilt immediately after the October fire, as was Johnny W. Thompson's Varieties/Bella Union, at that time housed in a new brick building at 44 Jefferson Street. John Henry soon learned that Johnny Thompson's served as headquarters for the majority of Dallas gamblers.[11]

Dallas's faro bankers welcomed the newcomer with open arms. They were not aware of the lessons that Sophie had given the young dentist back in Georgia. John Henry immediately appreciated the similarities between the old slave game of "Skinning" and the age-old gambling game of faro. Faro was easier to learn because the casekeeper kept track of the cards in the discard pile and there was no great advantage to the dealer, at least not in an honest game. He soon discovered that honest games were few and far between. His card-playing education from Sophie had not included any information about the vast number of cheating devices used by the professionals. He learned about these the hard way!

Will and Finck of San Francisco, the country's largest and best-known manufacturer of gaming equipment, prominently displayed the components of faro layouts in its national catalog. Ninety percent of the dealing boxes that they sold were rigged for "dealing seconds," one method of crooked dealing. Also included in their catalog was a fine line of card trimming shears, purportedly to be used to prolong the life of playing cards by trimming the frayed edges. The gamblers knew that the shears were primarily used for trimming certain denominations of cards to be a different width than others—giving the faro banker the advantage of knowing when particular cards were about to be dealt by the feel of their edges. Will and Finck also offered a vast assortment of other cheating devices that were used both by dealers and by players, including numerous varieties of marked cards, holdouts, nail pricks, and even vest cold-decking machines that allowed the wearer to exchange entire decks of cards without being noticed.[12]

The friendly but fierce competition of the games in the kitchen of Uncle John's house in Atlanta with Sophie, Robert, and George had taught John Henry to recognize a few of the sleight-of-hand techniques used by most of the faro bankers. Mechanics, as the trickery was called, was the most prevalent way in which dealers gave themselves an advantage in this game with fairly even odds. On the western frontier, cheating was commonplace and was regularly implemented in games with inexperienced players. This unethical conduct was only problematic when detected, and John Henry's good sense demanded that he practice until his talent precluded his being caught. His mathematical mind also made it easy for him rapidly to compute the odds for the appearance of the remaining cards. This young southern gentleman was quickly becoming a competitive gambler.

After introducing himself to the regulars as the new dentist in town, John Henry soon developed a reputation as a player to be respected in the sporting community. Before long, he was able to provide himself with a good supplemental income by being both a faro player and banker and a fine poker player. Bat Masterson later maintained that "gambling was not only the principal and best-paying industry in town [Dallas] at the time, but it was also reckoned among its most respectable."[13] These were also John Henry's sentiments as he acquired a faro layout, which included a casekeeper dealing box as well as a fine pair of Will and Finck card-trimming shears.[14] Fortunately, he had an advantage over many of the other players in that he had a small bankroll to use as a stake.

A southern aristocrat, John Henry knew that wealthy southerners used high-stakes wagers as a means to display their competitiveness, their courage, and their materialism. Great gains as well as great losses served as a symbolic testament to the postbellum cavalier lifestyle of the southern gentry. The Holliday men never allowed money, either gains or losses, to affect their demeanor. It would not have been gentlemanly! This precedent made a lifelong impression on John Henry. Therefore, it would have been an affront to the Holliday family in Georgia for a member to become anything more than a social gambler. As time went on, John Henry was forced to use the circumstance of his illness coupled with his difficulty in establishing a successful dental practice as the rationalization for allowing his avocation of gambling to become his newfound vocation. He was fast becoming a professional gambler, a man who made money by talent and wit from the greed of others.

On March 2, 1874, John Henry and Dr. Seegar dissolved their partnership by mutual consent. Presumably John Henry's new lifestyle conflicted with Seegar's professional image.[15] Seegar remained at the old office over Cochrane's Drug Store, while John Henry moved his practice to the second floor of the Dallas County Bank at the corner of Main and Lamar Streets, where he also took up temporary residence. He continued to pursue his dental career, but supplemented that dwindling income with increased devotion to his gambling pastime.

On May 12, 1874, John Henry was indicted along with twelve other gamblers following a sweep of Dallas's gambling dens.[16] The press periodically put pressure on the city's authorities to enforce the city's gaming codes. The *Dallas Weekly Herald* noted:

> There seems to be no settled policy looking to eliminate these elements. The thing goes on until it gets obnoxious and then there is a sudden burst of stage indignation, and the "sports" find themselves descended upon, arrested and hurried into court, where they

smilingly plead guilty, pay a nominal fine. . . . Whatever we do, let us stop the miserable sham of periodically jerking them up and fining them ten dollars, and then laying the flattering unction to our souls that we have vindicated the majesty of the law and protected society from the devil.[17]

On Friday, May 22, 1874, J. H. Holliday, D.D.S., appeared in court for the hearing. Accompanying him was T. M. Myers, as surety, who posted the absurd amount of one hundred dollars as bond for an offense that carried a routine ten dollar fine. This ensured that John Henry would return to face the charge of betting at a keno bank.[18] The residents of Dallas had been proclaiming the magnificence of their new courthouse, which had opened only three weeks earlier.[19] Surely the respected Dr. Holliday had not anticipated that he would first see the inside of the new courthouse in this manner.

He countered the shame of being arrested as a gambler by taking an even greater pride in his appearance. Every day he dressed to perfection with finely tailored imported clothing.[20] His manners matched his attire, even as he began to adopt the code of the West. He carried the revolver that his Uncle John had given to him, drank bourbon, and gambled—"but six-shooters, whiskey, and poker, however, were within the code; these things had no connection with morals; indulgence in them was neither moral nor immoral, but natural to the times."[21] John Henry had been taught the effective use of firearms under the watchful eyes of both his father and his Uncle John. Sophie had him well-schooled in card playing and wagering. He was now fast acquiring the ability to carry his liquor as well as any man on the frontier. Though the influence of his genteel upbringing never disappeared, it increasingly was overshadowed by his newly emerging western personality.

The 1874 tax rolls had been filed at the beginning of the year, listing J. H. Holliday; on June 1, 1874, he was assessed and promptly paid both a one dollar poll tax and a one and a half dollar personal property tax.[22] He was still trying to achieve a successful dental practice when another devastating fire broke out late Sunday evening, June 21, 1874. This time it was in the rear of the new brick building owned and occupied by Johnny Thompson's Varieties and Bella Union Saloon.[23] Two nights earlier an arsonist had attempted to start a fire one block south near Kingdon's Restaurant, but restaurant employees promptly doused the flames. This time the arsonist did a better job. The neighborhood's first warning was a loud explosion. The flames quickly spread through the buildings, most of which were wooden, consuming the block bounded by Main, Austin, Elm, and Market Streets. This included G. M. Swink's two-story building at 56 Elm Street, which housed Cochrane's Drug Store on the first floor and the dental offices of John A. Seegar upstairs.[24] When Dr. Seegar surveyed the ashes of what had been his office, he quickly set out to reestablish his practice by opening temporary facilities over the Dollar Store on the corner of Pacific and Market Streets.

John Henry decided to seek opportunity elsewhere due to Dallas's faltering economy.[25] Perhaps he was also hoping that a change might relieve the angers that plagued him—anger at the disease that had taken his mother's life and afflicted him, anger at his father for remarrying, and anger that he was unable to fulfill his commitment to his cousin Robert. He sold his large equipment to Dr. Seegar and notified his family of his change of address to Denison, Texas.[26] The mail addressed to Dr. Holliday that was sent to Dallas in September went unclaimed because by this time he had left town.[27] In the fall of 1874 E. E. Butterfield and C. M. Rundlett gathered information for the 1875 edition of the *Directory of the City of Dallas*.[28] They deleted the Holliday name from the list of entries both as a dentist and as a resident. Meanwhile, Dr. Seegar reached an agreement to share office space with a local physician, Dr. "Mac" McQueen.[29]

After leaving Dallas, John Henry relocated approximately seventy-five miles north in Denison, Texas. This small town was beginning to thrive as the terminus for the Missouri, Kansas and Texas Railroad. Located just five miles south of the Red River in Grayson County, Denison had a population of five thousand and was later described as the lowest of the low places in Texas with respect to bawdy houses, dance houses, and variety shows.[30] Though now a resident of Denison, John Henry periodically boarded the Houston and Texas Central Railroad, which offered daily rail service to Dallas. For several months he frequently returned to visit friends and to gamble. One of these trips was made at the end of December 1874 to celebrate the New Year.

January 1, 1875, found John Henry in Dallas ushering in the New Year at the St. Charles Saloon on Main Street, operated by Charles W. "Champagne Charlie" Austin, "a rollicking fellow . . . [who] fixes up the 'smiles' and hands them out smilingly."[31] Though the exact circumstances were not recorded, both John

Henry and Champagne Charlie were arrested that day because of an incident that occurred at three o'clock in the afternoon. The records show no bill of indictment naming Charles W. Austin, indicating that he was never charged.[32] He must have had some political clout to be released with no charge after the newspaper indicated equal fault in its rather lighthearted narrative of the event. "Dr. Holliday and Mr. [Charles W.] Austin, a saloon keeper, relieved the monotony of the noise of firecrackers by taking a couple of shots at each other yesterday afternoon. The cheerful note of the peaceful six shooter is heard once more among us. Both shooters were arrested."[33]

On Monday, January 18, 1875, a bill of indictment, charging Doctor Holliday with the crime of assault to murder, was issued by the Dallas County Grand Jury in connection with the shooting. One week later, on January 25, John Henry appeared in court on the charge. After hearing the evidence, the jury retired and soon returned with a verdict of not guilty.[34] John Henry Holliday's only shooting incident in Dallas occurred after he had moved to Denison.[35]

He returned to Denison, but soon determined that the town offered little promise. Its growth had subsided once it was learned that the extension of the railroad—which had entered Texas with the intent of building south through Waco and Austin to the Rio Grande and beyond—was not to be continued in the near future. The Panic of 1873 had again taken its toll, and the line did not extend farther into Texas until 1880. Increasingly peripatetic, John Henry once again made the decision to search for the elusive town that could cater to both his recuperation and his lifestyle. This time he decided to leave Texas and go to Colorado.

Before leaving the state, he returned to Dallas once again. On Tuesday morning, April 13, 1875, his gaming charge—outstanding for the previous eleven months—was brought before the court. J. H. Holliday, D.D.S., pled guilty to the charge. A jury of "twelve good and lawful men" heard the case and considered the evidence; the foreman, H. McDowell, read the verdict: "We the Jury in a plea of guilty assess the punishment as a fine of ten dollars."[36] John Henry immediately paid the standard ten dollar fine and thereby avoided being held in custody. He boarded an El Paso Stage Company stagecoach and began the trip to Denver, without taking the time to return to Denison. He left behind five unclaimed letters at the Denison Post Office.[37]

John Henry traveled about 160 miles in a westerly direction through Fort Worth, Weatherford, Jacksboro, and Fort Belknap to the town of Fort Griffin, in northeastern Shackelford County, Texas.[38] Before boarding another stage to continue on his way toward Denver, he stopped to take a look around this town, which was rapidly becoming known as one of the most notorious places in the West.

Fort Griffin was located along Collins Creek on a half-mile stretch of level land between the Clear Fork of the Brazos River and the military establishment that gave the town its name. The fort had been built on a mesalike hill in 1867. United States troops, consisting initially of four companies of the Sixth Cavalry and three companies of the Seventeenth Infantry regiments, were garrisoned here. The fort had grown into the largest government post in western Texas. Since 1873 the town had served as a source of supplies for the hunters who sought the southern buffalo herd that roamed the area. In 1875, when Kansas farmers overran the Chisholm Trail, Fort Griffin's location on the new Western Cattle Trail placed it at the center of a flourishing cattle industry. By the conclusion of the Red River War in the spring of 1875 and the defeat of the war bands of the Kiowas, Comanches, and southern Cheyennes, the town, commonly called "The Flat," had grown to over one thousand residents and was the largest town on the east-west stage route between Fort Worth and El Paso. An estimated two thousand transient hunters and cowboys annually frequented Fort Griffin.[39] Their presence and their money attracted drifters, gamblers, and prostitutes, and the settlement had a reputation as the wildest community on the Texas frontier.

The saloon that John Henry quickly sought was the Beehive, a two-room adobe building at the northern end of town fronting on Griffin Avenue, the main street. One of the two partners in the Beehive was his friend Owen Donnelly, the brother-in-law of the notorious John Selman. Donnelly also had recently arrived in Fort Griffin, having previously maintained a boarding house and saloon in Dallas where, as a bartender, he dispensed the potent "Red Eye and Forty Road" around the corner from John Henry's practice.[40] Donnelly, along with his partner Patrick Carroll, operated the Beehive, which had a dance hall in the rear and housed a saloon with some gaming tables in the front.[41]

After settling in for a round of gambling, John Henry once again found himself involved in a scrape with the law. On June 12, 1875, Sheriff Henry Jacobs arrested him along with another gambler, Mike Lynch, for "playing together and with each other at a game of cards in a house in which spirituous liquors were sold," a violation of both Texas state law and Shackelford

County's antigambling ordinance.[42] Mike Lynch had been indicted on the same charge only four weeks before.[43] While such indictments were commonplace and frequently were employed as a form of business taxation in other areas of the West, it is also likely that in closely knit Shackelford County the arrest was an inducement to encourage Dr. Holliday, a newcomer, to leave town.[44] Apparently anxious to avoid any further legal entanglements, he promptly left Fort Griffin, failing even to take time to clear up this minor gambling charge.[45] On June 30, 1875, an *alias capias* for John Henry's arrest was forwarded to the sheriff of Tom Green County at San Angelo, Texas, indicating that he had continued along the old stage route toward Fort Concho.[46]

John Henry's lifestyle in the past two years had not been conducive to recuperation, and he still had his tubercular cough. His cousin Robert had just completed his schooling in Philadelphia in May and was ready to begin their dental practice together. Though not yet twenty-four years old, John Henry did not know whether he would ever be well enough to return to his family in Atlanta. In fact, it was uncertain whether he would ever be able to support himself with the practice of dentistry. This frustrating situation must have been extremely depressing to the young dentist. Life continued to deal him disappointments as he tried to find a place where he could settle down, earn a living, and recuperate.

His route to Denver took him along the old stage road that had connected the various military posts between Fort Worth and El Paso. These military posts provided him with protection along the way from both Indians and outlaws as well as providing opportunities to ply his new trade of gambling. At El Paso, he turned north and crossed into the New Mexico Territory and passed through Las Vegas. He then crossed the Dick Wooten Pass into Colorado and continued on to Trinidad and Pueblo, eventually reaching Denver.

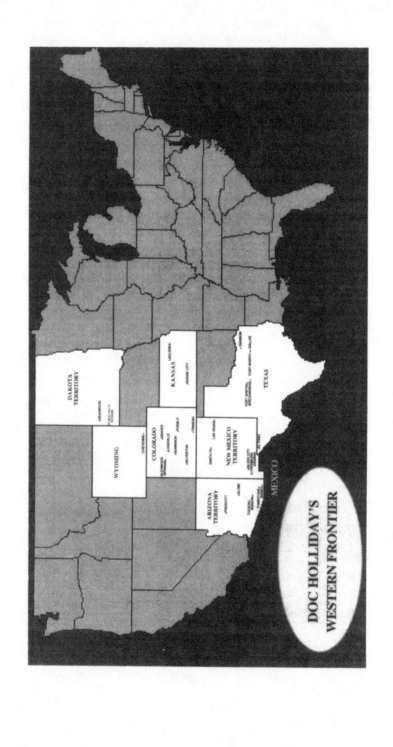

DOC HOLLIDAY'S
WESTERN FRONTIER

8

From Denver
to Dodge

When John Henry Holliday arrived in Denver in the summer of 1875, in an attempt to get off to a fresh start, he used the alias Tom Mackey.[1] In all probability, Charley Foster did not know, or care to know, the true identity of the young man he hired to work as a dealer in the Theatre Comique, which he managed. Owned by John A. Babb, the Theatre Comique at 357 Blake Street featured vaudeville acts and a saloon, as well as gambling.[2]

John Henry's attempt at a fresh start was successful: this sojourn in Denver was unmarked by any significant event—most notably there was no confrontation with the law. The following story in the *Denver Republican* (which appeared on Christmas Day in 1887, shortly after John Henry's death) was merely an invention by a journalist attempting to add some color to this rather uneventful period of Doc's life. "He [Doc] was a quiet, modest man, with a smile that was childlike and bland; he was generally regarded as very inoffensive, but one night he electrified the town by nearly cutting off the head of Budd Ryan, a well-known Denver gambler. 'Doc' Holliday alias Tom Mackey was a little better known in Denver after that."[3] Bat Masterson readily perpetuated the story:

> While Denver, in many respects in those days was a rough and ready town, it nevertheless enforced to the very letter the ordinance against the carrying of fire arms, and Holliday, for the nonce became prudent, put his cannister aside, but straightway went and bought himself a murderous looking knife. Thus heeled, he did not delay in getting into action, and in so doing carved up the face and neck of one Bud Ryan, a quiet and gentlemanly looking sport, in a frightful manner.[4]

Though the event never happened, many writers have repeated the story as fact.[5]

While dealing faro at the Theatre Comique, Doc certainly heard much discussion on the rush to the Black Hills in the Dakota Territory. Gold had been discovered there during an expedition led by Lt. Col. George A. Custer the year before. This also created a boom for Cheyenne, in the Wyoming Territory, which was the junction of the Union Pacific and the Kansas Pacific/Denver Pacific Railroads and therefore the primary point of departure for the gold fields near Deadwood in the Black Hills.[6] The stampede for gold prompted the opening of a myriad of saloons and gambling halls in Cheyenne as well as Deadwood. Both gamblers and miners came from fading mining towns throughout the West. John Henry's boss, John A.

Babb, decided to go to Cheyenne and open another variety theater, raising money for the venture by selling a partial interest in his Denver saloon to A. H. Grant. Babb left the business in Denver in the care of Grant and headed north to Cheyenne, where he and another partner, Thomas Miller, opened the new saloon, which they named the Bella Union. According to an editorial in the *Black Hills Pioneer*, the Bella Union was a saloon with gambling and a vaudeville show that was "a little naughty."[7] John Henry stayed in Denver dealing for Grant. In January 1876 Babb turned a quick profit by selling his interest in the Bella Union to Miller and returned to Denver.[8]

Upon his return, Babb presumably shared the news of booming Cheyenne, which would have added spark to Doc's already burning desire to leave. Babb lost a good faro dealer, for Doc was in the company of "a fresh invoice of Denver gamblers" when he arrived in Cheyenne on February 5, 1876.[9] By the summer, as people swarmed to the gold country, more than a quarter of Denver's dwellings stood vacant, sporting "For Rent" signs, while there was not an available dwelling in Cheyenne.[10] Tom Miller continued to operate the Bella Union Variety Theatre in Cheyenne until the fall of 1876, when he moved his production to Deadwood.[11] Doc managed to avoid any scrapes with the law in Cheyenne before following Miller.[12] He joined the cadre of gamblers in Deadwood, where he spent the winter of 1876–77. Wyatt Earp also arrived in Deadwood during that fall of 1876. Possibly it was here that Doc and Wyatt first learned of each other's existence.

In the spring of 1877 John Henry climbed aboard the Cheyenne and Black Hills stage and headed back to Cheyenne.[13] From there he traveled on the Denver

Pacific Railroad to Denver, where he boarded the Kansas Pacific Railroad headed toward Kansas City. He left the train at the railroad depot at Wamego in Pottawatomie County, Kansas, on the north bank of the Kansas River.[14] From Wamego, he rode eleven miles north to Laclede to the home of his aunt, Rebecca Annaliza Holliday McCoin, the youngest sister of Henry B. Holliday. "Aunt Annaleezie" and her husband, Alpheus, had left Georgia in 1872 along with their four children, her two from her previous marriage, Mattie and James Jones, and their two children, Hallie and William. John Henry had not seen his young cousins for five years. Aunt Annaleezie and Uncle Alf had since added another daughter, four-year-old Pearl.

Annaleezie's correspondence from her brothers had told her little about John Henry, who had always enjoyed "favored nephew status" among the family because of the difficulties he experienced after his surgery as a baby. She must have found it remarkable that John Henry, now twenty-five years of age, so strongly resembled her brothers. She had not seen him since his return to Atlanta following his graduation from dental college. Maturity had accentuated the high cheekbones and broad jawline that were shared by all of the Holliday men. He had become a very handsome young man. She could only assume the paleness of his cheeks was caused by his tuberculosis. In reality, his pallor was primarily caused by all the late hours spent in smoke-filled saloons and very few hours spent outside in healthy sunlight.

They had lots of family news to discuss. Cousin Robert had graduated from the Pennsylvania College of Dental Surgery the year before, which undoubtedly prompted speculation as to whether the two young dentists would someday be able to form their partnership. Four years had passed since the two cousins had accepted Uncle John's offer of financial assistance and had enthusiastically planned their future together. Another bit of news that was certainly a topic of conversation was Henry Holliday's recent election as the mayor of Valdosta on January 8, 1877. Surely Uncle Alpheus related his experiences as a schoolteacher, and John Henry learned that his cousin Mattie also intended to teach school. Though they all enjoyed this brief visit, John Henry must have been especially pleased to be among his family once again, after not having seen any relative for almost three years.

This visit between aunt and nephew was the last time that Annaleezie saw a member of her Georgia Holliday family. John Henry once again boarded the Kansas Pacific Railroad heading toward Kansas City. He most likely found a poker game on this train, which commonly catered to sport hunters as well as buffalo hunters. At Kansas City he transferred to the Missouri, Kansas and Texas Railroad, familiarly called the "Katy," and headed for Texas.

By June 1877 he had returned to Denison. The John Henry Holliday who came to Denison was not the same man who had departed two years previously. When he left Texas, his illusion of a successful dental career was dwindling and he was a budding gambler. In the interim, he had developed into a professional sporting man, considerably hardened to the ways of his new profession and to the lifestyle of the frontier. From Denison John Henry proceeded by train to Dallas then took the recently constructed Texas and Pacific to Fort Worth. By Wednesday, the Fourth of July, he was in Breckenridge in Stephens County, Texas.

Breckenridge had been founded in early 1876 as the county seat when the county court had auctioned off a 200-acre tract to establish a trading center for local residents. The new town soon attracted the sporting crowd, including Doc Holliday. On Independence Day in 1877, Doc was playing cards at a table with a local gambler, Henry Kahn. When an argument broke out, John Henry caned Kahn repeatedly with his walking stick. Both men were arrested and fined. Later that day they encountered each other again and renewed the argument, which quickly became violent when Kahn fired a shot, wounding John Henry.[15] The account of the feud was carried in the *Dallas Weekly Herald* on July 7, 1877, stating that John Henry had been killed. His friends in Dallas must have been relieved when they learned that the newspaper account was in error. Although the wound was extremely serious, it proved not to be fatal. A friend of Doc's telegraphed word of the shooting to Dr. John S. Holliday of Atlanta.[16] The Holliday family gathered to decide who would go to John Henry's assistance. Though Uncle John thought he should go because he was a physician, his sons prevailed upon him to stay home because of possible danger. Robert had commitments to fulfill with his dental career and his activities associated with the Georgia Dental Association. It was decided that George would go to help John Henry through his convalescence.[17]

George Henry Holliday was the only one of Dr. John Stiles Holliday's sons who was married at that time. His wedding to Mary Elizabeth Wright in 1869 had been attended by John Henry before his departure to dental school. Their first daughter, Mabel, had been born the following year and Ethel, their second, followed

George Henry and Mary E. Wright Holliday, Atlanta, Georgia, 1869. Collection of Mrs. Constance K. McKellar

in 1874. Though George was anxious to go to John Henry's aid, it must have been difficult to leave his family, which now included his first son, George, Jr., born less than three months earlier on April 22.

George boarded the train in Atlanta. Because of the completion of the Texas and Pacific Railroad to Fort Worth the previous year, he was able to travel by rail all the way to Fort Worth, quite unlike the route taken by John Henry almost four years earlier. On July 21, 1877, nineteen days after the shooting in Breckenridge, George reached Fort Worth. The reunion between the cousins was at Fort Worth's best hotel, the Trans-Continental on the southeast corner of Belknap and Houston Streets.[18] During this time together George had the opportunity to give a complete update on all of the family news. He helped his chagrined cousin through his recuperation and attempted to convince him to return with him to Georgia.[19] However, upon John Henry's recovery, George returned to Atlanta alone, and Doc returned to tension-filed Fort Griffin.

It was apparent from the moment of Doc's arrival that the atmosphere in Fort Griffin had changed in the past two years. In February 1876 John M. Larn, "a charmer with many attributes of a gentleman, but . . . an outlaw, a cowthief, and a killer," had been elected the second sheriff of Shackelford County, succeeding Henry Jacobs, who had been in office when Doc passed through in 1875.[20] Larn and his unofficial deputy, John Henry Selman, had cooperated with the vigilantes referred to as the Tin Hat Brigade. In their own way, they had cleaned up the countryside, usually by short-cutting the law. Hangings such as those of Houston Fraught, Charlie McBride, Bill Henderson, and Henry Floyd were commonplace. Posters were distributed that threatened Fort Griffin's ladies of the evening: "Leave or you are doomed. —VIGILANCE."[21] Eventually, the lawmen became leaders of the vigilance committee while stealing cattle and horses on the side. After securing a contract to supply beef to the army at Fort Griffin, Larn submitted his resignation as a lawman (March 7, 1877), finding it more profitable to devote full time to his new duties as a cattle inspector—and cattle rustler. The illicit activities of Larn, Selman, and their associates became more widespread, and killings were a frequent occurrence.

Ultimately, a reconstituted Fort Griffin Vigilance Committee emerged in an effort to thwart the lawlessness.[22] Shackelford County stockmen donned white sheets and became vigilantes themselves. They created their own lynch law to protect their herds as well as their lives. When Doc returned, Fort Griffin was at the height of this renewed vigilantism. It was a good time for him to remain in the background, stick to gambling, and stay on the right side of the law. He did precisely that.[23]

Doc checked into the new seventeen-room Planter's Hotel, run by Jack Schwartz and his wife.[24] Mrs. Schwartz "established a reputation second to none as a hostess" and assisted her husband in maintaining the friendly atmosphere for which the hotel was known.[25] Conveniently located on the southwest corner of Fourth Street and Parson Avenue, the Planter's Hotel was only one block east of John Shannsey's Cattle Exchange Saloon.[26] Here John Henry settled into a daily routine of poker and faro, and it was also at "Shanny's" that he encountered Kate Elder, a well-traveled, educated twenty-six-year-old of Hungarian descent.[27]

109

Kate was the eldest of the seven children born to Michael Harony, M.D., and his second wife, Katharina Baldizar Harony. The family had emigrated from Hungary before settling in Davenport, Iowa, in late 1860. In 1865 both parents died, leaving their five surviving children (Mary Katherine, Alexander, Wilhelmina, Rosa, and Louis) to be placed under the guardianship of Gustavus Susemihl, the husband of their older half-sister, Emelia.[28] In October 1867 Otto Smith petitioned the court to be the new guardian of four of the Harony children. According to the court records, Mary Katherine, now sixteen, "cannot be found anywhere because she went, it is said, to parts unknown and hence could not be found anywhere."[29]

In fact, Mary Katherine had stowed away on a Mississippi riverboat, traveled to St. Louis, and assumed the name Kate Fisher.[30] There she was befriended by Silas Melvin and probably shared his home and bed. The infant Melvin whose death is recorded in 1867 in St. Louis is presumed to be the child of Kate and Silas.[31] Before long, Kate realized that Melvin was not to be her lifetime partner. By 1870, still under the assumed name Kate Fisher, she was residing at Joseph Henry's Theatre Comique at the corner of 5th and Biddle.[32] Silas Melvin married a dressmaker, Mary V. Bust, in 1871.[33] Kate supported herself by assuming a lifestyle that was in direct conflict with her moral Catholic upbringing. Eventually she left St. Louis and traveled west, where the opportunities for "soiled doves" were more prevalent.

In the summer of 1874 Kate was arrested and fined in Wichita, Kansas, for working in a "sporting house" run by Sallie and Bessie (Mrs. James) Earp.[34] Here she must have met Wyatt Earp. The following year she left

Left, Mary Katherine Harony, "Big-Nosed Kate"; right, her sister Wilhelmina, ca. 1867. Photo courtesy of Albert Haroney and Hattie Haroney. Copyright Glenn G. Boyer, 1977

Wichita and was working in Tom Sherman's Dance Hall in Dodge City under her new name, Kate Elder.[35] By the summer of 1877 Kate had arrived in Fort Griffin, possibly as part of the entourage of James and Bessie Earp.[36]

James Earp. Glenn
G. Boyer Collection

John Henry had not met many worldly ladies since he left Dallas. He found Kate to be his intellectual equal. She was a stimulating companion possessed of a strong, independent nature. She, in turn, liked having an intelligent man with proper upbringing and mannerly ways, in marked contrast to the raucous, rough, unshaven, and crude men who were found in most of the cattle towns. Doc must have seen the way her circumstances had often forced her to support herself by means requiring tainted morals—much as his circumstances had often led him to deviate from the teachings of his youth. They spent a good deal of their time in Shannsey's, where she would accompany "Doc" as he set up shop at the faro table most evenings. According to Kate, Doc's days were spent in his hotel room office, practicing dentistry.[37] The two became a pair and lived together sporadically for the remainder of John Henry's life.[38]

Also in Fort Griffin at the time was beautiful, red-headed Lottie Deno, who had earned quite a reputation for herself as a faro dealer. Her beauty combined with her prowess at the faro table served as a magnet for Shackelford County's gambling element. Little was known of her background, which gave her an aura of mystery and only served to enhance her appeal. When Lottie encountered Doc Holliday at the faro table, two of the best faced off, laying a foundation for stories that would be repeated and enhanced for generations to come.[39] Doc always enjoyed keen competition.

Wyatt and Mattie (Celia Ann Blaylock) Earp arrived in Fort Griffin during the fall of 1877. Wyatt dropped in to see his old friend from Cheyenne, John Shannsey, at the saloon.[40] Wyatt and Shanny, a former pugilist, shared an interest in boxing. While at the Cattle Exchange, Wyatt also spent some time talking with the well-dressed faro banker, Doc Holliday, who was dealing at the time. By the time Wyatt left town, the seeds of friendship had been sown. This was the beginning of a relationship that would gradually bind the well-bred southern dentist to the raw-boned and weathered Earp brothers as though they were related by blood. The family bond that developed between the Earps and Doc, who must have desperately craved the familial ties that he had left in Georgia, would be strengthened a few months later in Dodge City and was to last for the rest of Doc's life.

According to Wyatt Earp, Doc and Kate's final departure from Fort Griffin was prompted by an event in

Wyatt Earp. Craig Fouts Photo Collection

Shannsey's Saloon. Doc was spending the evening playing poker with Ed Bailey, a local resident. As the story was related by Earp, Bailey was sitting to Doc's right "monkeying with the deadwood" (examining the discards). Doc warned him a couple of times to "play poker." The next time Bailey looked at the deadwood, Doc claimed the pot without showing his cards—an act well within the gamblers' code. Bailey started to "throw his gun" on Doc, who jerked out his knife and "caught Bailey just below the brisket."[41] The town marshal arrested Doc, but, unsure of the truth of his claim of self-defense, was reluctant to take him to the jail. Instead, he placed Doc under "house arrest" and ordered him confined for the remainder of the night in his room at the Planter's Hotel.[42] When Kate saw how the vigilantes "clamored for his [Doc's] blood," she immediately devised an escape plan.[43] As a diversion, she set fire to a nearby shed. While the townsfolk busied themselves in the bucket brigade to douse the fire, Kate entered the Planter's Hotel, pulled a six-shooter on the marshal, and freed Doc from his captivity. After hiding in the willows outside of town for the rest of the night, John Henry and his lady set off at daybreak.[44]

In early 1878 Doc and Kate headed north toward Dodge City.[45] They followed the Rath Trail, an important trace through the buffalo lands.[46] As they headed north, Doc wrote to his cousin Martha Anne Holliday from Texas: "[I] enjoyed about as much of this [Texas] as [I] could stand."[47]

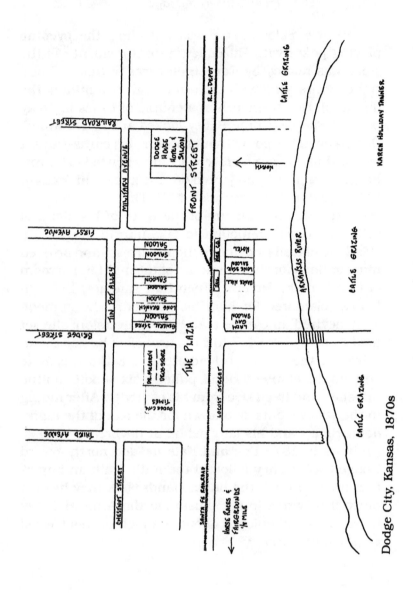

Dodge City, Kansas, 1870s

9

Following the Circuit

Dodge City was established when the Atchison, Topeka and Santa Fe Railroad arrived in 1872. In the heart of buffalo country, Dodge's major source of income was serving the needs of the hunters. In 1876 Hige Nail, the main trail boss for the Adams Brothers of Uvalde, Texas, blazed a trail with his herd northward across the plains of Texas to Dodge City.[1] This, the last great cattle trail in America, served to get the stock from the southwest part of Texas northeast to the railroad. Yards were created for grazing in the vast area south of the railroad, which was only a mile west of Dodge City. The arrival of this historic trail further enhanced the boom in Dodge City by bringing prosperity for the law-abiding citizens as well as for those who had little regard for law and order. The growth of the cattle industry in the area created such an impact that by 1878, a year and a half later, some 260,000 head of cattle were coming to Dodge—accompanied by thirteen hundred Texas cowboys flush with their pay from the long trail ride. The average drover earned about thirty dollars, or about fifteen cents per head of cattle, for each month spent on the trail. The wages, as well as the desire to spend it, built up during the drive.

Upon arrival at their destination, the trail bosses doled out the accumulated pay to the restless cowboys, who wasted no time heading into Dodge City with their new wealth burning holes in their pockets. They were seeking whiskey, women, and, of course, the excitement of the gaming tables. Always keeping a watchful eye for new areas of opportunity, the young Doc Holliday was also lured to these same gaming tables.

Prior to leaving Fort Griffin, Wyatt Earp had told his new friend John Henry about the activity of Dodge City.[2] Doc asked many questions and obviously liked Wyatt's responses. When Doc was faced with the need to leave The Flat, Dodge City beckoned. After traveling northward, he and Kate arrived in Dodge in the spring of 1878.

John Henry secured a room for them at the Dodge House, owned by George B. "Deacon" Cox and his partner, F. W. Boyd. Located on the northwest corner of Railroad and Front Streets, it was considered the finest hostelry in the city, containing fifty rooms, a restaurant, and a bar.[3] It also had facilities for buying, selling, and boarding horses, the "best billiard parlor in the city," and a "first class laundry."[4] Maintaining his reputation, John Henry continued to dress immaculately, each day wearing a freshly laundered, starched, and ironed shirt, usually pastel in color. He customarily finished off his attire with a cravat held in place by his diamond stickpin and a gray coat. The laundry in the hotel was conveniently located for his daily use. Once again Doc established a dental practice that, as always,

The Dodge House, looking west along Front Street, Dodge City, Kansas, 1874. Kansas State Historical Society, Topeka

helped him maintain his sense of professionalism, which remained an important part of his self-image. The town was very much in need of his services. Professional men were at a premium in Dodge City. There were three doctors in town but only one of them, Dr. Thomas L. McCarty, actually had attended a medical college and had a degree. Occasionally, when the heavy workload caused by the arriving cowboys became too great, the doctors were assisted by William S. Tremain, M.D., post surgeon at the nearby Fort Dodge. Because of the rapid growth of the town, the three local doctors were forced to do more than just try to heal the sick and wounded. McCarty served as the town coroner, and one of the others specialized in diseased animals as well as people. All three doctors practiced dentistry when needed.[5] Now, with the arrival of J. H. Holliday, D.D.S., Dr. McCarty shared with the newcomer the distinction of being the only two men in town who could legitimately call themselves doctor. Coincidentally, they both had received their professional education in Philadelphia.[6] Tom McCarty, twenty-nine years old, was only two years older than John Henry and had come west to Dodge City in 1872, the year before Doc had left Atlanta. Their similar educational backgrounds and their proximity in age made it very comfortable for Dr. McCarty to refer dental patients to John Henry. McCarty was an influential man in the community. He was one of the original founders of Dodge City, as well as one of the founders of the Catholic Church in town. The Methodists were also quite active, having the first organized congregation in Dodge—though it is doubtful that Doc felt a strong desire to attend.[7]

Living in the Dodge House, Doc was able to practice both of his trades—dentistry during the day and playing cards at night. The Dodge House gained local notoriety for the dances that it regularly held and was considered to be the social center for many community activities. Though it also had gaming, Doc frequented many of the other establishments as well. Among the regular patrons of the many sporting houses were members of the local law enforcement clique. It was in these places that Doc became acquainted with the sheriff and marshals of the area—including the Masterson brothers, Ed, Bat, and Jim.

The post of city marshal of Dodge was held by Ed Masterson. After he was gunned down on April 9, 1878, by Jack Wagner and Alf Walker, the job was given to Charles E. Bassett. Ed's brother Bat was sheriff of Ford County, having just been elected five months earlier on November 5, 1877. Soon after the assassination of Ed Masterson, Wyatt and Mattie Earp arrived back in town.[8] On May 12, 1878, Wyatt was appointed to be Bassett's assistant. Because of their rather meager wages, it was not uncommon for members of the law enforcement community to supplement their incomes by being house dealers or faro bankers. Therefore, the lawmen were sympathetic to the needs of the owners of the gaming establishments as well as to the activities of the gamblers. The sporting houses were located on Front Street north of the plaza and south of Dodge City's railroad tracks near the cattle's grazing area, conveniently welcoming the cowboys as they arrived in town from their long journeys on the trail. John Henry and the Mastersons were often seen at the gaming tables befriending cowboys with newly filled pockets. Doc easily helped them to empty those pockets while, at the same time, he developed a lasting relationship with many of the local peace officers.

John Henry appears to have avoided any scrapes with the law while in Dodge City. In fact, his close friendships garnered for him something of an identification as a shirt-tail lawman. Andy Adams, a trail cowboy from Texas, wrote that "the roster of peace officials of Dodge City . . . during the brief span of the trail days, were the brothers, Ed, Jim, and 'Bat' Masterson, Wyatt Earp, Jack Bridges, 'Doc' Holliday, Charles Bassett, William Tillman [*sic*], 'Shotgun' Collins, Mayor A. B. Webster, and 'Mysterious' Dave Mather."[9]

The springtime brought increased activity to the citizens of Dodge as they geared up for the anticipated arrival of the estimated thirteen hundred cowboys. The Texas trail bosses had rounded up their herds in preparation for the long trip north at the close of winter. Throughout the spring and summer, the cattle could be seen grazing along the trails during their occasional stops, before their eventual arrival at their destination south of Dodge City. John Henry decided to capitalize on the potential and remain in town through the summer of 1878. On June 28 the *Dodge City Times* carried the following announcement:

> DENTISTRY. J. H. Holliday, Dentist, very respectfully offers his professional services to the citizens of Dodge City and surrounding country during the summer. Office at Room No. 24, Dodge House. Where satisfaction is not given money will be refunded.[10]

By the time of the second annual Fourth of July festivities in 1878, the town was in full swing. The young men of the Dodge City Fire Company sponsored the celebration, which began at two o'clock in the afternoon with a parade displaying the volunteer firemen marching in full uniform. The parade was followed by horse racing held on a 500-yard course southwest of town, east of the cattle grazing pastures. The majority of the horses were quarterhorses, though there were some thoroughbreds in the area. Bill Tilghman, later one of the West's best-known lawmen, was a leading breeder and trainer and an active participant in the early races.[11] During the races, the firemen raised money by selling ice cream while bets were placed. The cowboys participated fully, taking advantage of what they hoped would be a lucrative opportunity. The horse races were followed by more races—of the foot and wheelbarrow variety. At this time, any further gambling activity moved into the gaming parlors. The final event of the scheduled festivities was a ball at the Dodge House with music supplied by Chalk Beeson, co-owner with William H. Harris of the Long Branch Saloon.[12] Beeson's orchestra provided the music until two o'clock in the morning, when the long day of celebration came to an end. No doubt Doc and the rest of the sporting community stayed busy all night.

About three weeks after the Fourth of July celebration, Sheriff Bat Masterson joined Doc for a game of Spanish monte at Ben Springer's Lady Gay Saloon and Comique Theatre on the southeast corner of Locust and Bridge Streets. It was three o'clock in the morning on July 26, 1878, and the renowned comedian Eddie Foy was spending his second summer in a row in Dodge City. Foy was in the middle of reciting a poem onstage when several cowboys rode by out front on their way back to camp after an evening of revelry. One of them let loose with his Colt's .45 pistol, shooting into the theatre.[13] Foy later wrote: "Everybody dropped to

The interior of the Long Branch Saloon, Dodge City, Kansas.
Kansas State Historical Society, Topeka

the floor at once, according to custom. . . . and I was
impressed by the instantaneous manner which they
[Masterson and Holliday] flattened out like pancakes
on the floor. I had thought I was pretty agile myself, but
those fellows had me beat by seconds at that trick."[14]
Fortunately no one was injured in that incident, though
Eddie Foy never forgot the quick reflexes of both the
gambler and the lawman. The unruly atmosphere of
these frontier towns had taught Doc that it was a
necessity of survival for a man always to keep an eye on
the door, an ear for the unexpected, and, often, his back
to the wall.

Two months later, on September 24, 1878, Wyatt
Earp supposedly let down his guard, which led to one
of the most often told tales concerning his life. Though
the versions are many and the details vary greatly, the
main theme of the event has never changed. As Wyatt

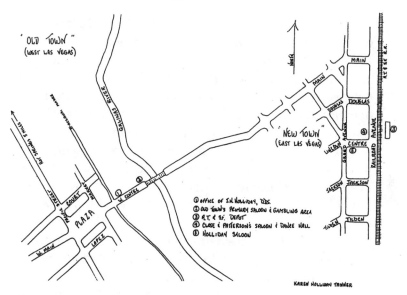

Las Vegas, New Mexico, ca. 1879

later told the story while testifying under oath in Tombstone, Arizona Territory: "I am a friend of Doc Holliday
because when I was city marshal of Dodge City,
Kansas, he came to my rescue and saved my life when
I was surrounded by desperadoes."[15] Following an
interview in 1896, a reporter related Wyatt's words:
"[Doc] saw a man draw on me from behind my back.
'Look out, Wyatt!' he shouted, but while the words were
coming out of his mouth he had jerked his pistol out of
his pocket and shot the other fellow before the latter
could fire."[16] The numerous versions of this episode
have so exaggerated the actual event that in all likeli-
hood even this account was overstated.[17] There remains
no doubt that Wyatt always credited Doc with saving
his life in Dodge City.

In the fall of 1878 Doc's health problems were causing him increasingly greater concern, so he and Kate left Dodge City bound for Las Vegas, New Mexico Territory, on the Santa Fe Trail, well known as a haven for people with tuberculosis. It is apparent from his decision to go to the then peaceful town of Las Vegas that Doc had decided to make a concerted effort to recover. Unfortunately, his health worsened while they were on the way, which necessitated a ten-day stopover in Trinidad, Colorado.[18] Wrote Kate: "Then we had to hire an outfit to take us [the rest of the way] to Las Vegas, New Mexico. We traveled with a big freight outfit."[19]

Doc and Kate, traveling as Dr. and Mrs. John H. Holliday, reached Las Vegas just a few days before Christmas of 1878, a full six months prior to the July 4, 1879, arrival of the Santa Fe Railroad.[20] At the time of their arrival, the town's main attraction was its hot springs, located several miles northwest of the plaza. Twenty-two springs were situated at the base of the mountains and produced water temperatures ranging from 110 degrees to 140 degrees.[21] Wealthy young tuberculars, who had come to Las Vegas seeking to cure their maladies, chose to reside in town, where they formed the Lungers Club.[22]

The first order of business in Las Vegas for Doc was the opening of a new dental practice on the north side of Bridge Street near the plaza. Also operating a business in the same building was William Leonard, a watchmaker and jeweler. Doc and Leonard developed a close friendship. At the time, Doc had no idea that it would later cause major problems.[23] Business proved slow as the region was experiencing its coldest winter in memory, with unprecedented snowfall and temperatures that sometimes plunged to below zero.[24]

The Adobe Hotel, Hot Springs, Las Vegas, New Mexico Territory, ca. 1879. Photo by James N. Furlong, Courtesy Museum of New Mexico, Neg. No. 138869

At about this time, the New Mexico Territorial Legislature introduced a measure that, if passed, would prohibit gambling within the territory. It was thought that the sporting fraternity would contribute a substantial amount of money to assure the bill's defeat. The gamblers did not meet the expectation and, remarkably, the bill was passed into law.[25] On Saturday, March 8, 1879, Doc was indicted under this new statute for "keeping [a] gaming table." *The Territory of New Mexico v. John Holliday* was heard in the San Miguel County District Court, Cause No. 931. On March 10, Doc plead guilty and paid the $25 fine, in reality a licensing fee, plus court costs of $1.75.[26]

This new law put a temporary damper on Doc's gaming business. Additionally, the extreme temperatures of the previous winter certainly had not helped either his health or his dental practice. All factors considered, he decided it was time to cut short his stay and leave Las Vegas. Doc left town aboard the Barlow and Sanderson stage bound for Otero then took the

"Hanging Windmill," Plaza, Las Vegas, New Mexico Territory, ca. 1879–80. Photo by James N. Furlong, Courtesy Museum of New Mexico, Neg. No. 14386

Santa Fe Railroad back to Dodge City. Contemporary accounts make no mention of Kate traveling with him, so she probably remained in Las Vegas.

Upon his return to Dodge City, Doc joined a group being formed by Bat Masterson, who was then a deputy United States marshal. During the early spring months of 1879 the Santa Fe Railroad was attempting to complete a rail route from Cañon City through the Royal Gorge to silver-rich Leadville, Colorado. The Denver and Rio Grande Railroad also claimed this right-of-way. It appeared that the Royal Gorge War, then being fought in the courts, was about to be fought on the tracks as well. On March 23 Masterson and his posse of thirty-three men, "armed to the teeth," boarded the Santa Fe train bound for Pueblo, the stronghold of the Atchison, Topeka and Santa Fe Railroad.[27] Among the recruits of this well-armed party was renowned Texas gunman Ben Thompson, who some claimed was actually in command.[28] Doc attempted to persuade his old friend Eddie Foy to take a break from his performances in Dodge and join them on their mission. Foy refused and later wrote:

> The Santa Fe, being "our own road," had Dodge's sympathy in the quarrel and, besides, there was a promise of good pay for the fighters. Doc Holliday suggested that I join them.
>
> "But listen, Mr. Holliday," said I, "I'm no fighter. I wouldn't be any help to the gang. I couldn't hit a man if I shot at him."
>
> "Oh, that's all right," he replied, easily. "The Santy Fee won't know the difference. You kin use a shot-gun if you want to. Dodge wants a good showin' in this business. You'll help swell the crowd, and you'll get your pay anyhow."[29]

Eddie Foy. Courtesy
Arizona Historical
Society/Tucson,
#28132

Bat and his posse got off the train at Pueblo, where
they settled in to guard the Santa Fe's interests. There
they remained for more than two and a half months,
eventually barricading themselves in the Santa Fe's
roundhouse. Gen. William J. Palmer, founder of the
Denver and Rio Grande, organized his own armed
party and enlisted the assistance of local county
sheriffs and Company B of the Colorado First Cavalry.
About three o'clock on the afternoon of June 11, the
Pueblo County sheriff, backed by about one hundred
and fifty deputized locals, headed toward the roundhouse where the Santa Fe force was still barricaded.
The leadership of the Atchison, Topeka and Santa Fe

force quietly surrendered, which disappointed some members of the posse who were looking for a good fight. However, they were all rewarded when Masterson reportedly doled out ten thousand dollars—bribe money paid by the Denver and Rio Grande![30]

Doc pocketed his share of the money, boarded "Dodge's own road," and returned to Otero, New Mexico, where he took the stage for the 100-mile return to Kate in Las Vegas. He knew the weather would have improved since the past winter and the climate for success at the gaming tables would also be improving with the imminent arrival of the railroad. He hoped that the peace officers of the town had relaxed their enforcement of the new gaming legislation and were now content with collecting licensing fees.

Prior to 1879, this quiet town was occupied mainly by Mexicans whose economy was based primarily on trade and barter. The Jesuits founded Las Vegas College in 1877, and, in his reminiscences, Father M. T. Hughes, S.J., discussed some of the personal aspects of the townsfolk's lives: "They live on coffee generally and that is one of the reasons they are generally so thin. They take very little substantial food, because they can't afford it. Give a Mexican 'chile,' 'buffalo meat,' 'frijoles' and coffee and he is happy. Their one redeeming trait is their piety."[31]

The Las Vegas to which Doc returned was rapidly changing from the community described by Father Hughes. It was already booming in anticipation of the arrival of the railroad. Doc's short period of rest and recuperation with the Lungers in Las Vegas soon came to an end. The Santa Fe finally arrived on July 4, 1879, making its grand entrance with a number of local dignitaries aboard, including Miguel Antonio Otero, later to be territorial governor.[32] Also aboard the train were members of the sporting element from Kansas and Colorado, who followed the railroads knowing that prosperity always arrived close behind the first train. New in town from Dodge City were some of Doc's past acquaintances. Perhaps most noteworthy was Hiram G. Neill, alias "Hoodoo Brown," a former buffalo hunter and saloonkeeper. Neill's moniker was hung on him by a dance hall girl at Close and Patterson's dance hall in Las Vegas. His shifty eyes convinced her that he was a jinx.[33] Other familiar faces included Dave Rudabaugh, Dave A. "Mysterious Dave" Mather, Dutch Henry, and John Joshua Webb.

When the final tracks were laid, the citizens of Las Vegas learned that the town had been bypassed by one mile. A town of tents and some hastily constructed clapboard buildings was quickly built by the money-hungry newcomers, anxious to reap the benefits of this new commercial center. This new part of town was full of restaurants and saloons, as well as gaming parlors and women of the night, ready to cater to all the desires of the new arrivals. It was named East Las Vegas, but the townspeople referred to it as New Town. Killings were common, often averaging one a month.

On July 19, 1879, a dance hall in New Town was the scene of a shooting. "Mike Gordon got drunk in a dance hall in Vegas and began a 'bluff' by drawing a 'pair of sixes' and firing promiscuously around the room. Some unknown person 'called the hand,' and Gordon was 'froze out.' He was buried at the expense of the county [the] next day. Vegas is a bad town to 'bluff.'"[34] Gordon had been drinking heavily when he walked into the dance hall on Centre Street and demanded that his girlfriend leave with him. She refused, and he stormed out. Suddenly he started firing randomly—some shots going in the direction of the dance hall. Other shots were heard, and a few hours later an injured Mike Gordon was found about forty yards away. He died before sunup.[35] As commonly happened in New Town, no witness could identify the shooter who "justifiably" killed the drunken Gordon before he could kill someone. This killing only became noteworthy when, in later years, it was claimed that it occurred in front of Doc Holliday's Saloon and that Doc was the killer. Impossible!—Doc had not yet built his saloon. The coroner's jury returned a verdict of excusable homicide by a person unknown.[36]

The day following the shooting of Mike Gordon, Doc sought to capitalize on the prosperity induced by the Santa Fe's arrival by establishing the Holliday Saloon and gambling concession in New Town. He brought in a limited partner in this venture, Jordan J. Webb. On July 20 Doc contracted with carpenter W. G. Ward for the construction of a one-story clapboard saloon, seventeen feet wide and thirty feet deep, at a cost of $372.50, to be built on land he had leased from Thomas L. Preston on the south side of Centre Street in the block due west of the railroad station.[37] The property commenced fifty feet east of the intersection of Centre Street and Grand Avenue, had twenty-five feet of frontage, and was just east of the Restaurant and City Bakery owned by Julius Graaf and immediately west of Sloan's Saloon.[38] Ten days later, on July 30, 1879, Doc purchased the eight-foot strip of land adjoining his saloon, probably to provide separate access to the gaming area at the rear of his business.[39] Hoodoo Brown, Doc's friend from Dodge City, became the first acting magistrate in New Town. Doc hoped that, at

Looking west along Centre Street, Las Vegas, New Mexico Territory, ca. 1881. The Holliday Saloon is on the left, beyond the second telegraph pole. Photo by F. E. Evans, Courtesy Museum of New Mexico, Neg. No. 14864

least temporarily, Hoodoo would eliminate the worry of any legal problems caused by gaming at his new saloon.

Apparently, Hoodoo did not help: Doc's name appears twice in the court records of the San Miguel County District Court within a month after opening. In Case No. 990, *The Territory of New Mexico v. John Holliday,* he was indicted for "keeping [a] gaming table" on August 12, 1879.[40] Bail was set at two hundred dollars. The next day Doc was indicted in Case No. 996 and charged with carrying a deadly weapon, a charge that carried a $100 bail.[41]

Doc and Kate were comfortable in Las Vegas and settled in for a permanent stay, as evidenced not only by his construction of the Holliday Saloon but by his purchase of the adjoining real estate. Their plans changed when Wyatt Earp arrived in Las Vegas on October 18, 1879. Wyatt told Doc about a new strike in

Arizona and invited him to join the Earp brothers and their families in trying out the new boomtown. The Earps were heading to Prescott to pick up Wyatt's brother Virgil, before continuing south through Tucson to Tombstone. After a meeting with Wyatt, Doc decided to join the Earps and leave Las Vegas. They promptly departed, leaving behind the Holliday Saloon.[42] Doc also left behind two unresolved court cases. Kate later wrote: "[Wyatt] persuaded us to go to Arizona with them. We pulled out the next afternoon. There were seven of us in that outfit: Jim Earp, his wife and stepdaughter, Wyatt Earp, his wife and Mr. and Mrs. John H. 'Doc' Holliday."[43]

The Holliday/Earp party arrived in Prescott in November 1879 and went straight to the home of Virgil and Allie Earp, who already had been in town for two years.[44]

Doc Holliday had come to the Arizona Territory.

10

Arrival in the Arizona Territory

Doc and Kate left the Earps at Virgil's house in Prescott and checked into a hotel.[1] Virgil and Allie already had plenty of help from their family to prepare for the trip south. Wyatt, Virgil, and James expected their brother Morgan and his wife to join them in Tombstone from Montana.

Prescott was founded in 1863 after gold was discovered in several of the region's creeks. Located along the banks of Granite Creek, it served as the capital of this new Territory of Arizona, which had been severed from the New Mexico Territory by an Act of Congress signed by President Abraham Lincoln in 1863. Prescott's main industry stemmed from the mines and the lumber mills. The few businesses, saloons, and gaming parlors in town easily served the needs of the miners and lumbermen of the area.

In no time at all, Doc found a faro game that was friendly to his financial well-being. About a week after

Montezuma Street,
Prescott, Arizona
Territory, ca. 1874.
Sharlot Hall Museum
Library/Archives,
Prescott, Arizona

their arrival in Prescott, the Earps had completed their preparations and were ready to leave for Tombstone. Holliday decided not to go with them because he wanted to continue to reap the benefits of the gaming tables.[2]

On March 2, 1880, the gaming parlors suffered a severe blow when the Village of Prescott passed Ordinance No. 20 requiring a monthly assessment on each gaming table or apparatus. Failure to comply would result in a fine of not less than $25 or more than $300.[3] At the same time, Prescott also passed Ordinance No. 21, requiring a fine of not less than $10 or more than $300 for discharging a firearm within the corporate limits of the town. Another blow to the gambling establishment would follow on April 1, 1880, when a territorial law was scheduled to go into effect requiring each gaming house to purchase a $500 license quarterly.[4]

When the Village of Prescott passed these anti-gaming ordinances, a damper was put on Doc's lucrative gaming business. Deciding that it was a good time to return to New Mexico and tend to his unfinished business, he boarded John A. Walsh's Star Line stage bound for Las Vegas. In addition to his business affairs, his pending legal charges needed to be settled. On March 12, 1880, Doc appeared in the San Miguel County District Court on his outstanding charges of keeping a gaming table and carrying a deadly weapon. The charges in Case No. 990 and Case No. 996 were dismissed at the request of Sidney A. Hubble, the acting district attorney. Doc recovered "his costs in this behalf"—the $300 bail that he had previously posted for the two cases.[5] Six weeks later, on April 24, Doc paid the debt he owed to W. G. Ward, the carpenter with whom he had contracted to build his saloon on Centre Street. With the outstanding lien against the Holliday Saloon paid, Ward had the payment duly recorded with the county.[6]

It was during this visit that Doc went into a saloon on the plaza in Old Town and once again met up with Charlie White, who was employed there as bartender.[7] Two years before, in 1878, the two had had a confrontation in Dodge City. At that time, Doc had accused White of theft and chased him out of town. Despite the passage of time, it is obvious that neither Doc nor White had forgotten the incident. As soon as he spotted Doc in the saloon, White drew his gun and started shooting. Doc immediately returned fire and dropped White to the floor. Convinced he had killed White, he left for New Town and the protection of Centre Street. Fortunately for Doc—and even more fortunately for White—the bullet had only grazed White, momentarily stunning him. The incident proved to be of such minor importance to Las Vegas officialdom that no arrests

John Henry Holliday,
Prescott, Arizona
Territory, ca. 1880.
Craig Fouts Photo
Collection

were made.[8] After quickly regaining his composure, White boarded the next train leaving for Boston, not wanting to press his luck and risk another meeting with Doc.

While in Las Vegas in the spring of 1880, Doc also crossed trails with young Miguel Antonio Otero, destined to become New Mexico's territorial governor. Twenty-one-year-old Otero was the manager of his father's wholesale and commercial merchants, Otero, Sellers and Co., located on the plaza in Old Town Las Vegas near the San Miguel National Bank, also owned by his father. When Miguel Otero met the twenty-nine-year-old dentist, the two immediately became friendly. Said the future governor: "Doc Holliday remained a few days in Las Vegas before taking his departure for Arizona, and I met him quite frequently and found him to be a very likable fellow."[9]

Doc returned to Prescott, where he shared living quarters on Montezuma Street with some friends, Richard E. Elliot and John J. Gosper.[10] Elliot, an early settler on Lynx Creek, was a single man and the owner of the Accidental Mine.[11] He was involved with the temperance movement, which certainly made him a rather unlikely friend for Doc. Gosper, a divorced man, was the secretary of state of the Arizona Territory and acting governor during the prolonged absence from Arizona of Governor John Charles Fremont.[12] John Henry's intelligence, wit, and social acumen continued to attract the influential members of society. The 1880 census enumerates only the three unmarried men living at the Montezuma address. Kate and Doc must have been going through one of their many turbulent periods, causing their estrangement.

According to Kate:

141

Richard E. Elliott, who was rooming with Doc Holliday in Prescott in June 1880. Sharlot Hall Museum Library/ Archives, Prescott, Arizona

In a short time Doc received a letter from Wyatt Earp stating that Tombstone was very lively and that Doc could do well there as there was no dentist there. A few days after the arrival of this letter, we started out together [in the late summer of 1880]. I didn't go to Tombstone. I said to Doc, "If you are going to tie yourself to the Earp brothers, go to it. I am going to Globe." He said, "All right, I will be in Globe in a few days too. I don't think I will like it in Tombstone anyway." We got as far as Jillet [Gillette] together and had to stay over night (where the old Tip

John J. Gosper, secretary of the Arizona Territory and acting territorial governor, when he was rooming with Doc Holliday in Prescott in June 1880. Courtesy of the Arizona Historical Society/Tucson, #44961

Top mills used to be). We had a time to find accommodations. There was no rooming house or any thing like it there. At last we went to the Superintendent, a Mr. Webber. He gave us a bed in his office. It was a good bed too. There was a store there, and we had a kind of a breakfast [the] next morning. We started out again: Doc to Tombstone and I to Globe.[13]

In spite of the fact that they left Prescott together, Doc and Kate's estrangement continued. Their paths separated as they traveled south through Arizona, though their relationship continued for the rest of Doc's life. Kate traveled to Globe, in Pinal County, where she claims to have made a five hundred dollar down payment and purchased a hotel.[14] As no deed was recorded, it is possible that she just leased a hotel or merely worked in one. She stated in a letter to her niece that when she periodically visited Doc in Tombstone she paid a friend to take her place in the hotel during her absence.[15]

Doc arrived in Tombstone in September 1880, about nine months after the Earps.[16] The Earp brothers had become well integrated into the community of Tombstone. Virgil was deputy United States marshal, a position he had secured on November 27, 1879, in Prescott, prior to departing for Tombstone.[17] In January 1880 Wyatt had been hired as a shotgun messenger for the Wells, Fargo Company. On July 27, 1880, he had also been appointed deputy sheriff of Pima County. James was employed as a bartender at Vogan's Bowling Alley on Allen Street, directly across from the Crystal Palace Saloon. He later opened a sampling room at 434 Allen Street.[18] Additionally, within six days of their arrival, the Earps had started to acquire mining claims and town lots.[19] Morgan and his wife, Lou, had arrived in the spring of 1880. Prior to coming to Tombstone, Morgan had been a policeman in Butte, Montana.[20] He joined in his brothers' business investments as well as the activities of the evening in the saloons and gaming parlors. Doc, finding his friends firmly entrenched in the economy of the town, wasted no time in joining them in various business dealings. In November 1880 he witnessed an affidavit of mining improvements for the Earps that was filed in Pima County.[21] In February 1881 Doc and Wyatt jointly purchased some water rights that were recorded with the Cochise County Clerk in Bisbee.[22] Doc and the Earp brothers regularly participated in the poker and faro games that could be found in almost every saloon in town as a means of supplementing their incomes.

Doc became a regular at the plush Oriental Saloon at the corner of Allen and Fifth Streets, owned by Milt E. Joyce. The grand opening on July 21, less than two months before Doc's arrival, had prompted the *Tombstone Epitaph* to hail the Oriental as the most "elegantly furnished saloon this side of the favored city of the Golden Gate."[23] It featured a carved bar finished in white and gilt on the right of the main entrance and a second club room in the rear set aside for the sporting element to ply their trade.[24] Lou Rickabaugh, Dick Clark, and William H. Harris leased the gambling concession from Joyce. Rickabaugh had learned the gambling trade in San Francisco, while Clark had acquired his experience in the gaming business in Denver; his credentials were considered to be among the most impressive in the West.[25] Harris had been a partner of Chalkley M. Beeson in Dodge City's Billiard Saloon, which they renamed the Saratoga. The two remained partners as operators of the renowned Long Branch Saloon.[26] The combined knowledge of the three men turned the Oriental's lavish gaming room into the most popular in Tombstone, causing the other gambling establishments in town to suffer. A cadre of the town's gaming people encouraged a small-time hood named Johnny Tyler to disrupt the Oriental's decorum, which, they hoped, would cause a decline in its successful business. In an attempt to thwart Tyler's harassment, Rickabaugh, Clark, and Harris sold Wyatt Earp a one-quarter interest in the Oriental gambling concession in August.[27] They believed that if Wyatt, along with his brothers and Doc Holliday, had a vested interest in the Oriental it would help to maintain order.

5th and Allen Streets, Tombstone. Courtesy Arizona Historical Society/Tucson, #60672

On Sunday night, October 11, 1880, Johnny Tyler entered the saloon and, when he began to stir up trouble, was promptly ejected by Wyatt. Doc stood nearby, showing obvious amusement and approval of Wyatt's action, and loudly berated Tyler. Angry over this public humiliation, Tyler fetched a pistol and returned to the Oriental. He confronted Doc, who issued a challenge, and both men angrily drew their guns. Perhaps to Tyler's relief, they were both quickly disarmed by mutual friends, and their guns were placed safely behind the bar. Milt Joyce intervened and made both men leave in an effort to avoid further trouble. Tyler vowed that he would someday get back at Doc for this public shaming.[28] Doc immediately went back to the Oriental and demanded the return of his gun. Joyce refused, and Doc stormed out, reappearing a few minutes later, now armed with a double-action revolver.[29] When Milt Joyce spotted Doc with pistol drawn, he struck him over the head with a revolver, knocking him to the floor. Joyce jumped upon Doc, and, as the argument continued, shots were fired.

Joyce was shot in the left hand and William C. Parker, Jr., a partner of Joyce's who was behind the bar, incurred a gunshot wound in the left foot.[30] That day Joyce filed charges against Doc for assault with a deadly weapon with intent to kill, and a warrant was issued to Tombstone city marshal Fred White. The next day, while in White's custody, Doc appeared before Justice James Reilly. The prosecution subpoenaed four witnesses, all of whom failed to appear.[31] Doc then entered a plea of guilty to a misdemeanor charge of assault and battery, and the charge of assault with a deadly weapon with intent to kill was dismissed. Doc paid a fine of $20 as well as $11.25 in marshal and court fees.[32]

Milt Joyce was unable to appear because of the severity of the gunshot wound. For the next ten days he remained in danger of losing his hand.[33] During this time, his feelings of contempt for Doc continued to seethe, fueled by his dislike for the entire Earp faction. He was unhappy that the gambling concession at the Oriental was partially under their control.[34]

In Tombstone Doc met up with another old friend, William Leonard, the jeweler whose business had occupied the same building as Doc's dental office on Bridge Street in Las Vegas. Leonard had opened and closed shops in both Las Cruces and Mesilla before coming to Tombstone. Wyatt wrote:

> Holiday [*sic*] was a friend of Leonard's, having known him in Las Vegas New Mexico where Leonard was established in the jewelry business. And was considered at-that-time a respectable citizen. And from Las Vegas he came to Tombstone and with Harry Head, Jim

147

Crane and Bill King and himself all went batching in a house two miles north from town, which was known as the Wells. And all three remained there for several months. Holiday would make them a visit now and then knowing Leonard so well which many people knew how friendly they were. Doc and Leonard had resumed their friendship in Tombstone.[35]

Neither Doc nor Billy had as yet opened a business in Tombstone.

On Tuesday, March 15, 1881, Doc decided to take a ride out of town to visit Billy at the Wells. The light snow that had fallen that morning was just enough "to whiten everything and it looked very pretty."[36] According to Wyatt:

Holiday [*sic*] went to the livery stable on this day, hired a saddle horse which he did quite often to visit Leonard at the Wells. The horse came from Dunbar's Stable. . . . Holiday remained there until 4 P.M. Old man Fuller was hauling water into Tombstone at-that-time and leaving the Wells with a load of water Holiday tied his horse behind the wagon and rode into town with Fuller and which many people knew. After Holiday ate his dinner, he went to playing faro. And he was still playing when the word came to Tombstone from Bob Paul to me that there had been a hold up.[37]

After dinner Doc, along with several of the other regulars, settled in for a long night of faro at the Alhambra Saloon.

That evening J. D. Kinnear's Arizona Mail and Stage Company's coach pulled out of Tombstone on its daily run to Benson, carrying nine passengers and eighty thousand dollars in silver bullion.[38] At about ten o'clock, as the stage neared Drew's Station about a mile north of Contention City, it was fired upon by robbers.[39] Eli "Bud" Philpot, the stage's usual driver, was feeling ill and handed the reins over to Bob Paul, the shotgun messenger employed by Wells, Fargo and Company. Philpot took over Paul's job and rode shotgun. The gunfire instantly killed both Philpot and passenger Peter Roerig, who was riding in the rear dickey seat on top of the coach. Bob Paul returned fire and heroically thwarted the robbery. When the horses bolted forward amid the firing, Paul skillfully regained control and drove the team north to Benson, where he reported the incident.

From Benson, a telegram was sent to Wells, Fargo agent Marshall "Marsh" Williams in Tombstone informing him of the robbery attempt. Williams immediately formed a posse that included three Earp brothers—Virgil, Wyatt, and Morgan—and Bat Masterson, who was also in Tombstone working as a dealer at the Oriental.[40] The posse left for the scene of the holdup and was joined by the courageous Bob Paul. Meanwhile, back in Tombstone, county sheriff John Behan called upon Frank Leslie and William Breakenridge to accompany him as a second posse. The Earp posse located a trail leading from the site of the holdup to the Dragoon Mountains at Helm's Ranch, then turned north to Tres Alamos. Three days later, after following the trail that led up the San Pedro River, they arrived at Len Redfield's ranch, where they were joined by Behan's group. Here Deputy Morgan Earp arrested

Luther King, who confessed that he had held the horses during the holdup attempt.[41] A frightened King named his accomplices as Harry "The Kid" Head, Jim Crane, and Doc's friend William Leonard![42] The *Tombstone Epitaph* on March 16 had stated that there were eight holdup men, which was the consensus of the passengers on the stage. Many Tombstone residents believed that the other four were Ike Clanton, "Curly Bill" Brocius, Pete Spencer, and Frank Stilwell. After King's confession, Behan insisted on taking custody of the prisoner and took him to Tombstone. The Earp party continued on the trail of the other three suspects named by King.

A rumor rapidly circulated that Doc Holliday was implicated in the attempted robbery because of his friendship with William "Billy" Leonard. The way to clear Doc's name from any suspicion was to catch those responsible so that the whole truth would be revealed. In Tombstone Luther King was placed in custody under the less than watchful eyes of Undersheriff Harry Woods. King easily escaped by walking out of the unlocked back door.[43] In addition to being undersheriff, Woods was also editor of the *Tombstone Nugget* and a crony of Johnny Behan's. He promptly published a self-serving account of the escape:

> [King] escaped from the sheriff's office by quietly stepping out the back door while Harry Jones, Esq., was drawing up a bill of sale for a horse the prisoner was selling to John Dunbar. Undersheriff Harry Woods and Dunbar were present. He [King] had been absent but a few seconds before he was missed. A confederate on the outside had a horse in readiness for him. It

was a well-planned job by outsiders to get him away. He was an important witness against Holliday.[44]

George W. Parsons, a conscientious resident who kept a diary throughout these years of lawlessness in Tombstone, recorded in his journal a somewhat different view of the escape: "King the stage robber escaped tonight early from H. Woods who had been previously notified of an attempt at release to be made. Some of our officials should be hanged. They're a bad lot."[45]

On March 24, the *Arizona Weekly Star* issued a report sympathetic with Woods's biased account. The Tucson newspaper reported that the three robbers (Head, Crane, and Leonard) were headed for Mexico by way of Tucson. "The fourth [alleged to be Doc] is at Tombstone and is well-known and has been shadowed ever since his return."[46] How quickly the *Star* forgot about Luther King! As the rumors of Doc's involvement continued, his hostility to the cowboys increased. Even Tombstone's Mayor John Clum heard Doc respond to the grapevine gossip by announcing that "he would make a sieve out of the next low-down blankety-blank who repeated the gossip."[47]

Doc's problems continued to mount as it became more obvious that Behan and his cronies were trying to implicate him in the double killing during the attempted stage robbery as a diversionary tactic designed to draw attention away from themselves. Apparently, they wanted to camouflage their own association with the criminal element that committed this and other stage robberies, as well as a number of other illicit acts. In addition, Behan was influenced by his close friend Milt Joyce, who had a well-known dislike for Holliday and the Earps. Behan's relationship with Wyatt was less than friendly: Behan had reneged on an agreement he had made in order to get Wyatt to pull out of the race for the sheriff's position.⁴⁸ The two were political rivals. Behan would love to have the notoriety of arresting Doc Holliday, the good friend of the Earp brothers, and charging him with the two murders. Finally, on a personal note, Behan's obvious antagonism toward Wyatt was fueled by the realization that his beautiful girlfriend Josie's eyes were wandering toward Wyatt.⁴⁹

Less than one month after the double killings, Doc was once more hauled into court as Oriental owner Milt Joyce continued the ongoing feud. On April 13, 1881, Doc was indicted in the court of Judge Albert O. Wallace, in *The Territory of Arizona v. J. H. Holliday,* for "threats against life" and for "attempting to kill a saloon-keeper who objected to his presence in the house."⁵⁰ When Joyce called Doc a stage robber, Doc took offense, and a scuffle ensued. The charges that resulted from this fight were dismissed when Doc agreed to pay the court costs.

Once again the Behan/Joyce faction and their cowboy friends laid the groundwork for Doc to be arrested. On May 27, 1881, he was indicted for a felony in the Federal Court of District Justice W. H. Stilwell. The charge stemmed from the Kinnear stage robbery attempt and the two murders. Because the stage carried mail for the United States government, the attempt to rob the stage became a federal offense. After posting a bond, Doc dutifully appeared in court with his attorney, A. G. P. George, on June 2, 3, 4, and 6, each time getting a continuance. Finally, the case was continued to the next session and, after still another continuance, was eventually stricken from the calendar.⁵¹

Doc's next entanglement with the law came from an unlikely source. Kate came to town from Globe to celebrate the 4th of July with Doc. Apparently the two argued, and Kate went "out on the town" with Doc's enemies. After a night of drinking with John Behan and Milt Joyce, Kate, in a drunken stupor, was persuaded by Behan to sign an affidavit stating that Doc had admitted to committing the two stage murders. Perhaps with glee, on July 5, 1881, Behan finally arrested Doc for murder. Bail for J. H. Holliday in the amount of five thousand dollars in *The Territory of Arizona v. John H. Holliday*, Case No. 30, was raised through the efforts of Wyatt Earp, in conjunction with Messrs. J. Meagher and J. L. Melgren as sureties.[52] Kate sobered up after she was charged with being drunk and disorderly and immediately regretted her actions.[53] After she repudiated her statement, Judge Wells Spicer dismissed the murder charge on July 9, saying there was no evidence whatsoever to show the guilt of the defendant.[54] Once more, Behan failed to implicate Doc. Kate promptly returned to Globe.

Doc had spent most of his summer thus far fighting the trumped-up charges concerning the murders and attempted stage robbery. Meanwhile, the real killers continued on their tempestuous trail. On June 10 Bill Leonard and Harry "The Kid" Head surfaced at a store in Eureka in the New Mexico Territory.[55] After a heavy bout with the bottle, they confided to the shopkeepers their intention to kill Ike and Bill Haslett in order to obtain the prosperous Haslett ranch in the nearby Animas Valley. The ranch was sandwiched between two ranches owned by Mike Gray, former Tombstone justice of the peace, who had strong connections with the lawless cowboy faction—one of whom was his son,

Dick "Dixie" Gray. With Gray controlling the three adjoining ranches, the cowboys would have plenty of room to hide either themselves or their "hot stock." Leonard and Head's plans were overheard by a friend of the Hasletts, who quickly located Ike and Bill at the nearby mine where the two were working. Warned of the impending attack, the Hasletts were prepared when Billy Leonard and Harry "The Kid" Head arrived. They hid behind the corral and ambushed and killed Leonard and Head. Billy Leonard, who had been suffering from the two gunshot wounds that he had received during the Kinnear stage holdup, was now out of his misery.[56] Word that the two had been killed appeared in the *Tombstone Epitaph* on Saturday, June 18, 1881. With the death of these two (and Luther King having fled the region) the only other known member of the Kinnear stage holdup gang remaining who could clear Doc's name was Jim Crane.

Crane, upon learning the news of Leonard and Head's killing, promptly organized a party of vengeful cowboys to pursue the Hasletts. On June 12 they arrived at Eureka and, following a twenty-five-mile chase, caught up with the brothers. The Hasletts succeeded in killing two of the cowboys and wounding a third, but in the end Ike and Bill were both killed.[57] The frequent killings created an urgency to catch Crane, before he, too, became a victim. Not only did Doc want him caught in order to end the vicious rumors, but the peaceful citizens wanted an end to these senseless killings. Lawlessness had reached such an extreme in the region and along the Mexican border that on June 21, 1881, the United States War Department forwarded reports of the criminal activities of the cowboys in the

Territories of Arizona and New Mexico to U.S. Attorney General Isaac W. MacVeagh.[58]

The United States government had become aware of the problem of the cowboys when the border was crossed to rustle horses and cattle from the Mexicans. The Mexicans retaliated whenever possible. The skirmishes near the border spread to the mountain ranges where the cowboys could easily hide the stolen stock. The border problems, ruthless killings, and frequent robberies brought the Southwest under the watchful eye of the federal, state, county, and local law enforcement agencies, as well as Mexican law enforcement officials. On August 5 U.S. Marshal Crawley P. Dake wired Attorney General MacVeagh informing him that he had sent a deputy and posse after the cowboys at an estimated cost of five to ten thousand dollars.[59] In addition to the funding that was expected from the federal government, Wells, Fargo had offered a reward of twelve hundred dollars each for the capture of Leonard, Head, and Crane.[60]

Wyatt Earp, at that time a detective on the Wells, Fargo payroll, secretly offered to give this reward money to Ike Clanton, Frank McLaury, and Joe Hill if they would reveal the whereabouts of the Kinnear stage killers. Wyatt not only wanted to clear Doc Holliday's name, but also wanted the glory of catching Crane in order to enhance his chances in the upcoming election for sheriff of Cochise County.[61] Leonard and Head were already dead when Ike Clanton and Joe Hill informed Wyatt that Crane had been seen at Newman Haynes "Old Man" Clanton's ranch near Cloverdale, New Mexico Territory. It is commonly believed that Wyatt Earp, armed with this information and deputized by his brother Virgil, headed the posse, which included his brothers Morgan and Warren and Doc Holliday, to pursue the fugitive Jim Crane as well as some of the other cowboys.[62] The posse left Tombstone and rode toward the region where the Arizona and New Mexico Territories met Mexico's states of Sonora and Chihuahua. In a canyon near the Mexican border they came upon a campsite. Some historians of the region and a number of local residents believe this camp was located in the Devil's Kitchen area of Skeleton Canyon. The contemporary newspapers reported that it was in nearby Guadalupe Canyon.

Jim Crane was camped for the night along with Old Man Clanton, Dixie Gray, Charles "Bud" Snow, William Lang, Billy Byers, and Harry Ernshaw. The cowboys had been heading toward Tombstone with a herd of cattle for market. At daybreak the group was awakened by gunshots. Determined not to become prisoners, they returned fire. The entire incident ended in a few minutes: though none were captured, five of the seven lay dead in the early morning light. Billy Byers, wounded in the abdomen and the arm, feigned death to escape capture. Harry Ernshaw fled amid a barrage of gunfire.[63] Notably, among the dead men was Jim Crane, the last of those named by Luther King who could have cleared Doc Holliday as a participant in the Kinnear stage robbery attempt.[64]

The posse had hoped to take Crane prisoner in order to extract from him the confession that would clear Holliday. All this bloodshed and the death of five cowboys, including Crane, removed Doc's last hope for vindication. To make matters worse, it is believed that Doc was shot in one leg, as was Warren Earp.[65] The others in the posse escaped injury during the exchange

Newman Haynes
Clanton. Craig Fouts
Photo Collection

of gunfire. Following this incident, Warren Earp returned to his parents' home in California to recuperate. When he returned to Arizona, he was still limping. John Henry probably spent his thirtieth birthday, August 14, 1881, nursing a gunshot wound from the day before. He was seen using a cane for some time thereafter.

About six weeks after Doc's injury, Kate took leave of the hotel in Globe and once again traveled to Tombstone. They had patched up their previous troubles, and Doc invited Kate to accompany him to the

157

San Agustín Fiesta in Tucson in October. It was to be a time of music, dancing, food, drink, and the ever-present faro game.

Doc had another reason for wanting to go to Tucson. The Federal Court there was scheduled to hear the case of Pete "Spence" Spencer and Frank Stilwell. The two were accused of robbing the Sandy Bob Stage on its way from Tombstone to Bisbee on September 8, 1881. The robbers had netted about twenty-five hundred dollars from the Wells, Fargo strong box and had relieved the passengers of an additional six hundred dollars. Fred Dodge, representing Wells, Fargo on the posse, had spotted fresh horse tracks and distinctive bootprints that were traced to Stilwell with the aid of a Bisbee bootmaker.[66] Pete Spencer was arrested with Stilwell, and charges were filed against the two by Marsh Williams. When they were released on a two thousand dollar bond each, they were then rearrested by Deputy U.S. Marshal Virgil Earp on federal warrants for robbing the mail.[67] The hearing was scheduled for October 20 in Tucson. Also attending the hearing, and ready to post additional bail for them, were cowboys Ike Clanton, William "Billy" Allen, and Ham Light.[68]

Doc and Kate had been at the fiesta in Tucson about four days. According to her:

> One evening at the Fiesta, Doc was bucking at faro. I was standing behind him when Morgan Earp came and tapped Doc on the shoulder and said, "Doc, we want you in Tombstone tomorrow. Better come up this evening." Doc said, "All right." He cashed in his chips. Morgan Earp did not want Doc to take me back with them; although he did not say anything. Doc said to me,

"You had better stay here. I will come after you tomorrow or in a day or two." I said, "No, I am going with you." Then he said, "We are going on a freight train." I said, "If you can go on a freight, so can I." Then he said, "We are going to Benson on a freight. Then we have to ride in an open buckboard." I said, "If you can ride in an open buckboard, so can I." They saw that there was no way of getting rid of me, so the three of us went back to Tombstone.[69]

At about ten o'clock on the night of October 25, 1881, Doc and Kate arrived at C. S. Fly's boarding house on Fremont Street. Doc immediately left for the Alhambra Saloon with Morgan Earp.

11

Gunfight in Tombstone

On Tuesday, October 25, 1881, the same day that Doc Holliday returned to Tombstone, Ike Clanton also returned. After leaving Tucson, Clanton had gone to his ranch near Charleston. He then proceeded to Sulphur Spring Valley, where he spent three days before eventually arriving in Tombstone.[1] Ike was becoming increasingly antagonistic toward Doc and the Earps. He believed Wyatt had disclosed their secret agreement regarding the reward money, which was to be confidentially given to Ike if he revealed the location of the Kinnear stage fugitives. In June Wyatt showed Clanton the telegram that Marsh Williams had received from Wells, Fargo stating the terms of the reward. Ike's paranoia led him to assume that Wyatt had discussed the secret with Williams.[2] As time passed, Clanton also convinced himself that Doc, too, was privy to the agreement. Now, two months after the still debated killings in which his father, Old Man Clanton, had died along with Jim Crane and three others, Ike was in a

161

panic. He feared for his life if any of the cowboys learned that he had sold out in hopes of receiving the reward. He felt it was demeaning that Doc and the Earps controlled his destiny: they could reveal the truth at any time.

That evening Clanton confronted Wyatt and in his high-pitched, squeaky voice accused him of revealing their secret.[3] Ike screeched that Doc Holliday had told him that he knew of the pact. Earp flatly denied the allegation, saying he could prove it when Doc returned from Tucson.[4] That evening at the Alhambra Saloon Wyatt angrily told Doc of his earlier argument with Clanton. He said that Ike had accused him of revealing the details of a secret business arrangement. Doc spent the next few hours drinking and playing faro, apparently not realizing the full importance of Ike's lie. At approximately one o'clock in the morning hunger eventually overcame him and he went to A. D. Walsh's Can Can Lunch and Eating Counter located in the front of the Alhambra, on the side opposite the bar.[5] There he came upon Ike Clanton, cursed, and called him a damned liar and "a son-of-a-bitch of a cowboy."[6] Clanton, believing that Doc already knew of the secret agreement, tried to cover his tracks by explaining in his shrill voice that he had told Wyatt of the whereabouts of Jim Crane in order to lure Doc and the Earps out of town so that the cowboys could fill them full of lead! This news must have shocked Doc, who did not mince words when he responded: "You son-of-a-bitch, if you ain't heeled, go and heel yourself."[7] It is likely that at this moment Doc revealed his involvement in the death of Clanton's father.

Virgil Earp, now Tombstone's City marshal, arrived and threatened to arrest both Doc and Ike if they did not stop quarreling.⁸ The two men parted, and Doc walked with Wyatt up Allen Street. Wyatt then went home to Mattie, and Doc returned to Kate at Fly's Boarding House. Ike went to the Occidental Saloon, where he drank and played poker until after the sun came up. Virgil Earp also joined in the game, which included Tom McLaury and Cochise County sheriff John Behan. At daybreak Virgil got up and left the game, saying that he was going to bed. Clanton stopped him and asked that he take a message to Holliday. When asked what the message was, Ike replied, "The damned son-of-a-bitch has got to fight." Virgil refused to be the courier, saying that he was an officer of the law and did not want any trouble. Ike stridently continued, the pitch of his crescendo rising, "You won't carry the message? You may have to fight before you know it."⁹

Later Clanton cashed in his chips, left the Occidental, and ran into Ned Boyle, a bartender from Kelly's Wine Room, on the street in front of the telegraph office. By that time it was about eight o'clock in the morning. He let it be known to Boyle and everyone else he encountered that Holliday had insulted him the night before and he wanted a fight. He then proceeded to Kelly's Wine Room, which was both a saloon and retail spirit shop, for another round. At about eleven, after also having stopped at the Capitol Saloon, he walked down Fourth Street—drunkenly bragging about his intention to kill Holliday and the Earps.¹⁰ A nearby policeman went straight to Virgil's house at the corner of First and Fremont and awakened him, carrying news of Ike's threats. At the same time, Ned Boyle went to inform Wyatt of the threats and told him that serious trouble was brewing.¹¹

Virgil Earp. Glenn G.
Boyer Collection

Later that morning, at approximately eleven o'clock, Virgil left his house and found Clanton between Fremont and Allen Streets, walking down Fourth with a Winchester rifle in his hand and a pistol stuck in his pants. Wyatt also arrived on the scene, and a fight ensued. Before Ike was able to get off any shots, Virgil pulled out his own gun and buffaloed Clanton.[12] After arresting the bleeding Clanton for carrying firearms, which was a violation of Tombstone's City Ordinance #9, Section 1, Virgil and Wyatt hauled him to Judge Albert Wallace's courtroom, where he was fined twenty-five dollars on a concealed weapons charge. Virgil left, after asking Ike where he would like his weapons deposited, and headed to the Grand Hotel, the designated spot for the weapons. Wyatt proceeded to berate Clanton: "You damned dirty cowthief, you have been threatening our lives and I know it. I think I would be justified in shooting you down any place I should meet you, but if you are anxious for a fight, I will go anywhere on earth to make a fight with you, even over to San Simon among your crowd."[13] As Wyatt left the courtroom, he encountered Tom McLaury, also suffering from lack of sleep because of last night's card game. Tension had grown within the cowboy camp, and all it took was an unfriendly comment for a scuffle to start between Wyatt and McLaury. Wyatt promptly buffaloed him across the left side of the head, dropping him to the ground, and walked away, muttering, "I could kill the son-of-a-bitch."[14]

Meanwhile, after tending to the head wound incurred in the fight with Virgil, a bandaged and hungover Clanton went seeking revenge against Doc. After retrieving his guns from the Grand Hotel, Ike arrived at Fly's Boarding House at about 1:30 in the afternoon. While Doc was sleeping, Mrs. Fly intercepted Clanton. She told him that she did not know if Doc was there. In spite of this, Clanton looked in both the gallery and dining room before leaving.[15] Mollie Fly alerted Kate to the fact that Ike was searching for Doc. When Kate relayed the message, Doc responded, "If God will let me live to get my clothes on, he shall see me."[16] As always, he dressed meticulously, putting on a black suit over one of his favored pastel shirts. He donned a broad hat and, because of the cold weather, slipped on a long gray coat. As he left, he told Kate he would be unable to take her to breakfast and that she would have to eat alone.[17]

Doc met up with Virgil, Wyatt, and Morgan at Hafford's Corner Saloon at Fourth and Allen Streets. They formed an imposing group, all about six feet tall and nicely attired in dark suits and coats. This intimidating foursome ranged in age from Virgil, the eldest at thirty-eight, down through Wyatt, who was thirty-three, Morgan at age thirty, and Doc, the youngest—also thirty, although four months younger than Morgan. Reuben Coleman, a local miner, approached the group and told them that he had just encountered Ike and Billy Clanton with Frank and Tom McLaury. He said that he had been standing in front of the O.K. Corral on Allen Street when the two Clantons and two McLaurys walked back through the corral, armed and obviously looking for trouble. Coleman had suggested to Sheriff Behan that he go to disarm the troublesome group before anyone got hurt. He made the same suggestion to city marshal Virgil Earp. Coleman, accompanied by one of the local gamblers, Billy Allen, then left and walked back through the O.K. Corral toward Fremont Street.[18] Virgil, in an apparent effort to appear more authoritarian, borrowed Doc's cane. In return, Doc was given Virgil's shotgun to carry. The four of them started walking.

Marshal Earp, carrying Doc's cane, had the air of a man who demanded respect. Escorted by his two brothers and Doc Holliday, acting as deputies, he went to disarm Ike and Billy Clanton and Frank and Tom McLaury, knowing full well that the four cowboys were looking for a fight and would not peacefully give up their guns. At about half past two on that cold afternoon of October 26, 1881, Marshal Virgil Earp, Deputies

Wyatt and Morgan Earp, and Deputy John Henry Holliday walked up Fourth Street. When they turned the corner onto Fremont Street, they saw that the two Clantons and the two McLaurys had been joined by Billy Claiborne and were standing in the vacant lot west of Fly's Boarding House.[19] The cowboys, unaware that Holliday was not still there, were waiting to catch him by surprise as he left Fly's. They planned to make good on Ike's threats of the night before to kill him.

As they approached the cowboys, Doc heard one of the Earps say, "Let them have it." Doc replied, "All right."[20] Then Marshal Virgil Earp called out to the cowboys: "Throw up your hands." Two shots were immediately heard.[21] It is not known, nor is it important to know, who fired the first shot, though most likely it was fired by Wyatt, hitting Frank McLaury in the stomach.[22] This fight was destined to happen, and it could have been any of the participants who pulled the trigger first. Doc had been the focus of Ike's wrath the night before as well as the object of his search earlier in the day, which culminated in the cowboys' taking their stance next door to Doc's residence. Certainly Doc needed to vent the many months of anger that had built up over the innuendos and gossip concerning the killing of Bud Philpot. Doc had the most justification to fire the first shot. However, armed with a shotgun, he awaited the opportune moment to enter the fray.[23]

During the next twenty to thirty seconds, as the shooting became general, Billy Clanton was struck by several bullets. Doc fired his shotgun, striking Tom McLaury, who ran down Fremont Street and fell dead from twelve buckshot wounds on the right side, all within a four-inch diameter.[24] Morgan Earp was shot in

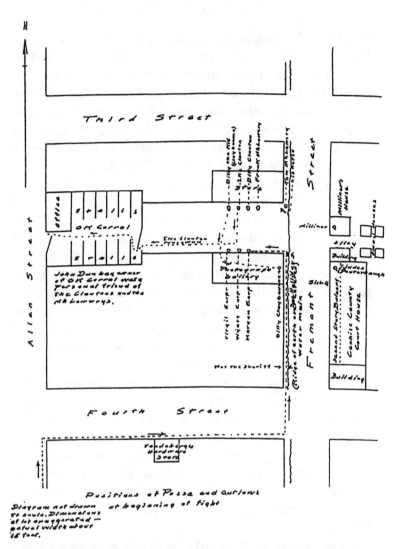

Positions of participants at onset of October 26, 1881, Tombstone gunfight, according to Wyatt Earp. Estelle Miller, Wyatt Earp's niece, said that Wyatt and John Flood drew maps at her kitchen table. This and the following map, drawn in colored ink, were published in *Wyatt Earp* by Wyatt S. Earp, commonly called the Flood manuscript. Copyright 1981 Glenn G. Boyer

the right shoulder. The bullet penetrated his shoulder muscle, continued across his back, clipping a vertebra, and exited through his left shoulder. Virgil was shot through the right calf. Doc then tossed the shotgun, drew his pistol, and started firing at the wounded Frank McLaury in the middle of Fremont Street.[25] About ten to twelve feet from Doc, Frank McLaury yelled, "I've got you this time." Doc responded, "Blaze away! You're a daisy if you have."[26] Both Morgan and Doc returned Frank McLaury's fire. Doc was struck on his holster and yelled, "I am shot right through."[27] Morgan Earp fell; when Frank McLaury also fell, Doc ran toward him yelling, "The son-of-a-bitch has shot me, and I mean to kill him."[28] Frank McLaury was in his final death throe and died from a head wound beneath the right ear and a wound in the abdomen.[29]

Within a minute, the months of tension climaxed and the shooting ended. The McLaury brothers and Billy Clanton were dead. Ike Clanton and Billy Claiborne had escaped death when they fled. Doc returned to his room at Fly's Boarding House. According to Kate, he came in, sat on the side of the bed, cried, and said, "Oh, this is just awful—awful." He was all broken up. She asked, "Are you hurt?" Doc said no, but when he removed his clothing there was a red streak about two inches long across his hip where Frank McLaury's bullet had grazed him.[30]

A coroner's inquest was held three days later on October 29. John Henry Holliday and the three Earp brothers were charged with the killings of Billy Clanton, Frank McLaury, and Tom McLaury.[31] Virgil and Morgan, due to their wounds, were not served, but Wyatt and Doc were arrested by Sheriff John Behan. Justice Wells Spicer set their bail at ten thousand

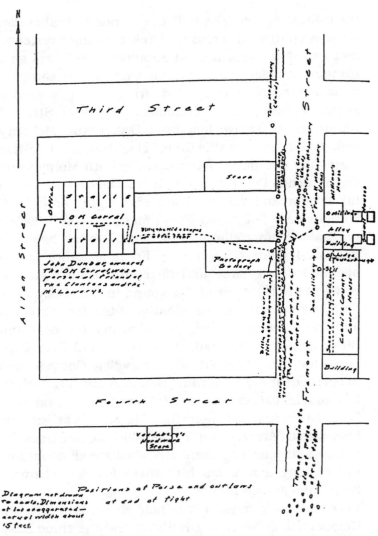

Positions of participants at conclusion of October 26, 1881, Tombstone gunfight, according to Wyatt Earp. Copyright 1981 Glenn G. Boyer

dollars each. Doc and Wyatt were both able to raise the bond money and leave the jail. During the inquest, attorney Will McLaury, the brother of the two dead McLaurys, arrived from Texas. After gaining admittance to the Arizona bar, he was able to make a motion in the courtroom that put pressure on Judge Spicer to reincarcerate Doc and Wyatt. They were rearrested and held without bond. A writ of habeas corpus dated November 7 was filed in the court of Judge J. H. Lucas. Justice Spicer was forced to set bond. This time he decided upon forty-two thousand dollars for the two combined.[32] With much assistance, Doc and Wyatt were able to raise bail. Many friends joined forces to raise the funds, including Wells, Fargo's undercover agent, Fred Dodge; Albert Billicke of the Cosmopolitan Hotel; William Hutchinson, later proprietor of the Bird Cage Opera House; Wyatt's mining partner, R. J. Winders; as well as James Earp. Once again, Doc and Wyatt were released.

The inquest was presided over by Justice Spicer and after some four weeks of testimony he gave his ruling on November 29. Spicer indicated that Virgil Earp, as chief of police, "committed an injudicious and censurable act" in employing Doc, Wyatt, and Morgan to assist him in attempting to control the Clantons and the McLaurys. He also determined that he could attach no criminality to the unwise act. In considering all of the conflicting testimony, Spicer found that Doc and the Earps were discharging their official duty and that they would not be convicted of any offense on the evidence by a trial jury.[33]

The verdict outraged the cowboys, who threatened to kill Doc and the Earps. Less than two weeks after the trial, on December 12, 1881, acting governor John J.

Gosper, Doc's acquaintance and former lodging-mate from Prescott, was compelled to telegraph President Chester A. Arthur informing him that arms were to be provided to Tombstone's Committee of Safety in order to assist in the peacekeeping efforts. Gosper sought the use of the military to protect the town against the new dangers that were anticipated because of the threats circulating throughout Tombstone. The talk was that a number of individuals had been marked for death by the cowboy faction.[34] The Earps and Doc Holliday took up secure residence in Billicke's Cosmopolitan Hotel.[35] Kate returned to the safety of the hotel in Globe.

Two days after Gosper sent the telegram to President Arthur, John Clum boarded the Benson stage on the initial leg of a trip to Washington, D.C. On December 12 the coach carrying the editor of the *Tombstone Epitaph* was fired upon.[36] Soon after, Justice Spicer received a message threatening his life if he failed to leave town. Less than two weeks later, late in the evening on December 28, there was an attempt to assassinate Virgi   p while he was crossing Fifth Street on his way back to his hotel from the Oriental Saloon. Shots were fired from the Huachuca Water Company building, which was then under construction. Buckshot struck him in the back and in the left elbow, which was badly shattered, leaving his arm permanently disabled. Immediately after the shooting, three men were seen running past the ice house on Toughnut Street, about one block away.[37] The belief in town was that Will McLaury was masterminding a vengeful attack against Holliday and the Earps. Using both legal and illegal means, he was working in conjunction with Ike Clanton and Curly Bill Brocius.[38] Wyatt also believed that Hank Swilling and Frank Stilwell were involved.

The tension carried over into the new year when Doc and John Ringo had a confrontation on Tuesday, January 17, 1882. The diary of George W. Parsons contained the following notation for that day: "Much bad blood in the air this afternoon. Ringo and Doc Holiday [*sic*] came nearly having it with pistols. . . . Bad time expected with the cowboy leader and D. H. I passed both not knowing blood was up. One with hand in breast pocket and the other probably ready."[39] Parsons later wrote: "I heard the latter [Holliday] say 'All I want of you is ten paces out in the street.' A few paces away was Wyatt, and across the street was a man with a rifle watching proceedings. The stage was complete for an encounter but it did not come off at that time."[40] The new chief of police, James Flynn (who had replaced the injured Virgil), quickly intervened, and both Doc and Ringo were arrested for carrying weapons on the street.[41] They subsequently appeared in Judge Albert Wallace's court and were each fined thirty dollars.[42]

On February 9, 1882, in an act of desperation, Will McLaury and Ike Clanton resorted to legal means and sought to reopen the case against Doc and the Earps. An order to arrest J. H. Holliday, Wyatt, Morgan, and Virgil Earp was issued by Justice J. B. Smith in Contention, Arizona. Doc and the Earps promptly sought a writ of habeas corpus, which was granted by Judge J. H. Lucas on February 11. Yet another charge was filed against Doc and the Earps on February 15 in Tombstone in Lucas's court. He promptly threw out the charges.[43]

The revenge continued, with little consideration for the law. On Saturday evening, March 18, 1882, Morgan Earp was fatally shot while playing billiards in

Letter of Ike Clanton to Billy Byers, February 14, 1882, which says, "I have got the Earps all in jail and am not going to unhitch." Craig Fouts Photo Collection

Morgan Earp. Glenn
G. Boyer Collection

Campbell and Hatch's Billiard Parlor on Allen Street.[44] The shots were fired from an alley through the rear window at ten minutes before eleven.[45] Wyatt, a spectator at the billiard game, held his wounded brother and heard Morgan utter his last words. Wyatt promised, "I'll get even Morg!"[46] Then Morgan breathed his final breath. When Doc got the news of his death he went berserk, kicking in doors of private homes looking for attorney Will McLaury and Sheriff Johnny Behan, believing that they were responsible for the murder of his good-natured, fun-loving friend.[47]

The following morning, the coroner held an inquest to investigate the shooting of Morgan Earp. Mrs. Marietta

Spencer testified that about midnight the night before her husband, Pete, had returned home accompanied by Frank Stilwell, "Indian Charlie" Florentino Cruz, and John Doe Freis.[48] This was only one hour after Morgan had been shot. Mrs. Spencer also testified that prior to coming to the inquest her husband had threatened her with violence if she related what she knew. In direct defiance of her husband, she stated that she believed her husband and Frank Stilwell had killed Morgan Earp with the assistance of Indian Charlie, who served as lookout. A grief-stricken Wyatt also testified on Sunday morning before joining the funeral cortege that was departing for the train depot in Contention shortly after noon. Wyatt, blaming the entire cowboy faction for his brother's murder, became obsessed with eradicating his enemies. Doc was fully in accord, and they began a vendetta that ultimately resulted in the deaths of Frank Stilwell, Florentino Cruz, Curly Bill Brocius, Johnny Barnes, and John Ringo.

Before beginning this path of vengeance, Wyatt had to arrange for the safe transport of Morgan's body to Colton, California, for burial near the Earp family home. Doc assisted in planning the train trip, which also included moving the wounded Virgil and his wife, Allie, along with Mattie and Morgan's widow, Lou, from Tombstone. Doc was confident that Kate was out of harm's way back at the hotel in Globe.

Prior to the conclusion of the coroner's inquest, Wyatt, accompanied by his brother Warren, Doc Holliday, and friends "Turkey Creek" Jack Johnson and Sherman McMasters, left the Cosmopolitan Hotel on Sunday, March 19. Wyatt and his posse escorted the wounded Virgil, the Earp wives, and the body of Morgan

Earp north to Contention. There they boarded a train bound for Tucson, where Virgil and the wives would accompany Morgan's casket on a train heading toward the Earp home in Colton. James and Bessie Earp, along with Wyatt's common-law wife, Mattie, boarded a subsequent train for Colton.

Coincidentally, aboard an earlier train to Tucson on Sunday was Frank Stilwell, about to be charged as one of the murderers of Morgan Earp.[49] He was scheduled to appear before the grand jury in Tucson on charges of having robbed the United States mail during the Bisbee stage robbery the previous September. Shortly after seven o'clock on Monday evening the train bearing Doc Holliday, the Earps, a few friends, and the body of Morgan Earp pulled into the train depot in Tucson. In the station awaiting the train's arrival were Ike Clanton and one of Morgan's murderers, Frank Stilwell![50] Upon spotting the entire Earp posse, Ike fearfully left the depot while Morgan's casket, accompanied by Virgil and the ladies, was transferred to the train bound for California. After Doc, Wyatt, and the remaining members of the funeral entourage left Tucson the following morning, a trackman for the Southern Pacific Railroad discovered the bullet-riddled body of Frank Stilwell alongside the tracks.[51]

Doc, Wyatt and Warren Earp, McMasters, and Johnson proceeded to the Papago railroad station nine miles to the east. There they flagged down a freight train for the return trip to Contention, where they were met by friends and taken to Tombstone.[52] When the group arrived home on March 21, Sheriff Behan informed Doc and Wyatt that a warrant had been issued in Tucson for their arrest. But, when he attempted to administer the warrant, Doc and Wyatt refused to be arrested.[53] Sheriff

Behan ignored the proclamation of John Carr, mayor of Tombstone,[54] who stated that he had been informed by Judge William H. Stilwell of the District Court that Wyatt Earp and his posse had been entrusted with warrants for the arrest of people charged with diverse criminal offenses. Judge Stilwell requested cooperation from the townspeople.[55] Though Wyatt, Doc, and the other posse members may have been acting within the law, they did stretch legality to its limit and possibly beyond. Wyatt never denied being on the revenge trail and savoring it. The code of the West took precedence over the laws of the Territory. Behan proceeded to deputize the area's toughest men, all enemies of Doc and the Earps, to assist in the arrest. Included in Behan's newly deputized posse were Ike Clanton and John Ringo.

Doc and his friends knew they were in great peril because their act of revenge had infuriated the remaining members of the cowboy mob, now also operating as a posse. For safety's sake, they decided to leave Tombstone immediately. Before departing, Doc, out of concern for his family back home in Georgia, instigated the writing of a letter to his father. He expected it to vindicate him in the eyes of his family. News of this letter was published in the *Valdosta Times*: "His father [Henry Burroughs Holliday] who is a quiet citizen, and who three or four terms was mayor of this town . . . received a letter signed by a large number of citizens of Tombstone entirely exonerating John from the charge of willful murder. Of the subsequent murder and outrages which are charged to 'Doc' Holliday his father knows nothing. We can but hope the charges are ill founded."[56] Fortunately for Doc's reputation, when the *Atlanta Constitution* reported news of the gunfight and deaths of the two McLaurys and Billy Clanton, it failed to mention the involvement of J. H. Holliday, D.D.S., formerly of Atlanta. This spared Doc's uncle, Dr. John S. Holliday, as well as his cousins back home, any immediate embarrassment.[57]

The arrangements for a swift departure from Tombstone were made easier because the rest of the Earp family was safely on its way to Colton. The vengeance seekers, including Doc, Wyatt and Warren Earp, Sherman McMasters, Turkey Creek Johnson, and "Texas Jack" Vermillion, left Tombstone in the early morning hours of March 22, only one day after the discovery of Stilwell's body. Later that same morning Doc, the Earps, and their posse rode into Pete Spencer's wood camp in the South Pass in the Dragoon Mountains seeking Spencer and Indian Charlie.[58] The following morning, March 23, the body of Indian Charlie was found riddled with bullets.[59] Another day passed before the slaying of Curly Bill Brocius in the midafternoon near Iron Springs in the Whetstone Mountains. Also gunned down in the struggle was Johnny Barnes, who later died from wounds incurred in this fight.[60]

The Earp posse spent that night camping in the Whetstones. In the morning they were joined by Dan Tipton, who brought both news and money from Tombstone. The posse then headed to the Dragoon Summit, where they flagged down an eastbound train on the afternoon of March 26. Seeking the rest of Morgan's assassins, they all boarded the train; after a fruitless search of every car, they got off the train and continued on toward the mountains.[61] The small group had dinner that day at Henderson's ranch and then camped in a grassy area one mile north.[62]

At seven o'clock on the morning of March 27 they left camp and proceeded north to Col. Henry C. Hooker's

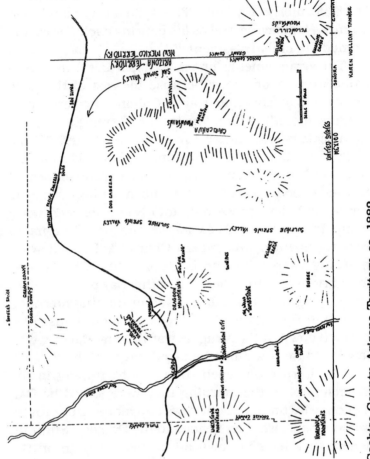

Cochise County, Arizona Territory, ca. 1882

Sierra Bonita Ranch in Graham County. The colonel showed them proper hospitality and provided them with food as well as feed for the horses.[63] The details of this portion of the trek were related in a letter dated April 4, 1882, signed "One of them" and addressed to the *Tombstone Epitaph*. Clearly, the purpose of this sarcastic letter was to ridicule and humiliate Sheriff Johnny Behan. The letter to the editor said: "Next morning, not being in a hurry to break our camp, our stay was long enough to notice the movements of Sheriff Behan and his posse of honest ranchers, with whom, if they had possessed the trailing abilities of an average Arizona ranchman, we might have had trouble, which we are not seeking." The chiding letter continued with a reference to the hot trail that the Holliday/ Earp party was following to find the lost Charley Ross. "We are confident that our trailing abilities will soon enable us to turn over to the 'gentlemen' the fruits of our efforts so that they may not again return to Tombstone empty-handed."[64] The tragic kidnapping of Charlie Brewster Ross on July 1, 1874, in Germantown, New York, had made the national press and the search for the boy remained a news item for many years. The writer's caustic wit, grammatical propriety, and awareness of national news clearly suggest the sense of humor and the education of John Henry Holliday.[65]

Presumably, the seven men never got to see this letter in print because they continued northeast toward New Mexico, probably by way of the Cedar Springs Road to the Gila River. They may have followed the river east as they were bound for Silver City.

12

Refuge in Colorado

On April 7, 1882, Doc, the Earps, and the rest of their group surreptitiously arrived in Silver City, New Mexico Territory. They found lodging in a private dwelling under assumed names. Their arrival in New Mexico was not known to the public until well after their departure, when the *New Southwest and Grant County Herald* published the following item:

Last Saturday evening at 10 o'clock, the Earp Boys' party and Doc Holliday were in Silver City. They went at once to the Exchange Hotel to find a stage agent to make arrangements to leave the next morning on the Deming coach. They slept in a private house up town and took breakfast the next morning in the Broadway restaurant, as they had not registered at any hotel, it was not known they were in town until after their departure. The party came on horseback, and put up at the Elephant Corral. They were all mounted and armed to the teeth. One of the men when asked his name, answered John Smith, and another Bill Snooks. This excited the suspicion of Mr. White, proprietor of the Corral, and the next morning when they offered to sell him their horses, he refused to buy them, fearing to get himself in trouble. They offered six of their horses for $300, but as the horses were worth more than that, this offer was also looked on as unfavorable to them. They finally sold the six horses to Mr. Miller, who is about to start a livery stable here.[1]

The *Las Vegas Daily Optic* reported that after riding the stage to Fort Cummings they boarded the Santa Fe Railroad at nearby Deming. From Deming, they journeyed through Socorro to Albuquerque, where they remained about ten days with Frank McLane, a close friend of Wyatt's from Dodge City, who loaned them two thousand dollars.[2] Again boarding the train, the seven men traveled through Las Vegas and into the new state of Colorado, getting off the train at the station near Trinidad in the small town of El Moro. They spent several days in Trinidad with Bat Masterson, then the city marshal.[3] There they decided to separate. McMasters and Johnson split from the group and ended up in Utah. Vermillion's path eventually led him to Virginia.[4] Before continuing on their way, they split the two thousand dollars among themselves.[5] About May 7 Doc arrived in Pueblo aboard the Denver and Rio Grande Railroad. Shortly thereafter, the Earps and Tipton left Trinidad for Gunnison, Colorado, clandestinely establishing their camp outside of town near the Chinery Ranch.[6] It was obvious that they were attempting to create difficulty for any pursuing deputy armed with an arrest warrant from Arizona.[7] Doc stayed in Pueblo to spend time with some old acquaintances, a decision that proved to be unfortunate.

A few days after his arrival in Pueblo, Doc, feeling comfortable that he had safely escaped the ire of the cowboys in Arizona, was in Tom Kemp's Comique Variety Theatre. He was approached by a stranger who called himself Perry M. Mallen. Mallen claimed that Doc had once saved his life in Santa Fe, New Mexico, and, desiring to return the favor, told Doc that Stilwell's brother was in Pueblo to avenge Frank's death.[8] Doc responded that he had never been in Santa Fe so could not possibly be the person who previously had saved Mallen's life, but thanked him for the Stilwell information. Though Mallen acted in a suspicious manner, apparently Doc temporarily forgot the incident.[9]

The following Sunday, May 14, 1882, Doc joined up with Bat Masterson, Sam Osgood, and another friend known only as Texas George. The four men left Pueblo to attend the races scheduled to be held the following Tuesday in Denver. After the races Doc planned to put more distance between himself and the cowboys and travel on toward the Wood River country.[10] The foursome arrived in Denver on Monday and registered at the recently constructed Windsor Hotel, managed by Maxcy Tabor and Bill Bush.[11] Located on the northeast corner of Eighteenth and Larimer Streets, the five-floor, 300-room Windsor had floors of white marble with plush red carpeting and a sixty-foot mahogany bar. The lavish decor along with its Russian and Turkish baths made the hotel the talk of Denver.

About nine o'clock on Monday evening, Doc walked back toward the hotel after dinner. He passed under an

electric street lamp in front of Daniels and Fisher's Dry
Goods and Carpet Shop on the southeast corner of
Sixteenth and Lawrence Streets. Hearing his name
called, he turned and was ordered to hold up his hands.
He was arrested and handcuffed by Perry Mallen, now
claiming to be a Los Angeles County deputy sheriff.
Accompanied by Arapahoe County deputy sheriffs
Charles T. Linton and Bernard G. "Barney" Cutler,
Mallen alleged that he had an Arizona warrant for the
arrest of John H. Holliday for the killing of Frank
Stilwell. As a crowd gathered, they immediately walked
Doc to the nearby sheriff's office, where a cab was
summoned to transport him to the county jail.[12]

It can be presumed that Mallen must have been a
paid envoy sent by Behan and his cohorts back in
Tombstone. He would go to any extreme just to get Doc
back in the Arizona Territory and into the clutches of
the discredited Sheriff Johnny Behan, who was still
chagrined by having allowed Doc and the Earps to
escape Tombstone and the outstanding warrant seven
weeks earlier. At the jail Doc issued a call for help to
Sheriff Bat Masterson. Masterson, with the assistance
of Denver attorney Frank A. Naylor of the law firm of
Naylor and Richardson, promptly set out to secure a
writ of habeas corpus for Doc. At half past three the
next morning, District Judge Victor A. Elliot signed the
writ and ordered Arapahoe County sheriff Michael
Spangler to have Holliday appear before the court later
that morning.[13]

The newspapers in Colorado, as well as Arizona,
carried the headline news of the arrest of Doc Holliday.
Typically, the newspapers were partisan. Many of the
journalists rallied behind Doc, and their papers carried
articles of the depredations of the Arizona cowboys.

Others portrayed Holliday as a murderer who deserved to be behind bars. Though their points of view often differed, they all described him as a handsome gentleman of tall, slender stature with a sophisticated, softspoken manner and piercing blue eyes. On May 22, 1882, the *Denver Republican* wrote: "His features are well-formed and there is . . . a well-defined look of determination from his eyes. . . . Holliday was dressed neatly in black, with a colored linen shirt. The first thing noticeable about him in opening the conversation was his soft voice and modest manner." The *Pueblo Daily Chieftain* stated on May 17, 1882, that "Doc Holliday is a man of light weight, rather tall, smoothly shaven, and is always well dressed. Streaks of gray can be seen in his hair. . . . His eyes are blue, large, sharp and piercing. He is not over thirty five years of age, and as straight as an arrow. He is well educated, and his conversation shows him to be a man of considerable culture." That same day Denver's *Rocky Mountain News* indicated that "Holladay [sic] is a delicate, gentlemanly-looking man, slightly built and with prematurely gray hair. He wears a heavy sandy mustache." The *Denver Daily Times* noted on May 16, 1882, that Doc was "a delicate, gentlemanly man, . . . perhaps thirty-five years of age."

While Doc languished in jail, Perry Mallen, the center of press attention, wove an outrageous tale of a seven-year pursuit. He claimed that Doc had murdered Mallen's friend Harry White in Utah and had then led him on a chase that involved cattle theft, stage robbery, and many more killings. While Mallen regaled reporters with outrageous claims, Doc busily attempted to set the record straight. He maintained that he had never been to Utah and had never robbed a stage. The warrant was obviously a phony because Frank Stilwell had been killed in Pima County, and Mallen's warrant was from Cochise County. Doc asserted that this claim was merely a plot to return him to Arizona and certain death at the hands of the cowboys. In an interview with the *Denver Republican* he stated: "We hunted the rustlers, and they all hate us. John Behan, Sheriff of Cochise County, is one of the gang, and a deadly enemy of mine, who would give any money to have me killed. It is almost certain that he instigated the assassination of Morgan Earpp [sic]. Should he get me in his power my life would not be worth much."[14] Many respectable citizens backed Holliday and defended his character. Bat Masterson also rose to his defense: "I tell you all of this talk is wrong about Holliday. I know him well. He is a dentist and a good one." Bat went on to claim that Mallen was a fraud "and a friend of the cowboys, whose only object is to get Holliday back in order that he might be killed."[15]

Also stepping in to defend John Henry was Lee Smith, an old friend of the Holliday family from Georgia. Smith had been a liquor and tobacco merchant in Griffin and had known both Henry and Alice Holliday.[16] He later became an investment banker and was now living in Denver overseeing his investment in some gold mines. Smith met with John Henry and assured him that he would help in any way possible. Additionally, he was soon leaving on a trip to Atlanta and promised to contact Dr. John S. Holliday to ensure that he heard an accurate report of this Denver ordeal. Smith met with Governor Frederick W. Pitkin and attempted to persuade him to intercede in favor of John Henry. Upon his arrival in Atlanta, he granted an interview with the *Atlanta Constitution,* which twisted the story of John Henry's life and troubles in the West.[17] Smith met with Dr. Holliday and delivered some letters and an article from his nephew.[18] Dr. Holliday, a *Constitution* reader, must have been infuriated by the way his newspaper had fictionalized the story and shaded its portrayal of John Henry's character. Presumably Henry Holliday was equally livid when the *Valdosta Times* reprinted the same *Constitution* article about his son three days later. In an interview with the *Atlanta-Post Appeal*, Lee Smith described Doc as "one of the best boys that ever lived, if he is left alone, but you mustn't impose upon him or you will smell burning powder."[19]

After his visit with Smith, John Henry was named on another warrant. On Wednesday, May 17, Pueblo County charged him with operating a confidence game that resulted in the loss of one hundred and fifty dollars by his victim. The following day City Marshal Jamieson of Pueblo walked into Sheriff Spangler's office with the warrant for Holliday's arrest, seeking custody of the prisoner. It was immediately evident that this charge was fabricated by Bat Masterson and other Holliday supporters to keep him safe from the wrath of the cowboys should he be released under the writ. Jamieson was refused custody until the completion of the habeas corpus hearing.

While Doc was incarcerated awaiting the hearing, Sheriff Behan in Tombstone received notification from the office of Arizona's Governor Frederick A. Tritle. The governor would not issue a requisition order to Colorado asking for the return of Holliday because the warrant was issued by a county other than the one in which the murder of Stilwell had occurred. Behan quickly contacted Pima County sheriff Bob Paul, asking him to issue a warrant from Pima County and to request a requisition from the governor for the return of John H. Holliday. After complying with Behan's request, Sheriff Paul realized that the arrest and ensuing return to Arizona would place Holliday's life in jeopardy. He immediately left for Colorado so that he could personally oversee the extradition to Arizona. Doc's friends in Colorado agreed with Sheriff Paul and knew that if Doc were extradited to Arizona the cowboys would never allow him to see the light of another day. Sheriff Paul arrived in Denver on Friday, May 19, with his proper warrant in hand but did not have the necessary requisition from Governor Tritle to take custody of Holliday and remove him from the state of Colorado.

The following Monday, Judge Elliot postponed the hearing on the writ of habeas corpus until the next day, in hopes of receiving the requisition before having to make a ruling. On Tuesday morning at ten o'clock he surprised the court when he discharged the case after it was revealed that Perry Mallen had admitted that his entire story was a ruse. Doc's delight quickly vanished when Deputy Sheriff Charles T. Linton immediately rearrested him, this time under the auspices of the authentic warrant from Sheriff Paul. Doc's attorneys promptly applied for a second writ of habeas corpus. Another hearing was scheduled for the coming Friday, and John Henry Holliday remained in jail.[20]

The requisition from Governor Tritle of the Arizona Territory was received in Denver by Sheriff Paul on Thursday, May 24. Paul promptly presented it to Governor Pitkin, who took it under advisement. After a further delay, on Monday, May 29, the parties, along with Governor Pitkin, gathered in Judge Elliot's courtroom. They heard the arguments from the Honorable Isaac E. Barnum on behalf of the authorities and Judge Westbrook S. Decker and Col. John T. Deweese representing John Holliday. It has always been assumed that the governor also heard influential private testimony offered by some of Doc's prominent friends. Pitkin determined that the Arizona requisition failed to authenticate the warrant. Additionally, because there was another outstanding warrant in Colorado, that state had priority over Arizona. Holliday would be freed in order to give Pueblo the opportunity to exercise its warrant. Judge Elliot released Doc, and two weeks of incarceration came to an end.[21] As quickly as Doc was released, he was once again rearrested by Pueblo city marshal Jamieson on the outstanding warrant charging larceny.[22] Denverites recognized that this charge had been created by his friends, and John Henry was almost a free man. Accompanied by Bat Masterson and Sheriff Paul, he made the trip to Pueblo—feeling safe in the custody of the hands of the law in the state of Colorado. Sheriff Paul claimed that he wanted to be available in case the Pueblo authorities released Doc. Paul enjoyed the reputation of being a fair and honest man who publicly spoke well of Doc.[23]

Perry Mallen, the cause of this entire uproar in Denver, had admitted that he was not a sheriff from Los Angeles and had lied about having spent the past seven years in pursuit of Holliday. In reality, he was a bounty hunter after the reward that had been offered by Johnny Behan in Tombstone. Mallen defrauded several Denver residents out of hundreds of dollars and quietly slipped out of town.[24]

On Wednesday, May 31, Doc, Bat, and Sheriff Paul, along with Deputy Sheriff Linton, arrived in Pueblo on the morning train. That afternoon Doc appeared before Justice McBride on the larceny charge of having obtained one hundred and fifteen dollars from Charles White of Pennsylvania under false pretenses. The case was bound over to the July term of the district court, and Doc was released on three hundred dollars' bail. He appeared jubilant and celebrated his freedom with his many friends in Pueblo.[25] Doc took advantage of the celebrity status created by his arrest in Denver by emphasizing to the press that he was not a bunco man.[26]

Three days after Doc's release on bail in Pueblo Wyatt Earp granted an impromptu interview with a reporter from the *Gunnison News-Democrat*. Wyatt indicated that Doc might be joining them in Gunnison.[27] He went on to speak of the death of Curly Bill. When he was asked if Doc Holliday had killed Frank Stilwell, Wyatt quietly remarked, "Well, Stillwell [*sic*] was killed at Tucson," but then added that at least he had heard that Stilwell had been killed. He continued, "I promised my brother [Morgan] to get even, and I've kept my word so far. When they shot him he said that the only thing he regretted was that he wouldn't have a chance to get even. I told him I'd attend to it for him."[28]

The newspaper in Pueblo reported on June 14 that Doc Holliday was still in town awaiting action of the grand jury.[29] However, by June 16 he had arrived in Gunnison and reunited with the Earps.[30] The reunion was occasioned by another newspaper interview, this time with the *Gunnison Daily-News Democrat*.

An intrepid journalist approached Holliday; he described Doc as "dressed in a dark close fitting suit of black, and wore the latest style of round top hat. His hair was seen to be quite gray, his mustache sandy, and his eyes a piercing dark blue." Spotting the approaching reporter, Doc employed his own brand of sardonic humor: "I'm not travelling about the country in search of notoriety, and I think you newspaper fellows have already had a fair hack at me." Obviously in a good mood, he cooperated with the journalist and freely answered questions. He allowed that he had been born in Georgia, had been educated at the Pennsylvania College of Dental Surgery, and had practiced dentistry in Texas. Doc admitted that he had been a member of the Methodist Church there as well as belonging to a temperance organization and explained that he had also lived in Fort Griffin and Denison and in Denver in 1875 and 1876. He then dismissed Perry Mallen as "some crank trying to gain notoriety" and indicated with a smile that Mallen had left Denver four days before his release. Doc indicated his intention to mind his own business and "let other people do the same."[31]

A discerning reader of Colorado newspapers in June 1882 would have noticed a plethora of interviews, news articles, and sightings of Doc Holliday and Wyatt and Warren Earp. With the exception of Doc's recent headline-making legal entanglement in Denver and Pueblo, one would assume that this group of Tombstone emigrants would attempt to stay clear of publicity. Quite the contrary: apparently they wanted to be noticed and have their whereabouts firmly established.[32] A Leadville newspaper reported that Doc was headquartered in Gunnison on July 1.[33] A news item in the *Salida Mountain Mail* dated July 8, 1882, reported the arrival of Doc Holliday the day before and that he had made it known that he planned to stay several days.[34] At this time, Doc and the Earps seem to disappear into thin air.

It is possible that after his brief newspaper interview on July 7 Doc slipped out of Salida and joined Wyatt and Warren Earp and Dan Tipton, who were waiting for him just west of town. The four men rode south in quest of another of Morgan's presumed assassins, John Ringo.[35] It is likely that the determined riders traveled through Poncha Pass before following the San Luis Creek roughly seventy-five miles to Alamosa. From Alamosa they probably boarded the Denver and Rio Grande to Española then continued on to Santa Fe, where their worries of being recognized would have lessened as they boarded the trunk line to Lamy. There the Santa Fe Railroad was the logical choice to go south to Deming via Albuquerque. At Deming a transfer to the Southern Pacific would have allowed them to continue their trip west.[36] Presumably, they got off the train upon reaching Lordsburg because continuing by train into the San Simon Valley of Arizona risked revealing their presence. As described, the entire journey from Salida could be done in three to four days, allowing the foursome to arrive in the Lordsburg area on July 10 or 11. This would have allowed sufficient time for Wyatt and his party to reach Cochise County by July 13.

Significantly, on that very day, July 11, the District Court of Pueblo County in Colorado issued a writ of *capias* for Doc, indicating that he was not present in court and that the sheriff of Pueblo County should advise him that the bail would be five hundred dollars. Later that same day, attorney W. G. Hollins learned of the writ and appeared in court on behalf of his client, the absent J. H. Holliday.[37] As the court proceedings were taking place, it appears that Doc was with the Earps, eager to find Ringo and complete their mission.

Sunday, July 9, found John Ringo at the cowboy hangout of Galeyville having dinner and drinking heavily.[38] On Thursday morning, July 13, Bill Sanders, whose ranch was at the mouth of Turkey Creek Canyon, passed a still-drunken Ringo wandering past a nearby string of watering holes called the Tanks.[39] Later that day at about three o'clock in the afternoon Mrs. Will Smith, who lived near the mouth of neighboring Morse Canyon, heard a gunshot. The logical conclusion is that Ringo was taken by surprise while camping and was shot and killed by Wyatt Earp.[40] After moving Ringo's body to a spot below the Smith ranch along the road into Morse Canyon, his killers quickly dispersed, ensuring that they were not seen by anyone. Thus, they avoided the mistake that had been made in Tucson when Stilwell was shot. Before dusk on the afternoon of July 13, 1882, not a living soul could be seen on the road leading to Morse Canyon.

On July 14, John Yoast, a local teamster, came to the Smith house and announced that while hauling lumber down the canyon he had come across the dead body of John Ringo. Fourteen of the local citizens viewed Ringo's remains before they buried him beneath the tree under which he was found. The Statement for the Coroner and Sheriff of Cochise County, Arizona Territory, was signed by the fourteen citizens on July 14. They indicated that the body had been in a sitting position when it was discovered, "facing west, the head inclined to the right." The sole wound on the body was a "part of the scalp gone including a small portion of the forehead and part of the hair." The coroner's inquest supposed that it was a gunshot wound, but determined that the cause of death was unknown.[41] A newspaper account further detailed the nature of the

John Ringo
(1850–82). Jack
Burrows Collection

wound, indicating that the hole was "large enough to admit two fingers about halfway between the right eye and ear, and a hole correspondingly large on top of his head, doubtless the outlet of the fatal bullet."[42] His feet were wrapped in a torn undershirt, though he did not appear to have gone any distance in this unusual footwear. He held a Colt's .45 SAA revolver (serial no.

Wallet and Colt's .45 revolver (ser. no. 222) found on Johnny Ringo. Jim Earle Collection

222—manufactured in 1874) in his right hand, and his new Winchester Model 1876 .45-60 rifle (serial no. 2189—manufactured in 1882) was leaning against the same tree that supported Ringo.[43] Remarkably, one of his two cartridge belts, the one containing .45 cartridges for his revolver, was found belted on his body upside down.[44]

The July 18, 1882, issue of the Tombstone Epitaph reported Ringo's death, stating that "many people who were intimately acquainted with him in life have serious doubts that he took his own life, while an equally large number say that he frequently threatened to commit suicide." The *Epitaph* leaned toward the suicide theory.[45] No one in Tombstone knew with certainty the true circumstances of Ringo's death.

Also on July 18 the district attorney of Pueblo County moved that the case of the still-absent John H. Holliday be continued until the court's next term.[46] According to the *Pueblo Daily Chieftain,* Doc was in Leadville on July 18—the first report of his whereabouts since he was last seen in Salida on July 7.[47] With the Arizona murder warrant still hanging over his head, Doc would have had no desire to leave the safe haven of Colorado.[48]

Downtown area, Leadville, Colorado, 1882

13

The Final Years

The 1877 discovery of a rich outcropping of silver ore gave birth to the boomtown of Leadville. Formerly bearing the undistinguished name of Slabtown, the community was renamed when Harrison Austin Warner "Haw" Tabor met with other civic leaders in George L. Henderson's cabin and decided on the new name of Leadville.[1] On January 14, 1878, another meeting was held and the new, more sophisticated name was officially approved.[2] The success of Tabor's Little Pittsburg mine and his many other profitable mining ventures made him the wealthiest man in the region. He was referred to as one of Colorado's Silver Kings. The community had no problem naming him the first mayor of the newly created town. Tabor repaid the citizens of Leadville by building the Tabor Opera House, which soon housed grand opera performances that could rival those of any large city in the country.

By 1879 the population had soared to some fifteen thousand residents, and a local census revealed that

Harrison Avenue, Leadville, Colorado, looking north. Hyman's Saloon is immediately to the left of the Tabor Opera House. Colorado Mountain History Collection, Lake County Public Library, Leadville, Colorado

there were one hundred and twenty saloons in town, half of which were on Harrison Avenue. Also located on Harrison and nearby Chestnut and Second Streets were most of the retail stores and restaurants. It was common for landlords in the downtown area to demand rents of three hundred to five hundred dollars a month. For a time, Leadville challenged Denver as Colorado's most populous city. By the time Doc was lured to Leadville in July 1882 the mine production was already in decline and the economy was slowing down.

Upon his arrival, John Henry arranged to receive his mail at the Western Union telegraph office at 106 East Second Street.[3] He wasted no time finding employment as a faro dealer at Cyrus "Cy" Allen's Monarch

Saloon at 320 Harrison Avenue. His employment at the Monarch did not last. Cy Allen soon discharged him, probably because of his growing dependence on alcohol. Before long, Doc was the faro dealer in one of the clubrooms at Hyman's Saloon, owned by his landlord, Mannie Hyman.[4] After purchasing the building from Adolph Newsitz, Hyman remodeled the saloon and added a second floor. It was located at 316 Harrison, next door to the Tabor Opera House and three doors south of the Monarch. Doc's room was upstairs on the northwest corner of the building. The seven-by-fourteen-foot room, one of nine rooms Hyman let out, had a view of the snow-covered peaks of the Rocky Mountains.[5] Though Doc both dealt and played faro for Hyman's, he was frequently seen on the player's side of the table across the street at John G. Morgan's Board of Trade Saloon playing stud poker.[6] He developed a friendship with the owners, John Morgan and Col. Samuel Houston.

At 216 Harrison, one block south of Hyman's, stood the renowned Texas House, reputed to take in "more money in a day than the Carbonate Bank."[7] Operated by John F. H. Chapman and Samuel D. Harlan, the Texas House was open twenty-four hours a day.[8] Baily Youngston, an interior decorator from Galveston, had transformed the gambling hall into a "palace of beauty" with many highly polished bars generously spaced around the entire first floor, which also held a dozen or more faro and keno tables.[9] The high rollers used a separate side entrance that led to an ornate stairway at the top of which were three elaborately furnished apartments, a dining room, and a separate gaming parlor. The upstairs gambling room was run by "Con" Featherly, described as a mechanic of the game who was a "debonaire [*sic*] little fellow with soft slender hands . . . who could operate a faro box as occasion demanded."[10] This upper gaming room had a lavish buffet, always fully stocked and ready to feed hungry players at any time of the day or night. Overseeing all of the gaming activity was John Pentland, a New York gambler who attained much notoriety when he earned over eighty thousand dollars for the house in the first few months of his employment.[11]

Doc, aware of Leadville's most lucrative gaming opportunities, was frequently seen during the day or night at different establishments on Harrison Street, though his dwindling pocketbook did not allow him to mingle with the big spenders playing upstairs with Con Featherly.

The card playing at the Texas House came to a screeching halt during the early morning hours of December 6, 1882. Joseph Dreichlinger, an employee sleeping next door in Herman Brothers clothing store, was awakened about three in the morning when he heard a loud explosion.[12] He ran out to the street to discover flames leaping from the windows of the Texas House. Dreichlinger quickly issued a call for help to the fire department. Within five minutes the firemen evacuated the building and had five hoses pouring water on the burning structure. The frame floors and walls fueled the fire, which rapidly spread to the second floor. Two firemen collapsed from the suffocating smoke and the furnacelike heat. As the flames stretched into the sky, they decided that they needed more manpower to help in controlling the fire so that the neighboring structures would not ignite. Without hesitation, a few of the townsmen who were still awake at that hour pitched in to aid the weary firefighters. The fire destroyed the building and almost everything it contained. Thanks to the firemen and the brave volunteers, no lives were lost and the adjoining buildings were saved. The lavish furnishings of the formerly elegant Texas House were turned into a pile of charred ruins. Only the front bar and cigar counter remained, a sad testimonial to the grandeur that had existed just a few hours earlier. The following day, Leadville's *Chronicle* told of the inferno and listed the names of the men who had fearlessly volunteered to assist the firemen. One of them was Dr. John Holliday, who had not hesitated to join in and fight the fire, apparently giving no thought to how the smoke and exertion would affect his already damaged lungs.[13]

Doc's tuberculosis was no longer in remission. In addition, he was losing the battle against Leadville's most common ailment, pneumonia, which he contracted several times in 1883 and 1884. The primary medication that he used to fight his illness was whiskey. He self-medicated himself up and down Harrison Street at the many saloons. With increasing frequency, Doc was seen suffering the effects of the overmedication. He was in a vicious circle. The more he suffered, the more he drank, and vice versa. His skills were no longer as sharp as they once were. He rarely practiced his dentistry anymore. His expertise at the card table was failing to be as lucrative as it once had been. The abundance of liquor combined with his lack of attention to a proper diet caused his weight to decline. The once handsome and suave dentist began to look like the sick man that he was.

Doc's physical condition continued to deteriorate. He was befriended by a local druggist, Jay Miller, who worked at the apothecary at the corner of Sixth and

John Henry Holliday. Courtesy Colorado Historical Society

Harrison Street. Miller felt compassion for Doc, and when whiskey failed to do an adequate job laudanum was provided free of charge.[14] During the next year and a half Doc remained in the Leadville area, minded his own business, and managed to stay out of trouble. He accumulated a good number of friends and was generally well liked. His tuberculosis and bouts with pneumonia, combined with his growing dependency on laudanum and his heavy whiskey swilling, made it increasingly difficult to earn a living. He sustained his meager existence with an occasional win at the card table and some help from Mannie Hyman. His continued efforts to avoid confrontation were put to the test when two of his old Tombstone enemies arrived and conspired for revenge against him.

William "Billy" Allen, a former Leadville policeman, had been associated with Ike Clanton back in Tombstone.[15] Allen had served as a prosecution witness during the Tombstone shooting inquest and hearings, testifying that he had accompanied Reuben Coleman on the day of the gunfight in Tombstone. They had walked down Allen Street through the O.K. Corral to the front of Camillus S. Fly's Gallery (behind Fly's Boarding House). It was believed by some, and certainly by Doc, that during the fracas Allen had fired a number of shots aimed at both Holliday and the Earps from the passageway between Fly's buildings.[16] After coming to Leadville, Allen had been a part-time policeman and had been hired by Cy Allen (no relation) as a bartender at the Monarch Saloon. Another of Doc's enemies from Tombstone, Johnny Tyler, was also living in Leadville. Now dealing at the Casino Gambling Hall, Tyler had not forgotten the humiliation he had suffered in 1880 when he was evicted from Tombstone's Oriental Saloon by Wyatt Earp with Doc looking on, laughing and taunting him. Tyler harbored tremendous anger and resentment toward Doc and now prepared to vent it.

Johnny Tyler and Billy Allen plotted their vendetta. Many members of Leadville's sporting fraternity recognized that this hatred traced back to the cowboy feuds of the Tombstone days.[17] The existence of this bad blood was also well known to the police, who were keeping tabs on Tyler and Allen, as well as on Doc.[18] In late July 1884, when several of Tyler's cohorts came into Hyman's bar and called upon Holliday to pull his gun, he announced that he did not have one. After having been stopped and searched several times by the police, he was very careful not to violate the city ordinance by carrying a gun. Doc's determination to stay on the right side of the law caused Tyler's cronies to insult him, with liberal use of profanity and vulgarity. A local newspaper reporter interviewed Doc and ran the story of his humiliation: "Words passed between he and the clique at Hyman's bar, and several of them called him to 'pull his gun.' He said he had none, and as he passed out was called filthy names. This rankled. Next day he told the writer, tears of rage coming to his eyes as he talked, that they were insulting and humiliating him because they knew he could not retaliate."[19] The paper clearly sided with Doc, labeling the Tyler faction "would be bad men" and asserting that there was "this much to be said for Holliday—he has never since his arrival here made any 'bad breaks' or conducted himself in any other way than a quiet peaceable manner."[20] Obviously John H. Holliday's efforts to be a law-abiding citizen were noticed by both the lawful and the lawless citizens of Leadville.

In August 1884 Doc found himself in the unenviable position of owing Billy Allen five dollars. Allen, knowing of his dire straits, had willingly loaned the money, assuming that he would have difficulty repaying the debt. This would give Allen justification to goad the weak, sick Holliday into a gunfight. Doc had borrowed the money with the promise to repay it in less than a week. Seven days later he had to go to Billy and humbly explain that he had not been able to collect an outstanding debt and therefore did not have the money. Doc said that his "jewelry was in soak" and he would pay the five dollars as soon as he was able.[21] Allen, who had been waiting for this opportunity, issued an ultimatum—Doc would have to pay the debt by noon of the following Tuesday or face the threat of violence.[22]

When Tuesday arrived, some of Doc's friends went to his room and told him that Allen was looking for him with a gun. About three o'clock in the afternoon Doc started downstairs toward the saloon and met Mannie Hyman on the stairway.[23] They chatted and Doc asked him to get an officer for protection. Doc continued into the saloon but did not find Allen. He asked his friend and fellow boarder Frank Lomeister, who was working the day shift as bartender, to get Capt. Edmond Bradbury of the Leadville Police Department or Marshal Harvey Faucett, adding that he did not want to sit around for the afternoon unprotected. Doc then returned to his room, where he stayed until about five o'clock in the afternoon. He sent a friend down to the saloon to conceal his Colt's .41 revolver behind the end of the bar.[24] Doc could not afford the fine if he were found carrying a weapon. Soon thereafter, he arrived and stationed himself by the cigar case, near the end of the bar and the hidden gun.

When Billy Allen entered Hyman's saloon, Doc saw Allen's hand in his pocket. Assuming that he was holding a gun, Doc grabbed his pistol and fired. The shot struck Allen in the fleshy part of the upper arm

Mannie Hyman's Saloon at 316 Harrison Avenue in Leadville, Colorado, before addition of the second floor. Photo by the Denver Public Library, Western History Collection

and severed an artery. He fell to the floor as Doc got off a second shot that barely missed his head, and the bullet lodged in the door sill.[25] Henry Killerman, now bartending, grabbed Doc and prevented him from firing any more shots. Assuredly, this saved the life of Billy Allen. Captain Bradbury, who was outside on the sidewalk, upon hearing the shots rushed in and arrested Doc. He escorted him to the jail, where he was charged with assault with the intent to commit murder. A reporter from the local paper obtained Doc's version of the gunfight, which was published the following day: "Well, Allen had told me he intended to do me up this evening. I was standing behind the counter when he came in and I saw that he had both hands in his pocket and that the handle of a pistol protruded from one of them. Of course I couldn't let him murder me so I fired."[26] Captain Bradbury put Doc in a cell, and bail was set at five thousand dollars. John G. Morgan and Samuel Houston, co-owners of the Board of Trade Saloon, arrived the next day and posted the bond for their friend, guaranteeing that he would appear in court the following Monday for the preliminary hearing.

The courtroom of Justice of the Peace William W. Old was full when it convened at two o'clock in the afternoon on August 25, 1884. Doc was represented by Charles F. Fishback and Judge Milton R. Rice. Presenting the people's case was District Attorney William Kellogg assisted by C. A. Franklin. The first witness called by Judge Old was Captain Bradbury. His testimony included the statement that Doc had requested protection. Frank Lomeister, Doc's friend and the afternoon bartender, was called to the stand and testified that Doc had been in the saloon earlier on the day of the shooting wanting the police to protect him from Allen. Also corroborating the story that Doc's life had been threatened by Allen was Henry Killerman, the bartender. Friends of Allen testified that Billy had harbored no ill feeling toward Doc and was not going to Hyman's to cause trouble. Conversely, friends of Doc related Allen's threat and told how killing Holliday would have enhanced the reputation of the gunfighter. Finally, Doc took the stand on his own behalf. After detailing the background of the loan and subsequent threat, he testified: "I saw Allen coming in with his hand in his pocket, and I thought my life was as good to me as his was to him; I fired the shot, and he fell on the floor, and [I] fired the second shot; I knew that I would be a child in his hands if he got hold of me; I

211

weigh 122 pounds; I think Allen weighs 170; I have had the pneumonia three or four times; I don't think I was able to protect myself against him."[27]

After hearing all of the witnesses, Judge Rice made a statement on behalf of John Holliday. He restated Doc's desperate pleas for protection and his fear of assault by Allen. District Attorney Kellogg gave a strong closing plea stating that the shooting of William Allen by John Holliday was premeditated murder. Judge Old was apparently convinced by Kellogg's speech: he bound Doc over for trial and increased the bail to eight thousand dollars.[28] Doc was remanded into the custody of the sheriff and jailed until the additional three thousand dollars' bond could be posted. He was not released until September 6.[29] The trial was set for November.

When the November session convened in the courtroom of District Judge George Goldthwaite, the docket was full. Because of the full schedule, the judge asked that *The People v. John Holliday* be continued to the December session and both sides agreed. After several more postponements, Doc's trial finally began on Saturday, March 28, 1885. Doc and his attorneys were present in the courtroom of Judge Goldthwaite and heard the sworn depositions of eight witnesses read to the jury. Noteworthy was the fact that no deposition by Billy Allen was read. When the attorneys completed their arguments, the jury retired to deliberate. They arrived at their verdict in short order. When the jury returned to the courtroom, the foreman, R. S. McCleod, informed the court of the decision. They found John Holliday not guilty.[30] After seven months of waiting, Doc was finally a free man—there would be no more shootings.[31]

Reports have persisted that following his acquittal in the Billy Allen case Doc took the opportunity to leave Colorado. Frank Scotten, later El Paso County, Texas, tax assessor, related that he observed Doc and Wyatt in El Paso on April 14, 1885, when the two men were playing faro in Lou Rickabaugh's casino at the rear of Taylor and Look's Gem Saloon. Sometime lawman and oftentimes gambler Will Raynor entered and created a drunken disturbance. Another faro player, Bob Rennick, also suffering from the effects of too much liquor, drew his gun and attempted to quell the ruckus. The incident abruptly ended when Rennick fatally shot Raynor. About thirty minutes later the drunken Buck Linn staggered in, incensed at the shooting of his friend Raynor. He accosted Bob Cahill, the faro dealer, to whom he erroneously attributed Raynor's death. Again guns were pulled, this time resulting in the death of Buck Linn. Scotten, a witness to the shootings, related how Doc and Wyatt managed to avoid the trouble and remained only interested spectators in the evening's deadly proceedings.[32] However, a letter supposedly written by Wyatt Earp regarding the 1885 El Paso incident stated: "No, Doc Holliday was not in El Paso while I was there."[33] One fact is certain: by the middle of June Doc was making his usual rounds of the gaming halls of Leadville.[34]

During the winter of 1885–86, Doc escaped Leadville's bitter cold and traveled to Denver, where he spent several months. The climate there was only a slight improvement, but the significant decrease in altitude was much easier on his weak lungs.[35] He was often seen at both the Arcade and the Argyle, as well as Patrick O'Connell's Missouri House on Blake Street.[36] One of the more noteworthy of the gaming halls where

Doc spread his business was the Chucovitch Saloon, where proprietor Vaso Chucovitch maintained a gambling room upstairs.[37] He was an associate of Denver's underworld czar Ed Chase in the saloon and vice business. Later, upon Chase's retirement, Chucovitch inherited his dubious distinction as king of the underworld.[38]

In February 1886 Doc received a letter from his cousin Robert. Mary, Robert's wife, had recently given birth to their first child, Robert Fulton Holliday, on January 26. John Henry must have felt homesick and wished that he could be with the family in Atlanta to share in the happiness and drink a toast to Robert's firstborn. Instead, he had to settle for sending a hearty letter of congratulations to Mary and Robert. This lengthy letter was evidence that John Henry did not want his family to be aware of his declining health. He failed to mention the status of his rapidly advancing tuberculosis.[39]

In the spring the cold weather broke and the warmer temperatures were more conducive to travel. Doc went on to Silverton, where he granted an interview to a reporter from the *New York Sun* on June 1, 1886. This report was picked up by the *Denver Daily Times* and Henry Holliday's hometown paper, Valdosta's *South Georgian Times*.[40] The lengthy article was represented as Doc's own words, but the hand of an imaginative journalist definitely shows through:

> I've had credit for more killings than I ever dreamt of. . . . down in Tombstone . . . that sort of thing couldn't go in a well-regulated community, and then, just to restore order, I gave it to a couple of them. That settled the whole trouble. Down on the border I had two or three

little scrapes, but they didn't amount to much. A party of drunken greasers came climbing over us one night, and I had to fix one or two . . . but it had to be done in the interest of peace. The claim that I make is that a few of us pioneers are entitled to credit for what we have done. We have been the forerunners of government. As soon as law and order are established anywhere we never had any trouble. If it hadn't been for me and men like me there never would have been any government in some of these towns. When I have done any shooting it has always been with this in mind.[41]

It is apparent that Doc believed that he had justification for the shootings in which he had participated. He had acted either under the guise of law enforcement or for purposes of self-protection. Neither allowed room for feelings of guilt. This newspaper interview would not have been missed by Henry Holliday in Valdosta. The uncultured subject matter of this article must have been a bit shocking for Major Holliday, although it left room for a reader to consider Doc's acts heroic.

Late that summer Doc again returned to Denver. He took up residence at Robert P. Newkirk's Metropolitan Hotel at 1325 16th Street.[42] The local police department was not thrilled when Holliday reappeared in town. His reputation as a gunfighter, enhanced by his heavy drinking and gambling, precluded his being welcomed by the law enforcement community. On August 3, 1886, while Doc stood outside of the hotel with two friends, bartender Kenneth McCoy and watchman J. S. Smythe, Officer Michael B. Norkett approached and hauled the trio off to jail.[43] Norkett said they were going to be charged with vagrancy. No charges had been filed when they appeared in Police Court the following day.[44] The *Denver Tribune-Republican* reported that the case against Holliday and McCoy was continued. In reality, there was no case as there was never a charge. Smythe let it be known that he had fifty dollars available if needed. The three men were freed, but not before Doc was made aware of the fact that he was not welcome in Denver.[45] The ploy of the police department worked: they were getting rid of the notorious Doc Holliday.

Doc left Denver before the city's police could cause any more trouble for him.[46] He went to Leadville, where his old friend Mannie Hyman had taken on a partner, Theodore Schultz, who was the new club room manager.[47] The winter in Leadville took its toll on Doc's already frail body. His spirits were low, and he decided to contact Kate. He wrote to her in Globe, telling her of his plans to go to Glenwood Springs to partake of the curative sulfur springs and asking her to join him.

Doc arrived via stagecoach in Glenwood Springs in May 1887.[48] He attempted to support himself by doing some dental work, but his violent cough made that effort unsuccessful.[49] Doc was hired by Judd Riley to help guard a coal claim at a nearby mine. The mine owner paid them ten dollars a day to hold down the claim until he could consummate a sale.[50] By the time this temporary work ended, Kate had arrived. She had no trouble convincing Doc to accompany her to her brother Alexander's cabin in Penny Hot Springs in the nearby Crystal Valley.[51] Alexander and his wife, Eva, helped Kate care for Doc. Unfortunately, the better diet and lifestyle did not stop the progression of his consumption. They soon agreed that Doc should return to Glenwood Springs and its mineral baths.

Alexander Harony cabin at Penny Hot Springs, Colorado. Glenn G. Boyer Collection

Doc, looking "like a man well advanced in years, for his hair was silver and his form emaciated and bent," once more went to the springs.[52] The sulfur springs, revered by the Ute Indians for their curative powers, had given the town some fame, and it had become the home of four hundred kindred souls, most of whom were in search of a cure for their varied ailments. Doc and Kate took rooms at the Hotel Glenwood on the northeast corner of Grand Avenue and Eighth Street. Completed in 1886, the hotel boasted both electrical lighting and hot and cold running water in every room.[53]

For a short period Doc dealt faro in several of the gambling houses. However, the sulfur vapors generated by Glenwood's hot springs had a debilitating effect on his consumptive lungs. A man who saw him in

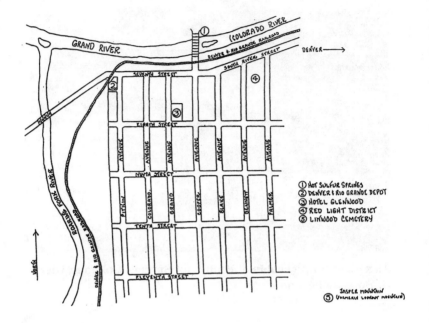

KAREN HOLLIDAY TANNER

Glenwood Springs, Colorado, ca. 1887

Glenwood Springs offered the following description: "He walked down the street with a feeble tread and a downcast look. If he heard a shot, he raised his head with eager attention and glanced this way and that."[54] As his health worsened, Glenwood Springs residents respected his fortitude in the face of adversity and found him to be a quiet man with a gentlemanly demeanor. It was also observed that Doc was "breaking to pieces" and was obviously a dying man.[55]

On Wednesday morning, October 5, 1887, the first Denver and Rio Grande Railroad train reached Glen-

Glenwood Springs, Colorado, looking east from Red Mountain, ca. 1886–87. Frontier Historical Museum, Glenwood Springs, Colorado

wood, resulting in an enthusiastic celebration. Unfortunately, Doc was not well enough to take Kate to the festivities. He had become bedridden several weeks earlier. Kate stayed with him and tried to ease his suffering. She used her small savings to sustain them when Doc could no longer work. The effects of the many years of drink, late hours, thin air, pneumonia, and tuberculosis finally caught up with him. During the last fifty-seven days of his life, he rose from his bed only twice.[56] They relied on the bellhop to serve them so that Kate did not have to leave his bedside. In spite of the fact that their funds were nearly exhausted, Doc was always generous when he tipped, as recalled by Art Kendrick, the bellman at the Hotel Glenwood.[57] During

219

Hotel Glenwood, Glenwood Springs, Colorado. Site of the death of John Henry Holliday, D.D.S. Photo by the Denver Public Library, Western History Collection

the third week in October Doc became delirious. By Monday, November 7, he was unable to speak.

About ten o'clock on the morning of November 8, 1887, Doctor John Henry Holliday died at the Hotel Glenwood in Glenwood Springs, Colorado, of miliary tuberculosis.[58] He was buried near Palmer Avenue and Twelfth Street in the Linwood Cemetery that afternoon at four o'clock at a service attended by many friends.[59] Kate arranged for the eulogy to be delivered by the Reverend W. S. Rudolph of the Presbyterian Church.[60]

After the brief service, Kate returned to the Hotel Glenwood and gathered together John Henry's few

Grave of John Henry Holliday, D.D.S., Linwood Cemetery, Glenwood Springs, Colorado. Collection of Karen Holliday Tanner

belongings. These possessions, along with a brief letter, were shipped in a small trunk to the Holliday family in Atlanta in care of Sister Mary Melanie of the Order of the Sisters of Mercy. Upon notification of the trunk's arrival, Sister Mary Melanie, concerned with the propriety of her situation, prevailed upon her uncle, Dr. John Stiles Holliday, to collect the trunk and its contents. Dr. Holliday grimly went to the train station from which he had bid John Henry good-bye fourteen years earlier. Upon receiving the articles, he gave Sister Mary Melanie the letter that she had written to John Henry. Dr. Holliday wrote to his brother, Maj. Henry Burroughs Holliday, in Valdosta, seeking guidance concerning the disposition of the remainder of John Henry's belongings. As there was nothing of personal interest to him among the belongings, Major Holliday asked his brother

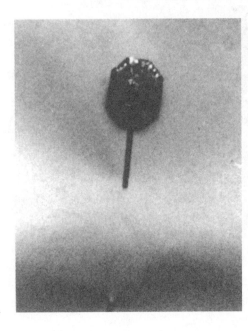

John Henry
Holliday's stickpin.
Collection of Carolyn
Holliday Manley

to handle the disposal. The clothes were given to the
needy. Dr. Holliday's son Robert requested and received
the remaining possessions.[61] Significantly, the trunk
contained no dental equipment or guns. In addition to
the Sheffield straight razor found among his personal
toilet items, only a small knife, a gold stickpin from
which the diamond had been removed, and a few gambling devices testified to the real career of John Henry
Holliday, D.D.S.[62]

Epilogue

Four days after the death of John Henry Holliday, the *Ute Chief* of Glenwood Springs carried a eulogy: "He represented law and order at all times and places. . . . 'Doc' Holliday had his faults none will attempt to deny; but who among us had not, and who shall be judge of these things?"[1] During his brief stay there, John Henry had made many friends. It was apparent from the local newspaper that the town's residents had forgiven the past sins of this man, known as a notorious gunfighter.

Kate soon left Glenwood Springs, with its sad memories. She remained in the Crystal Valley region of Colorado, where, less than two and a half years later, she met George M. Cummings. She was almost forty years old when she married him in Aspen on March 2, 1890.[2] Eleven years her senior, George Cummings had been born in New York in 1839. Now a respectable married woman, Mary Katherine Harony Cummings discontinued the use of the nickname Kate that she had assumed following her hasty departure from home while still a teenager. Once again using her birthname of Mary, she reverted to a life of hard work and rectitude. George and Mary Cummings lived in Rock Creek, Colorado, before settling in Bisbee, Cochise County, Arizona, in 1895. Two years later they moved to a nearby mining camp in the Pierce district, where he was employed as a blacksmith and she cooked for the mining camp. By the spring of 1899 their marriage had ended, and Mary left her alcoholic husband.[3]

She was briefly employed at a hotel run by John J. Rath at Cochise, Arizona. On June 2, 1900, she accepted employment as a housekeeper for John J. Howard of Dos Cabezas, Arizona, for twenty dollars a month and board. She remained in his employ until Howard's death on January 3, 1930. On June 13, 1931, she wrote to Governor George W. Hunt requesting permission to live in the state-owned Arizona Pioneers' Home in Prescott. Governor Hunt granted her request, and she remained in the Pioneers' Home until her death on November 2, 1940.[4] She is buried at the Pioneer Cemetery, Prescott, Arizona.

During the last few years of her life, Mary Cummings made it very clear that she considered herself to have been married to Doc.[5] Almost half a century had passed since his death when Kate wrote her recollections of Doc:

> He was considered a handsome man. He was a gentleman in manners to the Ladies and everyone. Being quiet, he never hunted for trouble. If he was crowded, he knew how to take care of himself. He was also known as the tubercular dentist. He was not a drunkard. He always had

Mary Katherine Cummings (née Horony), "Big-Nosed Kate," ca. 1890. Copyright A. W. Bork and Glenn G. Boyer

a bottle of whiskey but never drank habitually. When he needed a drink, he would only take a small one. He never boasted of his fighting qualities. He was a neat dresser, and saw to it that his wife was dressed as nicely as himself.[6]

Although many experiences and even more years now separated them, Kate's opinion of Doc, probably the only man she had truly loved, never wavered. In Georgia the Holliday family never knew the woman who proudly referred to herself as Mrs. Mary Holliday, widow of John H. Holliday, D.D.S.[7]

John Henry's father, Maj. Henry B. Holliday, spent the remainder of his life in Valdosta. He maintained his nursery, sold carriages and furniture, and remained very active in local political affairs as well as the Confederate Veterans Association. During the winter of 1893 the major's health began to fail and on Friday, February 17, 1894, he was stricken with paralysis. Dr. and Mrs. John S. Holliday, accompanied by Dr. and Mrs. Robert A. Holliday, immediately traveled to Valdosta. They were with Henry Holliday when he died on Wednesday, February 22, 1893, two weeks before his seventy-fourth birthday.[8] More than nineteen years had passed since he had said good-bye to his only son. Presumably, his guilt-ridden sorrow over his son's tragic life was what kept him from uttering his son's name after 1887, the year of John Henry's death.[9] His true feelings will never be known.

Dr. John Stiles Holliday continued to be an integral part of Atlanta's society and commerce. In 1879, while working with associate Joel Hurt to rebuild the Atlanta Savings and Loan Association, he was elected clerk of the Superior Court for Fulton County.[10] After his term

John Stiles Holliday, M.D., Atlanta, Georgia, 1885. Collection of Mrs. Constance K. McKellar

as clerk, he remained associated with the County Clerk's office as deputy. In 1884 he formed a partnership with Samuel H. Perkins, founding Perkins and Holliday, a planing mill and lumber yard on Nelson Street. On January 2, 1894, his beloved Permelia, his wife and companion of fifty years, died.[11] The following year Dr. Holliday retired from his position as deputy clerk when his health began to fail. He suffered from multiple sclerosis, which caused his death in Atlanta on April 27, 1897, at the age of seventy-four.[12] He never participated in any negative discussion concerning the lifestyle of his brother's son. Dr. John S. Holliday maintained that his nephew had been victimized by the desperados of the West. He always believed in the integrity of his namesake.

Dr. Holliday's son Robert refused to take on a dental partner during the lifetime of his cousin. He never forgot the plans that they had made to be partners in a dental practice and kept the spot reserved for his cousin.[13] As Robert's prominence in the dental field grew, he was asked to serve as recording secretary and publisher of the *Southern Dental Journal* between 1878 and 1881.[14] He was then elected to the board of the Georgia State Dental Association, serving as its vice-president in 1883. In 1884 he chartered the Atlanta Dental Supply Company. On October 21, 1884, Robert Holliday married twenty-eight-year-old Mary Cowperthwaite Fulton. In 1887 he founded a dental college in Atlanta.[15] In 1898, while living in New Orleans, Robert joined with several others in the establishment of the New Orleans College of Dentistry. In June 1906 he was again living in Atlanta when he was diagnosed as having stomach cancer. Robert Holliday died three months later on November 9, 1906, ending a long and prestigious dental career.[16] During his twenty-two-year marriage, he passed on to his wife all of the memories and dreams that he had shared with his cousin—childhood chum, gambling pal, best friend, debonair bachelor, and dental preceptor—John Henry Holliday.

Mary Fulton Holliday, a widow in her forties, perceived herself as a "woman of the new issue."[17] Prior to her marriage, she had attended finishing school in Philadelphia before studying art in France and Italy. Now, with Sophie Walton to care for the house and tend the three children, Mary pursued her cultural interests.[18] She wrote:

> [I] want[ed] to see the world. I want to know and
> to see what lies beyond these time-worked

Robert Alexander
Holliday, D.D.S.,
Atlanta, Georgia,
1882. Collection of
Karen Holliday
Tanner

farms, the life beyond these mountains. It's not idle curiosity, but the desire to see and know what others are doing, and to look into the minds and hearts of men. All is a riddle to me now, so I want to find the answer. There is no one in this community who can tell me. All I know [is] from school books, weekly papers, and our own library. I want to accomplish something, and here we seem to live, only for the day. I want to live beyond the day, and what would a life be without experience. It is hard to tell you what I feel, it is a feeling without a name.[19]

The free-spirited Mary and Sophie privately discussed John Henry's life in the West. Sophie was

Mary Cowperthwaite
Fulton Holliday,
Atlanta, Georgia, ca.
1895. Collection of
Karen Holliday
Tanner

secretly proud of her prize student as she heard tales of Doc's gambling expertise. She took credit for giving him his start. Mary Holliday was fascinated by the exciting adventures of her husband's cousin. When most of the Holliday family were unaware of the actual activities of their western relative, Mary devoured any newspaper articles written on the infamous gunfighter. She remembered many details that she heard about this intriguing relative.

Denial, shame, guilt, fascination, and pride—all of these emotions must have been felt by members of the Holliday family when the subject of their infamous relative was broached. This complex and paradoxical man had caused them to have a multitude of views as to his character. It would be many years before it

230

became apparent that the vivid contrasts in his known personalities must have been created by Doc himself. A stranger to the frontier, frightened and lonely, young Doc Holliday carefully nurtured the mystery that surrounded him. He embellished the stories of his youth in order to portray himself as having been an incorrigible ruffian as a youngster. He used this contrived reputation as the foundation for his newer image, which was a fundamental part of his self-protection. As his health declined, he further enhanced his image as a gunman. Bat Masterson wrote of John Henry's killing of several black youths in a swimming hole massacre as a teenager. There can be only one source for this grossly exaggerated story, based on a bland incident of John Henry's youth: Doc himself.

This is only one of the many falsified stories printed and reprinted about this notorious, allegedly cold-blooded killer, who had at times been called the most dangerous man alive. Contemporary testimony attributed as many as twenty-five graves to his blazing gun. Documentary evidence certainly disputes his fiery reputation as a gunfighter. He was involved in shooting scrapes with Charles Austin in Dallas, with Henry Kahn in Breckenridge, with Milt Joyce in Tombstone, and with Billy Allen in Leadville, none of which resulted in fatalities. He was indicted in the Austin case and found not guilty. In his case involving Milt Joyce, the charge of assault with a deadly weapon with intent to kill was dismissed. He paid a twenty dollar fine for the misdemeanor charge of assault and battery. He was fined in the Kahn case and acquitted in the Billy Allen shooting. No charges were ever brought against Doc for the killing of Ed Bailey at Fort Griffin or the shooting of Charlie White in Las Vegas, New Mexico. He probably pulled the trigger on Old Man Clanton in Tombstone, delivered one of the three fatal shots that killed Frank McLaury, and definitely fired the shot that killed Tom McLaury. He rode with the Earp faction during the vendetta that followed and may or may not have been responsible for the deaths of any of the victims.

Doc Holliday's career as "the most skillful gambler and the nerviest, speediest, deadliest man with a six-gun," while blood-stained, was principally isolated to some eighteen months and was generally confined to one location—Tombstone.[20] He was charged with murder once in his life. The judge refused to indict and dismissed the case. Of his seventeen known arrests, he pled guilty to two gambling charges, one charge of carrying a deadly weapon, and one misdemeanor assault charge. In each of the other instances, either he was found not guilty or the case was dismissed.

He carefully preserved and occasionally enhanced his reputation in the West while he used every effort to conceal this same reputation in the South. Additionally, he shared few details of his background with his frontier acquaintances—whether friend or foe. It is no wonder that his true persona went unknown. Yet he adapted and he survived. Ill, with a progressively weakening body, he maintained his sense of humor and his own sense of integrity. With his almost Dickens-like view of the world about him, he developed a form of what anthropologists currently describe as amoral familism. For those who befriended him—most significantly the Earps—he developed pseudo-family attachments, attempting to replace the ties that had been left behind in Georgia. He forged strong, perhaps even obsessive, bonds of loyalty to this new family. He allowed the family, not the community, the state, or the territory, to determine right and wrong. He was a complex man with a simple code of right and wrong. His adherence to that code makes for rattling good history.

Appendix: John Henry Holliday's Genealogy

The origin of John Henry Holliday's family in America dates back to the emigration from Ireland of his great-great-grandparents, William Holliday, Sr., and his wife, Ann, sometime after 1750. The Scotch-Irish Hollidays and their children first settled amid other Irish immigrants in Laurens County, South Carolina. They later moved to Augusta in Richmond County, Georgia, prior to the American Revolution.

In 1779 William and his son William, Jr., enlisted in Capt. Thomas Cole's Fifth Company of Col. Elijah Clarke's first regiment of mounted infantry.[1] On February 14 the two Hollidays saw action in the Battle of Kettle Creek in Wilkes County near Tyrone, Georgia. Following this service, William, Sr., moved his growing family to Wilkes County, Georgia, and settled at Little River on state bounty lands that he received for his service. Here his ten children all reached maturity. It is known that at least some of the children, possibly all, were born in Ireland. In addition to William (Jr.), the other children were Robert, Thomas, Abraham, Ayres, John, Jane, Mary, Ann, and Elizabeth. William Holliday, Sr., died during the summer of 1786.[2]

William Holliday, Jr., John Henry's great-grandfather, emigrated with his parents from Ireland. Following his father's death in 1786, William took his wife, Jane Cooper Holliday, and their children back to Laurens County, South Carolina, and settled about ten miles south of Tumbling Shoals. He died in 1826, and his will was proved in Laurens County on November 14 of that year. The children of William and Jane Holliday were William, Robert Alexander, Matthew, Martha Ann (nicknamed Nancy), and Margaret.[3]

Grandfather Robert Alexander Holliday was the first of John Henry's Holliday ancestors to be born in America, at Laurens County, South Carolina, in 1787. As a young man, Robert would accompany his father when William traveled the ten miles to the Masonic Lodge meetings held at the home of Henry Burroughs. Henry Burroughs (1750–1829) had emigrated from England, married Amy Stiles, who was twenty-seven years younger, and settled at Hickory Tavern, Laurens County, South Carolina. After serving in the American Revolutionary Army, Henry moved to Tumbling Shoals in Laurens County. He kept a public house (tavern) at both places. At Tumbling Shoals he also had a mill, store, blacksmith shop, and hotel. It was at the Masonic Lodge meetings that Robert became acquainted with Henry and Amy's daughter Rebecca, born in Laurens County on November 28, 1800.[4] On June 4, 1818, thirty-one-year-old Robert and seventeen-year-old Rebecca were married.

Following his father William's death in 1826, Robert and Rebecca resettled, along with his in-laws, Henry and Amy, in Anderson County, South Carolina. After the death of his father-in-law in 1831, Robert brought his wife, six children, mother-in-law, and eight slaves to Fayette County, Georgia. Five more children were born there.

Named for the Marquis de Lafayette, the notable French statesman and soldier, Fayette County had been created in 1821, following the signing of the Creek Indian Treaty in January of that year. In 1823 the Georgia Legislature incorporated the City of Fayetteville as the county seat.[5] With its loblolly pines, cotton fields, and red Georgia clay, Fayette County was depicted by Margaret Mitchell (*Gone with the Wind*) as "a savagely red land, a pleasant land of white houses, peaceful plowed fields and sluggish yellow rivers, . . . of brightest sun glare and densest shade."[6]

In 1832 Robert paid $320 for a 405-acre farm about three miles southwest of the city of Fayetteville.[7] Over the next two years, through purchase, he doubled the size of his farm to 810 acres.[8] Although he produced cows, poultry, and vegetables, cotton was king in this area of Georgia and was the foundation of his economic activity. However, Robert was not content simply to grow cotton. Presbyterian and raised with the ethic of stewardship, he had acquired from Henry Burroughs experience in operating small businesses. Robert developed a philosophy that the secret of economic success and respectability was in commerce, built upon an agricultural foundation. This is the philosophy that he later instilled in his sons. In 1836 he began buying city lots in Fayetteville. In 1837 he founded what would become a thriving hotel business. By 1850 Robert Holliday had accumulated 1,125 acres of agricultural land in Fayette County and 10 lots and 23 acres of commercial and residential property in Fayetteville—ten thousand dollars' worth of real estate.[9] While his head was always in his account books, his feet remained rooted to the soil. Therefore, while he maintained a Glynn Street house in Fayetteville, his farm remained his home and served as the focal point of Holliday family activities for almost two decades.

Henry Burroughs Holliday, the father of John Henry Holliday, was the firstborn child of Robert and Rebecca. Henry was born on March 19, 1819, and was twelve years old when his father moved the family to Georgia.[10] In 1838 he served in the Cherokee Indian War as second sergeant in John D. Stell's Corps of Stokes' First Georgia Volunteers. Henry also served as a second lieutenant in Company I, known as the Fannin Avengers, of the First Georgia Volunteers during the Mexican War and was discharged at Jalapa, Mexico, effective June 1, 1847.[11]

On January 8, 1849, the Reverend Jonathan W. Wilson married Henry B. Holliday and Alice Jane McKey of Henry County, Georgia.[12] Born in South Carolina on April 21, 1829, Alice was the daughter of William Land McKey (1800–1856) and Jane Cloud McKey (1804–53).[13] Henry and Alice settled just north of the railroad tracks in the city of Griffin, Georgia. Henry purchased the house, located on the south side of Tinsley Street, between Hill and Eighth Streets, just two weeks before the wedding.[14]

Henry had six younger brothers, only three of whom lived to adulthood. Of his four sisters, only two survived to maturity.

Henry's brother William Cooper Holliday was born on December 16, 1820, at Laurens County, South Carolina, and married Jane Holcomb on November 1, 1842. He died on April 2, 1868, and had no children. He was a farmer and tavern owner.

The second brother of Henry Holliday was John Stiles Holliday. He was born on December 4, 1822, and was eight years old when the family moved to Fayetteville.[15] Three months after his twenty-first birthday John married Permelia Ellen Ware on March 17, 1844.[16] Permelia was born in Danielsville, Georgia, on February 3, 1825, the daughter of George Washington Ware and Mildred Sorrells Ware.[17] John's new father-in-law had settled in Fayette County in 1823 and represented the county in the Georgia State Legislature in 1839. Soon after his marriage, John S. Holliday graduated from the Medical College of Georgia at Augusta, founded in 1829 as the Medical Institute of the State of Georgia. The wife of the new Dr. Holliday gave birth to their first child, Ellen, on December 28, 1844. Ellen died on May 25, 1846. In 1846 Dr. Holliday and his wife set up housekeeping in a home on Lanier Avenue, one-half block west of the courthouse in Fayetteville.[18] In this home their first son, George Henry Holliday, was born on September 26, 1846.[19] Robert Alexander Holliday (II), their second son, arrived four years later on October 14, 1850.[20] John Stiles Holliday, Jr., their third son and last child, was born on February 12, 1857.

Another of Henry's brothers, Robert Kennedy Holliday, was born on April 6, 1829, the sixth child and the last of Robert and Rebecca Holliday's sons to survive to adulthood and to raise a family.[21] He was only an infant when the family left South Carolina for

Georgia. Robert married Mary Anne Fitzgerald of Fayetteville on March 6, 1848.[22] She was the daughter of James and Mary Ann [O']Carew Fitzgerald and was born on November 6, 1831, in Fayette County, Georgia. Mary Ann's father and his brother, Philip Fitzgerald, had emigrated to America from Ireland in 1825. They both taught school in Fayetteville and later became shopkeepers. Philip Fitzgerald was the great-grandfather of Margaret Mitchell, who later immortalized the region's history in *Gone with the Wind*. The eight children born to Robert and Mary Anne Holliday were Martha Anne "Mattie" (Sister Mary Melanie, Sisters of Mercy), born December 14, 1849, and died April 19, 1939; Lucy Rebecca, born in 1850 and died in 1912; Mary Theresa, born in 1852 and died in 1896; Roberta Rosalie, born in 1857 and died in 1893; Catherine Clara, born in 1859 and died in 1902; James Robert "Jim Bob," born in 1864 and died on December 25, 1943; Frances Marie, born in 1867 and died in 1955; and Philip Bernard, born in 1868 and died in infancy.

Martha Holliday, Henry's oldest sister and Robert and Rebecca's fourth child, was born on December 1, 1824, in Laurens County, South Carolina.[23] She married Col. James Franklin Johnson on November 23, 1840, in Fayetteville.[24] Nearly eight years her elder, Colonel Johnson was already a successful attorney, planter, and merchant when he married Martha. James Johnson later served as clerk of the Fayette County Superior Court in 1847. Their three children were Thomas Daniel, born in 1841 and died in 1884; Martha, born and died in 1844; and John Allen, born in 1846 (death date unknown).

Tragedy struck in the spring of 1834 when an epidemic hit the Robert Holliday household and took the lives of three of Henry's younger brothers and sisters in one week. The family Bible sadly reveals that the fifth child of Robert and Rebecca, Amy Holliday, born on November 7, 1826, died on May 15, 1834. Their seventh child, George Washington Holliday, born on February 16, 1831, died on May 22; and their eighth child, Jane, born on December 13, 1832, died on May 19. The next five years brought three more births and two more deaths to the household of Robert and Rebecca Holliday. Their ninth child, Matthew Calhoun Holliday, was born on November 25, 1834, and died on September 2, 1836. Their tenth child, Thomas Jefferson Holliday, was born on November 11, 1836, and died on April 6, 1839. The children were all buried in the Fayetteville City Cemetery.

Henry Holliday's youngest sister was Rebecca Annaliza, born in Fayetteville on March 15, 1839.[25] She married Joseph H. Jones in 1858. They had two children, Martha, born in 1859, and James, born in 1861. Following Joseph's death, presumably in the war, Annaliza married her second husband, Alpheus W. McCoin, in 1864. In 1872 she and her husband moved to Laclede, in Pottawatomie County, Kansas, with her two children, Martha and James, and their two children, a daughter, Hallie, born in 1865, and son, William, born in 1867. After their move to Kansas, one more daughter, Pearl, was born in 1873.

The year after the birth of Henry's last sister, Rebecca Annaliza, Gen. Lewis Lawrence Griffin, president of the Monroe Railroad Company. founded the city of Griffin, twenty miles southeast of Fayetteville. He believed that Georgia's north-south railroad and east-west railroad would ultimately intersect there. By 1842 the north-south line from Macon had reached Griffin;

in 1843 it had arrived in Jonesboro and was headed toward Marthasville (now Atlanta).

The population of Fayette County drastically declined as many of its citizens moved closer to the railroad's route. Henry's brother Dr. Holliday retained his residence in Fayetteville as did his brother William, but Henry, his brother Robert, and brother-in-law Col. James Johnson sought opportunity closer to the railroad.

As Robert and Rebecca's children pursued their own fortunes in the world, they remained within a twenty-mile radius of the family home when beginning their own households. Fayetteville continued to serve as the magnet that frequently drew their expanding family together.

Notes

Chapter 1. Farewell

1. "Recollections of Sophie Walton Murphy; 1930–1932, as told to Carl Birger Olson" (hereafter cited as "Recollections, Sophie Walton Murphy"), typed MS, signed, author's collection.

2. "Recollections of Mary Cowperthwaite Fulton Holliday (Mrs. Robert Alexander Holliday, DDS) 1935–1940, as told to Carl Birger Olson," typed MS, signed, author's collection (hereinafter cited as "Recollections, M. F. Holliday"). The stickpin is presently in the possession of Frank and Carolyn Holliday Manley of Decatur, Georgia. Mrs. Manley is the granddaughter of John Henry's cousin James Robert Holliday.

Chapter 2. Birth of a New Holliday

1. Henry B. Holliday Family Bible.
2. Ibid.

3. "Recollections, M. F. Holliday."

4. Mary Fulton Holliday, Atlanta, Georgia, to Mary Holliday Olson, April 1, 1940, Chicago, Illinois.

5. First Presbyterian Church, Griffin, Georgia, Record Book. "Alice Jane Holliday joined the church and was baptized. Died, date unknown."

6. Ibid.

7. This pendant was inherited by Permelia Ware Holliday upon the death of her mother-in-law. It was later inherited by Permelia's daughter-in-law, Mary Fulton Holliday, then by Adeline Hooper Holliday, followed by Mary Holliday Olson. The pendant is now owned and worn by the author.

Chapter 3. Early Childhood

1. Amy Burroughs died on June 13, 1852, as evidenced by her tombstone in the Fayetteville City Cemetery.

2. Anderson County, South Carolina, Will of Henry Burroughs dated October 12, 1829, and proven December 21, 1829.

3. Henry Burroughs Holliday, Valdosta, Georgia, to Robert Alexander Holliday, D.D.S., Atlanta, Georgia, May 7, 1884, author's collection.

4. "Recollections, M. F. Holliday."

5. Albert S. Pendleton, Jr., and Susan McKey Thomas, *In Search of the Hollidays: The Story of Doc Holliday and His Holliday and McKey Families*, p. 13.

6. Mary Fulton Holliday, Atlanta, Georgia, to Mary Holliday Olson, April 1, 1940, Chicago, Illinois.

7. "Recollections, M. F. Holliday."

8. Will of William L. McKey, Spalding County, Georgia, Will Book A, p. 26.

9. In addition to his farm Henry B. Holliday purchased a number of town lots in Griffin and West Griffin between 1851 and 1855; see Spalding County, Georgia, Deed Book A, pp. 52, 53, 56, 62, 457, 458, and 615; Deed Book B, p. 167.

10. Uncle Philip, many years later, gained worldwide renown. He was the great-grandfather of Margaret Mitchell, who patterned the character of Gerald O'Hara in *Gone with the Wind* after him.

11. Stephens Mitchell, "Fitzgerald History," in Joseph Henry Hightower Moore, *A History of Clayton County, Georgia: 1821–1983*, ed. Alice Copeland Kilgore et al. (Clayton County, Ga.: Ancestors Unlimited, 1983), pp. 241–46.

12. Will of Henry Burrow [*sic*], Anderson County, South Carolina, Will Book 1, p. 367, probated December 21, 1829.

13. "Recollections, M. F. Holliday."

14. Mattie also attained a degree of fame in later years when she was used as a role model in *Gone with the Wind*. Most literary historians consider Melanie in the book to be patterned after Mattie Holliday (later Sister Mary Melanie).

15. Hugh M. Dorsey, Sr., "Fayette County's Only Ante-bellum Home Still Standing," in Carolyn C. Cary, ed., *The History of Fayette County: 1821–1971*, pp. 121–23. This is still believed to be the only unaltered antebellum home remaining in Fayette County.

16. Their younger son, John, was the same age as his cousin George (Dr. John and Permelia's eldest son). No child was ever without a companion of comparable age during these large gatherings of the mid- to late 1850s.

17. The Fayetteville Academy, referred to as the Fayetteville Female Academy in Margaret Mitchell's *Gone with the Wind*, numbered among its graduates Anne Elizabeth Fitzgerald (1844–1934), Miss Mitchell's grandmother.

18. The Griffin Male and Female Academy was located on land originally prepared by General Griffin, with Quilly Street on the north, Chappell Street on the south, and Sixth Street as its eastern boundary.

19. Spalding County, Georgia, Minute Book A (1852–70), pp. 62, 100, and 132; Docket Book A (1852–79), p. 27.

20. Will of William L. McKey, Spalding County, Georgia, Will Book A, p. 26.

21. Spalding County, Georgia, Letters of Guardianship (1857–84), p. 43.

22. Pendleton and Thomas, *In Search of the Hollidays*, p. 13.

23. On March 30, 1926, eighty-four years after his first successful use of ether to perform an operation, Dr. Long's statue was unveiled in Statuary Hall at the National Capitol, where each state has the privilege of honoring its two most distinguished citizens. On April 8, 1940, the United States Postal Service paid tribute to Dr. Long by issuing a stamp numbering him among the scientists of the Famous Americans Series.

Chapter 4. The War Years

1. Cary, *The History of Fayette County: 1821–1971*, pp. 344–46.

2. Roster of the Twenty-seventh Georgia Volunteer Infantry, Georgia State Archives, Civil War Records Section. The Twenty-seventh Georgia was attached to Col.

Alfred Colquitt's Brigade, Gen. Robert Hoke's Division, First Corps, of the Army of Tennessee.

3. Payroll Records, Twenty-seventh Georgia Volunteer Infantry, Georgia State Archives, Civil War Records Section. On June 14, 1862, Maj. Henry B. Holliday was paid $112.00 for his twenty–four days of service as a captain and $785.00 for five months and seven days of service as a major.

4. Ibid.; Lillian Henderson, *Roster of the Confederate Soldiers of Georgia: 1861–1865*, vol. 3 (Hapeville, Ga.: Longino and Porter, n.d.), p. 285; Muster Rolls, Henry B. Holliday

5. Commission Appointment, Robert K. Holliday, collection of Carolyn Manley Holliday. The commission was offered on May 17, 1861.

6. Moore, *A History of Clayton County, Georgia: 1821–1983*, p. 25.

7. Quoted in Cary, *The History of Fayette County: 1821–1971*, p. 345.

8. Maj. H. B. Holliday to Col. L. B. Smith, July 27, 1862, Records, Twenty-seventh Georgia Volunteer Infantry, Georgia State Archives, Civil War Records Section.

9. Roster, Twenty-seventh Georgia Volunteer Infantry.

10. Pendleton and Thomas, *In Search of the Hollidays*, p. 15.

11. Spalding County, Georgia, Deed Book C, pp. 641, 649, 692, and Deed Book D, p. 218.

12. Lowndes County, Georgia, Deed Book B, p. 499.

13. On January 10, 1859, guardianship for Margaret Ann McKey transferred from Henry B. Holliday to Dr. James Taylor McKey, Margaret's older brother. Henry

ceased to file an accounting balance for Margaret in 1859. However, she continued to live with the Henry Holliday family, as evidenced by the 1860 census. With her brothers serving in the Confederate Army, it is probable that she remained part of the Henry Holliday household at the time of the move. Spalding County, Georgia, Minute Book A (1850–70), p. 100; Spalding County, Georgia, Docket Book A (1852–79), p. 41; Spalding County, Georgia, Annual Returns, vol. 1, pp. 359–60; United States Government, 1860 Census, Spalding County, Georgia, pp. 25–26.

14. $3,150, Lowndes County, Georgia, Deed Book B, p. 505.

15. Martha Anne Holliday, "Memoirs," from Pendleton and Thomas, *In Search of the Hollidays*, appendix, p. 11.

16. Robert L. Rodgers, "Roster of the Battalion of the Georgia Military Institute," *Southern Historical Society Papers* 33 (1905): 306–7, 314.

17. Martha Anne Holliday, "Memoirs," pp. 11 and 12.

18. Ibid.

19. Carolyn Holliday Manley, Decatur, Georgia, interview by John D. Tanner, Jr., June 25, 1995.

20. Mary Holliday Olson, Fallbrook, California, interview by the author, August 1, 1994.

21. Robert Lee Holliday, New Orleans, Louisiana, interview by the author, January 14, 1995; "Memoirs of Robert Lee Holliday, Sr.; May 19, 1915 to Only God Knows, part 1 (1915–1973)," typed MS, 1995 (photocopy), pp. 4, 8.

22. "Recollections, Sophie Walton Murphy."

23. Records, Georgia Soldier Roster Commission, March 12, 1929, collection of Carolyn Holliday Manley.

Chapter 5. Reconstruction

1. United States Government, 1870 Census, Lowndes County, Georgia, p. 662.

2. United States Government, 1860 Census, Fayette County, Georgia, p. 167; United States Government, 1870 Census, Fulton County, Georgia, p. 70.

3. Clayton County, Georgia, Probate Court, Robert K. Holliday Probate #1890-2451.

4. *History of Lowndes County, Georgia: 1825–1941* (Valdosta, Ga.: General James Jackson Chapter, D.A.R., n.d.), p. 109.

5. Pendleton and Thomas, *In Search of the Hollidays*, p. 10.

6. Henry B. Holliday had returned from the Mexican War with a young orphan, Francisco Hidalgo. The boy, then thirteen years old, was last known to be living in the Holliday household in 1850, at the time of the United States Census; United States Government, 1850 Census, Spalding County, Georgia, p. 889. He married Martha Freeman in Butts County, Georgia, on June 12, 1854, and later served in the war from Butts County, with his name anglicized to Edalgo. He died on January 13, 1873, of tuberculosis (Pendleton and Thomas, *In Search of the Hollidays*, pp. 5–6). The contagious nature of tuberculosis suggests that he may have contracted the disease from Mrs. Holliday. It is also possible that he may have been the source of the disease and introduced it into the Holliday household.

7. Obituary; ibid., p. 11.

8. "Recollections, M. F. Holliday"; *Gunnison (Colorado) Daily-News Democrat*, June 18, 1882.

9. Pendleton and Thomas, *In Search of the Hollidays*, pp. 12, 55.

10. Deeded to Rachel Holliday on February 12, 1875; Lowndes County, Georgia, Deed Book, p. 410; ibid., p. 12.

11. "Recollections, M. F. Holliday."

12. *History of Lowndes County, Georgia: 1825–1941*, p. 73.

13. Fayette County Deed Book I, p. 225. The property included "that land enclosed by fencing and known in the village as the J. S. Holliday Town property," lots 37, 38, 53, 54, 69, 70, and part of lot 4.

14. This is presently the site of the Atlanta Civic Center.

15. "Nanny" (as Sophie came to be called) not only taught these games to the Holliday boys of the 1860s and 1870s but taught Robert Alexander's children, Lewis, Clarence, and Mary Adele. She later lived with and raised the five children who were born to Lewis Ware and Adeline Hooper Holliday. One of those children, Mary Holliday Olson, taught these games to her daughter, the author.

16. The rules of these games as learned by the author are basically the same as those taught to John Henry.

17. The younger Robert A. Holliday eventually became the owner of six of his father's diamonds. Some years later in Chicago, his widowed wife, Mary, was forced by her lack of finances to sell five of the six diamonds, the sixth having been passed to her only surviving son, Lewis Ware Holliday. The purchasers of the five diamonds were the Hon. John K. Prindiville and his wife, Mary, who was a first cousin of Lee E. Hooper, father of Mrs. Lewis Ware Holliday. Mary Prindiville, who had no children, eventually reunited the Holliday diamonds with the family of her surrogate daughter, Mrs. Lewis Ware Holliday.

Lewis Ware Holliday was very much a Holliday male—tall, good-looking, very athletic, and a high stakes gambler. He never wore a diamond stickpin. He had his diamond, the largest of the Holliday diamonds at 2.49 carats, fashioned into an engagement ring for his fiancée, Adeline Hooper (1888–1988). In 1919 he took it from her to have it cleaned. Before returning the diamond, he died of kidney failure at the age of thirty–two. Mrs. Holliday had no idea where her ring was located. Sophie Walton, then an elderly woman working for the Holliday family in Chicago, uncovered a pawn ticket. Lewis, unbeknown to his wife, had pawned the diamond to cover gambling losses. Mrs. Holliday eventually reclaimed it. That diamond is presently owned and worn by the author. The other five remain in the possession of members of the family.

18. Pendleton and Thomas, *In Search of the Hollidays*, p. 33: "the tale of killing a negro and running away she [Miss Lillian McKey of Valdosta, daughter of William H. McKey and John Henry Holliday's cousin] thinks not true. However, he did fire a gun into the air to scare some negro boys who were in swimming to see them run"; J. F. DeLacy, Havana, Florida, to Robert N. Mullin, Toledo, Ohio, January 9, 1949, Stuart N. Lake Collection, Letter Box 10, Huntington Library, San Marino, California.

19. Bat Masterson wrote that Holliday had killed two and wounded several others. There is no foundation for this statement; Bat Masterson, "'Doc' Holliday," *Human Life* (May 1907), reprinted in *Famous Gunfighters of the Western Frontier*, annotated by Jack DeMattos (Monroe, Wash.: Weatherford Press, 1982), p. 77. Walter Noble Burns in *Tombstone: An Iliad of the Southwest*, placed the number of fatalities as high as three but allowed that it had been written that possibly they were only wounded (p. 49). John

Myers Myers in *Doc Holliday* reduced the number of fatalities to one (p. 19). The unfounded story of fatalities was in no way helped by Glenn G. Boyer's celebrated spoof, *The Illustrated Life of Doc Holliday*, which was taken seriously by many recent writers.

20. At this time, Robert Kennedy Holliday was working as a clerk at Tidwell and Holliday in Atlanta. He remained at Tidwell and Holliday through 1870; *Atlanta City Directory* (Atlanta: William Hanleiter, pub., 1871), p. 227.

21. "Recollections, M. F. Holliday."

22. Ibid.

23. Thannie Wisenbaker diary, quoted in Pendleton and Thomas, *In Search of the Hollidays*, p. 33.

24. *Seventeenth Annual Announcement of the Pennsylvania College of Dental Surgery*, pp. 2, 4, 5, 10, and 11.

25. Robert G. Kesel, D.D.S, "The Teeth and Their Care," in *Family Medical Guide*, ed. Donald G. Cooley (New York: Better Homes and Gardens Books, 1973), p. 526.

26. Ronald D. Allison, D.D.S, interview with the author, July 25, 1995, author's collection. In 1961 Dr. Allison had occasion to provide dental services to this former patient of John Henry Holliday's. He confirmed her story with the Pierre Fouchard Academy in 1963.

27. *History of Lowndes County, Georgia: 1825–1941*, p. 249.

28. United States Government, 1870 Census, Valdosta, Lowndes County, Georgia, p. 33. Dr. Frink practiced in Valdosta from 1869 until 1879.

29. Pendleton and Thomas, *In Search of the Hollidays*, p. 42.

30. *Seventeenth Announcement of the Pennsylvania College of Dental Surgery*, p. 12. The Pennsylvania College of Dental Surgery merged with the University

of Pennsylvania in 1909. Presently, "the University of Pennsylvania claims 'Doc' Holliday as an alumni [*sic*]" (Gail M. Pietrzyk, public services archivist, University Archives and Records Center, University of Pennsylvania, to the author, March 20, 1995).

    31. "Recollections, M. F. Holliday."

Chapter 6. Atlanta Dentist

    1. "Recollections, M. F. Holliday."

    2. Mary Cowperthwaite Fulton Holliday, "Love's Lament, 1933," typed MS (photocopy), pp. 98–99.

    3. "Recollections, Sophie Walton Murphy."

    4. "Recollections, M. F. Holliday"; Dr. Samuel Hape remained a family friend, later serving as a pallbearer at the funeral of Robert A. Holliday, D.D.S.

    5. H. Herbert Johnson, ed., *Biographies of Past Presidents of the Georgia State Dental Society*, p. 20.

    6. Ibid., p. 2.

    7. *Atlanta Constitution*, August 15, 1872.

    8. Johnson, *Biographies*, p. 20. Arthur C. Ford died in Palatka, Florida, in 1883.

    9. Spalding County, Georgia, Deed Book F, p. 1.

Grantee: Holliday, John H.
Grantor: Holliday, John H. by Guardian
Recorded 12 Nov. 1872

State of GA, Lowndes County; Indenture, 10th of September 1872, by Henry Burroughs Holliday as natural guardian for his son John H. Holliday of the first two parts and John Henry Holliday of Fulton County and city of Atlanta of the second part. For the sum of $10 paid, conveys a certain house and Lot No. 10 in the plan of the Baptist Church Lot survey, City of Griffin, 28 feet fronting Solomon St. and owning back 90 feet to the adjoining lot of Miss McKey on the east side and on the west side adjoining the building known as "Alama's Hall" [Alama's Hall was an arcade of stores]. Recorded 12 Nov. 1872.

Several authors have concluded that John Henry Holliday owned two parcels of land in Griffin. This is in error. A copy of the September 10, 1872, deed was recorded on March 28, 1873, due to the original deed having been misplaced. The copy conveys the same Lot 10.

10. Spalding County, Georgia, Deed Book F, recorded March 28 1873, p. 95. N. G. Philips died in 1882, still in possession of the property. His estate bequeathed it to Paul Cook of Louisiana.

11. "Recollections, M. F. Holliday."

12. Ibid.

13. *Nineteenth Annual Announcement of the Pennsylvania College of Dental Surgery*, p. 12.

14. Obituary abstract from "Garrett's Necrology," MS, Roll No. 6, Frame 642, Atlanta History Center, Atlanta, Georgia. When Robert K. Holliday's estate was appraised on February 8, 1878, it was valued at $553.75 and consisted of one lot valued at $400 and personal property valued as $153.75. Clayton County, Georgia, Probate Court, Robert K. Holliday Probate, #1890–2451, Inventory—8 Feb. 1878.

15. His wife, Mary Anne, survived him by almost twenty years. She died in Atlanta on May 29, 1892, and is buried beside her husband in Fayetteville Cemetery.

16. After the 1860s tuberculosis was increasingly thought to be caused by a germlike agent, but it

was not until 1882 that Robert Koch, who had already identified the bacterial cause for anthrax, identified the tubercle bacillus as the agent responsible for tuberculosis. Meanwhile, George Bodington (1799–1882) continued to call for country air and a nutritious diet—a regime first suggested about 1800 by the renowned Dr. Benjamin Rush of Philadelphia. George Bodington, M.D., *An Essay on the Treatment and Cure of Pulmonary Consumption* (London: Longman, Orme, Brown, Green, and Longmans, 1840). Dr. John Stiles Holliday *did not* prescribe late nights, smoke-filled rooms, or an abundance of whiskey.

17. Ibid.

18. Charles Nordhoff, *California: For Health, Pleasure and Residence: A Book for Travellers and Settlers* (New York: Harper and Brothers, 1872), p. 110.

19. This volume, inscribed "J.S.H. Nov. 12, 1872," is presently in the possession of the author.

20. "Recollections, M. F. Holliday."

21. Ibid.

22. Ibid.

23. "Recollections, Sophie Walton Murphy."

Chapter 7. Gone to Texas

1. *Dallas Weekly Herald*, February 28, 1874.

2. Ibid., March 13, 1869.

3. Published on December 1, 1873, the directory was released in February of 1874; *Dallas Daily Commercial*, February 13, 1874.

4. United States Government, 1880 Census, Dallas County, Texas, vol. 9, E. D. 56, Sheet 30, Line 81.

5. The office was located at the present site of the Dallas County Community College.

6. *Dallas Weekly Herald,* October 9, 1873.

7. John Henry wrote to his Uncle John about his prizes; "Recollections, M. F. Holliday."

8. *Gunnison (Colorado) Daily-News Democrat,* June 18, 1882.

9. *Dallas Weekly Herald,* October 11, 1873.

10. *Fort Worth Democrat,* December 6, 1873.

11. Ibid., November 1, 1873. Thompson's was not universally popular. Several years later the *Frontier Echo* (Jacksboro) would report: "The Dallas *Commercial* has commenced war against John Thompson's Varieties, and for the good name of Dallas, we trust the hell-hole may be abated" (February 15, 1878).

12. Robert Will Burton, great-grandson of Frederick A. Will, co-founder of Will and Finck, interview with the author, September 28, 1996, Fallbrook, California; Will and Finck, *Gambler's Cheating Equipment Catalog* (San Francisco, 1896); Barnard R. Levine, *Knifemakers of Old San Francisco* (San Francisco: Badger Books, 1977), pp. 91–93.

13. Masterson, " 'Doc' Holliday," p. 36.

14. "Recollections, M. F. Holliday."

15. *Dallas Daily Commercial,* March 2, 1874. John Henry accepted responsibility for the two outstanding debts against the firm, most likely for the major dental equipment purchased for his use when the partnership was formed.

16. *State of Texas v. J. H. Holliday,* Dallas County, Court Minutes, 1874–78, Case #2236, May 12, 1874, pp. 209, 256–57. The others were booked under case numbers 2237 through 2248.

17. *Dallas Weekly Herald,* November 21, 1874.

18. The resolution of the charge in Dallas County Criminal Court did not occur until the following year.

19. *Dallas Weekly Herald*, May 2, 1874.

20. "Recollections, M, F. Holliday"; Mary Katherine Cummings (Kate Elder), "The O.K. Corral Fight at Tombstone: A Footnote by Kate Elder," ed. A. W. Bork and Glenn G. Boyer, *Arizona and the West* 19 (Spring 1977): 83; *Pueblo (Colorado) Daily Chieftain*, May 17, 1882.

21. J. Frank Dobie, *A Vaquero of the Brush Country* (Boston: Little, Brown and Co., 1929), p. 189.

22. The only appearance of J. H. Holliday's name was in the Assessment Roll of Precinct No. 1, 1874, p. 20. Having moved from Dallas prior to January 1875, he does not appear on the 1875 tax rolls.

23. *Dallas Daily Commercial*, June 22, 1874.

24. *Dallas Weekly Herald*, June 27, 1874.

25. As an indication of Dallas's declining prosperity, the sum of Dallas County's occupation tax for 1874 was $13,177. In 1875 it dropped to $5,860; *Fort Worth Democrat*, April 1, 1876.

26. *Gunnison Daily-News Democrat*, June 18, 1882; "Recollections, M. F. Holliday."

27. *Dallas Weekly Herald*, September 12, 1874, list of unclaimed letters.

28. February 16, 1875; *Directory of the City of Dallas* for 1875—Dr. Holliday's name does not appear.

29. On September 30, 1874, yet another fire struck and destroyed the office shared by Dr. Seegar and Dr. McQueen; *Dallas Weekly Herald*, October 3, 1874. Dr. Seegar reopened over the City Bank of Dallas in the Block and Jett Building at the corner of Elm and Lamar several days later; *Dallas Daily Herald*, October 10, 1874.

30. *Denison Daily Cresset,* April 1, 1875; *Fort Worth Democrat,* November 13, 1875.

31. *Dallas Daily Commercial,* August 12, 1874. "It is admitted by all that Charlie beats the world mixing drinks; and from our own experience, unqualifiedly assert that Charlie 'understands his gait'" (ibid., August 14, 1874).

32. Austin had been previously charged with an assault with intent to commit murder on Maj. G. W. Campbell, ex–marshal of the City of Dallas. He was judged to be not guilty (ibid., March 6, 1874).

33. *Dallas Weekly Herald,* January 2, 1875.

34. *State of Texas v. J. H. Holliday,* Dallas County, Court Minutes, 1874–78, Indictment #2643, January 18, 1875, pp. 486 and 516.

35. The details of this rather mundane shooting were embellished by Stuart Lake, who made the erroneous assertion that "Doc's first fight in the West ended a row over a Dallas card-game. He shot and killed a top notch gunman, and as Doc was comparatively a stranger where his victim had many friends, Doc had to emigrate" (*Wyatt Earp, Frontier Marshal,* p. 196). John Myers Myers accepted Lake's inaccurate account and added to the myth by stating that Holliday killed a second prominent citizen (*Doc Holliday,* p. 45).

36. *State of Texas v. J. H. Holliday,* Dallas County Court Minutes, 1874–78, Case #2236, April 13, 1875.

37. *Denison Daily Cresset,* May 28, 1875.

38. Bat Masterson claimed that John Henry was involved in a scrape with a soldier in Jacksboro, Texas, on his way to Denver, resulting in the soldier's death ("'Doc' Holliday," p. 36). Stuart Lake added that "Doc tangled with

three or four more gunmen successfully, but eventually killed a soldier" (*Wyatt Earp*, p. 196). John Myers Myers placed John Henry in Jacksboro for about a year, involved him in three gunfights with civilians, and stated that "Doc killed his second man in that town. . . . a member of the Sixth Cavalry Regiment" (*Doc Holliday*, p. 56). There is no foundation for these stories. Neither the Jack County court records nor the *Frontier Echo* (Jacksboro) mention Holliday.

39. Carl Coke Rister, *Fort Griffin on the Texas Frontier*, p. 132.

40. Located on Jefferson Street, between Main and Elm; see advertisement, *Dallas Daily Commercial*, March 6, 1874, and August 20, 1874. Most certainly John Henry and Donnelly were acquainted in Dallas.

41. Lester W. Galbreath, *Fort Griffin and the Clear Fork Country*, p. 38. Donnelly's wife was Lucinda Selman, the gunman's sister.

42. *State of Texas v. Mike Lynch & Dock [sic] Holliday*, Shackelford County, Minutes of the District Court, vol. A, 6-7 [18]75 to 3-1 [18]84, Case #34, June 12, 1875, p. 16.

43. *State of Texas v. Mike Lynch*, Shackelford County, Minutes of the District Court, vol. A, 6-7 [18]75 to 3-1 [18]84, Case #14, May 17, 1875, p. 3.

44. Interview with Ty Cashion, author and assistant professor, East Texas State University, Commerce, Texas, October 31, 1995.

45. Shackelford County, Texas, District Court Docket, vol. 1, no pagination, in Pat Jahns, *The Frontier World of Doc Holliday*, p. 61. This record has since disappeared from the courthouse of Shackelford County; Frances Wheeler, county and district clerk, interview with the author, Albany, Texas, September 12, 1995. On May 17, 1876, a second order for a *capias* was issued for J. H.

Holliday due to his failure to appear; Shackelford County, Texas, Minutes of the District Court, vol. A, 6-7 [18]75 to 3-1 [18]84, Case #34, p. 49.

46. Shackelford County, Texas, District Court Docket, vol. 1, in Jahns, *The Frontier World of Doc Holliday*, p. 61.

Chapter 8. From Denver to Dodge

1. *Denver Republican*, May 22, 1882. His uncle, Thomas Sylvester McKey of Valdosta, Georgia, was the source of the name that John Henry created for this subterfuge.

2. Jahns, *The Frontier World of Doc Holliday*, p. 87, note 2. In 1875 Babb's Saloon was located at 357 Blake Street. At the time of Holliday's 1882 interview with the *Denver Republican* (May 22), Edward Chase operated his Palace Theatre at 357 and 359 Blake Street. *City Directory, Denver* (Denver: Corbett, Hoye and Co.), 1875, p. 71; 1877, p. 68; 1882, p. 151.

3. *Denver Republican*, December 25, 1887.

4. Masterson, "'Doc' Holliday," p. 37.

5. Walter Noble Burns (*Tombstone*, p. 49) also perpetuated the story, and Stuart Lake (*Wyatt Earp*, p. 196) elaborated on it. There is no record on the Denver Police Magistrate's Docket of this stabbing, nor was it mentioned in the newspapers at the time of the supposed occurrence. Pat Jahns speculated that the *Denver Republican* confused the story of a waiter with a bad reputation named "Kid" Ryan who was arrested for the stabbing of a barkeeper, John H. Brogan, in Moses' Home Saloon on Larimar Street; (*The Frontier World of Doc Holliday*, p. 84); *Denver Republican*, June 22, 1887; *City Directory, Denver* (Denver: Corbett and Ballenger, 1886), p. 155.

6. The Kansas Pacific had purchased the Denver Pacific in 1872. The Union Pacific purchased both lines in 1880.

7. *Black Hills Pioneer*, September 23, 1876. Babb and his partner A. H. Grant continued to operate the Theatre Comique at the Blake Street address in Denver.

8. *Cheyenne Daily Leader*, January 6, 1876.

9. Ibid., February 6, 1876; *Wyoming Weekly Leader*, February 12, 1876, in Ben T. Traywick, *John Henry: The "Doc" Holliday Story*, p. 48.

10. Neither the *Cheyenne Daily Leader* and *Daily Sun* nor the *Black Hills Pioneer* make mention of Doc. City of Cheyenne criminal records and Police Department records have not survived from this era. The surviving Laramie County records indicate that Doc was not charged with any criminal offense. John C. Thompson wrote in "In Old Wyoming," *Wyoming State Tribune* (Cheyenne), August 4, 1940, that Jeff Carr, the big Cheyenne town marshal, did not choose to take on a killer of Holliday's ruthless character. However, there is no reference to Doc in the papers of Jeff Carr; Thomas Jefferson Carr (1842–1916), Vertical File, Wyoming State Archives, Cheyenne, Wyoming. The *Daily Leader* of July 18, 1876, details the shooting of Dr. John Holliday, but the reference is to John A. Holliday, M.D., of Barry County, Missouri, who was gunned down by Bud Crawford on July 10, 1876. Crawford died awaiting charges; *Goodspeed's History of Barry County* (Goodspeed's Publishing Co., 1888; reprint, Cassville, Mo.: Litho Printers, 1995), p. 72.

11. *Black Hills Pioneer*, September 9, 1876.

12. Dodge City sutler Robert M. Wright recounted a humorous tale of John Henry's involvement in a confidence game during this time. Wright's account of Doc's

Heidelberg education and his diving down into mountain lakes to retrieve phony gold bricks is bizarre; Robert M. Wright, *Dodge City: The Cowboy Capital and the Great Southwest*, pp. 249–51.

13. J. H. Holliday of St. Louis was aboard the Cheyenne and Black Hills stage on June 26, 1877, when the stage and its passengers were robbed of twelve thousand dollars by the Bill Blevins Hat Creek gang; *Cheyenne Daily Leader*, June 28, June 29, and July 8, 1877; *Cheyenne Daily Sun*, June 28, 1877. However, this J. H. Holliday was Joseph H. Holliday, a representative of J. H. Weir and Co. of St. Louis; *Daily Sun*, July 15, 1877; *Gould's St. Louis City Directory, 1876* (St. Louis: Gould, 1876), p. 430.

14. "Recollections, M. F. Holliday."

15. *Dallas Weekly Herald*, July 7, 1877. Kahn was cleared of charges following an examination. All case records concerning this incident have disappeared from the Stephens County Courthouse; interview, Charise Johnson, deputy clerk, Stephens County, October 12, 1995, Stephens County, Texas. One case file concerning Henry Kahn remains in Stephens County; Stephens County, Texas, State Docket, County Court, 1877–97, File #23, *State of Texas vs. Henry Kahn, Keeping a Gaming Table*, filed on April 30, 1877. Records indicate that following the transfer of this case to the district court in May of 1877 it was continued in May and June, July's record is blank, and in August there was a judgment against the sureties who had posted Kahn's bond. The case was continued again in November and dismissed in December. At no time after April does Henry Kahn physically appear before the court. Also, at this time Kahn was under indictment in Shackelford County for forgery; June 27, 1877, Shackelford County, Texas, Minutes of the District Court, vol. A, 6-7 [18]75 to 3-1 [18]84, *State of Texas v. H. Kahn and Geo. Clay*, Case #96, p. 90. There is no record indicating his

appearance on this charge. Kahn seems to have left the area following the shooting of Holliday.

16. Apparently Doc wanted his uncle, rather than his father, contacted. Due to John Henry's estrangement from his father, many of his associates in the West, including Kate Elder, believed that Dr. John Stiles Holliday was Doc's father (Cummings, "The O.K. Corral Fight at Tombstone," p. 84).

17. "Recollections, M. F. Holliday."

18. *Fort Worth Democrat*, July 21, 1877.

19. "Recollections, M. F. Holliday."

20. Watt R. Mathews, quoted in Frances Mayhugh Holden, *Lambshead before Interwoven: A Texas Range Chronicle, 1848–1878*, p. 157; *Frontier Echo* (Jacksboro), March 3, 1876.

21. *Frontier Echo* (Jacksboro), April 28, 1876; June 9, 1876; June 30, 1876.

22. Larn was arrested in June 1878 and taken to Albany, Texas, for trial and was shot by vigilantes on June 23 of that year. Selman escaped to West Texas. Two years later, under the alias of Captain Tyson, he was arrested by Texas Rangers at Fort Davis and was returned to Shackelford County. Local citizens, tired of the Larn affair, turned a blind eye when Selman's guards fired into the air, allowing him to escape. Selman later became a peace officer in El Paso. In 1884 he killed former Texas Ranger Baz "Bass" Outlaw. On August 19, 1895, he killed gunman John Wesley Hardin. Selman, who turned to heavy drinking and gambling, was killed in an alley outside the Wigwam Saloon at El Paso on April 6, 1896, by Deputy U.S. Marshal George Scarborough.

23. A wealth of apocryphal stories of Doc's escapades at Fort Griffin have been written, based primarily on John Cloud Jacobs's letter of July 17, 1928, to Marvin

Hunter, who published the tales; J. Marvin Hunter, *The Story of Lottie Deno: Her Life and Times*, p. 58. Many writers, as well as residents of Fort Griffin, have used Hunter's stories to glorify Doc and bring fame and notoriety to Fort Griffin. Most contemporaries of Doc's in 1877 were not even aware of his presence. G. W. Robson, the insightful and witty publisher of the *Frontier Echo*, wrote of "deviltry at Fort Griffin" (March 10, 1876), a "shooting bee at Fort Griffin" (January 19, 1877), horse thieves (June 2, 1876), hangings (June 9, 1876), and damsels of spotted virtue (February 19, 1876). However, he never wrote of Doc Holliday. Robson founded the *Frontier Echo* on June 30, 1875, and it served the community of Jacksboro and the Clear Fork country until December 6, 1878. Robson reestablished his paper as the *Fort Griffin Echo* on January 4, 1879, and continued to publish in Fort Griffin until January 21, 1882. On January 6, 1883, he founded the *Albany Echo*. If Robson had any knowledge of Doc Holliday committing any illegal wrongdoing, he certainly would have printed it. Significantly, contemporary Sallie Reynolds Mathews also failed to mention Doc Holliday when she chronicled her experiences growing up on the Clear Fork of the Brazos (*Interwoven: A Pioneer Chronicle*). Don H. Biggers likewise neglected to note the presence of the notorious dentist in his *Shackelford County Sketches*, a history of Shackelford County. The only explanation for the obvious exclusion of John Henry Holliday by these noted writers is that Doc minded his own business and stuck to his dentistry and card playing. However, Doc's paid-up account with Conrad & Rath, merchandisers, then located at the post at Fort Griffin, indicates that during the week of September 14 to September 21, 1877, his drinking had not abated; "Day Ledger, Conrad & Rath, Fort Griffin, Texas," Hank C. Smith Collection, Panhandle-Plains Historical Museum, Canyon, Texas. Abstract by Chuck Hornung, Odessa, Texas.

24. Rister, *Fort Griffin on the Texas Frontier,* p. 195. Jack Schwartz came from Fort Worth. Schwartz, also formerly of Jacksboro, founded the Planter's Hotel sometime after February 9, 1877, at which time he was still a resident of Fort Worth; *Frontier Echo,* February 9, 1877; October 18, 1877.

25 *Fort Griffin Echo,* January 4, 1879.

26. Lester W. Galbreath, Fort Griffin State Historical Park, interview, Fort Griffin, Texas, August 9, 1995; Galbreath, *Fort Griffin and the Clear Fork Country,* p. 36. John Shannsey, formerly of Jacksboro and Fort Worth, came to Fort Griffin with Jack Schwartz and founded the Cattle Exchange Saloon at the same time Schwartz founded the Planter's Hotel. The *Frontier Echo* has both the Planter's and the Cattle Exchange in existence by October 18, 1877. Shannsey left Fort Griffin at the end of 1878, moving to Palo Pinto, Texas. "'Shanny' is a gentleman and a good man and we wish him success in his new location"; *Frontier Echo,* February 9, 1877; October 18, 1877; January 4, 1879.

27. It is possible that Doc and Kate had met previously in Deadwood. They are both thought to have spent the winter of 1876–77 there. Mary Katherine Harony, alias Kate Fisher and Kate Elder, was born on November 7, 1850, in the Pest section of Budapest. All information except as elsewise noted is from Cummings, "The O.K. Corral Fight at Tombstone," pp. 65–84.

28. Horony Family Record, compiled and supplied by Sharon Horony Osborne, 1997 (the Harony family currently spells the name "Horony"); Mrs. Ernest L. Beckwith (grandniece of Mary Katherine Harony), McDonough, New York, to Glenn G. Boyer, Bisbee, Arizona, January 22, 1977 (photocopy supplied by Glenn G. Boyer). The information was provided to Mrs. Beckwith's mother, Christine Harony Owens,

by Mary Harony Cummings. Two children were born of Michael Harony's first marriage, and two from his second marriage predeceased him.

29. Scott Co., Iowa, Petition of Otto Smith, October 7, 1867, Book 9, p. 186; copy supplied by Glenn G. Boyer.

30. Horony Family Group Record; Beckwith to Boyer, January 22, 1977.

31. Kate later claimed to have married Silas Melvin in St. Louis and that her husband and their infant son died in 1871. This was a fabrication on her part, probably to make herself appear more respectable. Silas H. Melvin was born about 1848 in Missouri. In 1870 he was an attendant at the St. Louis County Insane Asylum.

32. *St. Louis City Directory* (St. Louis: Edward's, 1870), p. 321.

33. They were married on October 10, 1871. Silas H. Melvin was living in St. Louis, at 1020 W. Brooklyn Street, in 1876; United States Government, 1870 Census, St. Louis County, Missouri, M593, Reel 808, p. 191; Recorder of Deeds, Marriage Record, vol. 15, p. 173; *St. Louis City Directory* (St. Louis: Gould, 1876), p. 605.

34. Kate Elder appears on the fine list in June 1874 and, as Kate Earp, on the list in August (Ed Bartholomew, *Wyatt Earp: The Untold Story*, p. 96).

35. The 1875 Ford County, Dodge City, Kansas, Census lists "entry no. 5, living at Tom Sherman's saloon: Kate Elder, age 24, female, white, no occupation given, born OH [sic], came to Kansas from Iowa" (ibid., p. 102).

36. J. Erb, quite probably James Earp, arrived at Jacksboro and registered at the Hotel Southern on June 14, 1877; *Frontier Echo*, June 15, 1877. Shortly thereafter, James Earp was employed at the Cattle Exchange Saloon in Fort Worth.

37. Cummings, "The O.K. Corral Fight at Tombstone," p. 75.

38. In 1935 Kate falsely claimed that she had married Doc in Valdosta, Georgia, on May 25, 1876. No record of any marriage for John Henry Holliday has surfaced anywhere. Frank Waters presents an equally spurious claim that Kate married Doc at the Planter's Hotel in St. Louis in 1870 (*The Earp Brothers of Tombstone: The Story of Mrs. Virgil Earp*, p. 44). The United States Census of 1880 shows that John H. Holliday considered himself single at that time. The tempestuous nature of this relationship—coupled with frequent moves in Texas, Kansas, New Mexico Territory, Arizona Territory, and Colorado—makes it doubtful that there could even have been the basis for a common-law marriage.

39. The dentist and the red-headed lady gambler served as the foundation for many tales. Author and newspaperman Alfred Henry Lewis (1857–1914) visited west Texas in 1881 and later wrote a colorful collection of tales, *Wolfville Nights* (1902), in which he used Lottie as a role model for the fictitious Faro Nell, a lovely female gambler who takes on Doc Holliday at the faro table. Doc's name also appears in several of Lewis's other fictional tales, which were not written until 1902, after Doc had attained a degree of local notoriety; Alfred Henry Lewis, *Wolfville Nights* (New York: Grosset and Dunlap, 1902), p. 63; *New York Times*, December 24, 1914. The story of Faro Nell and Doc was used as the foundation for the equally apocryphal story written by former Shackelford County sheriff John Cloud Jacobs. In a 1928 letter to J. Marvin Hunter, editor of the *Frontier Times*, Jacobs related the story, substituted Lottie's name for Nell's, and changed the amount of money involved; John C. Jacobs, San Antonio, Texas, to Marvin Hunter, Bandera, Texas, July 17, 1928, quoted in Hunter, *The Story of Lottie Deno*, p. 58.

Jacobs also related another disingenuous tale that occurred during a faro game at the Beehive Saloon. Doc and Lottie were in the midst of a game when Kate arrived in a jealous rage. When an argument ensued in which both women pulled their guns, Doc stepped in and stopped the fight. Hunter further perpetuated the stories. For a thought-provoking discussion of the role of Jacobs, Rye, and Hunter in concocting the tall tales that later emerged as fact in the legend of Lottie Deno, see Ty Cashion, "Rewriting the Wild West for a New History," *Journal of the West* 34 (October 1995): 54–60.

40. Wyatt later stated that he was following some cattle thieves who had crossed the border into Texas; *San Francisco Examiner*, August 2, 1896. Stuart Lake claimed that Wyatt was tracking down Dave Rudabaugh for the Santa Fe Railroad (*Wyatt Earp*, p. 198). This is impossible because Rudabaugh robbed a train at Kinsley, thirty-five miles east of Dodge City, on January 27, 1878—two months after Wyatt's departure from Kansas. Rudabaugh was arrested by Bat Masterson on February 2, 1878, at Harry Lovell's ranch on the Kansas–Indian Territory line (Bartholomew, *Wyatt Earp: The Untold Story*, pp. 211, 216).

41. *San Francisco Examiner*, August 2, 1896.

42. Lester W. Galbreath, Fort Griffin State Historical Park, interview with the author, August 9, 1995.

43. *San Francisco Examiner*, August 2, 1896.

44. This event cannot be substantiated by Shackelford County Court records because the supposed file containing all items relating to John H. Holliday disappeared prior to 1988. Neither is it mentioned in the *Frontier Echo*. Joan Farmer, archivist of the Old Jail Art Center in Albany,

Texas, claimed in an interview with the author on September 19, 1995, that she has the original court documents ordering Kate's arrest. Upon questioning, she admitted that the records do not mention Kate by name, merely an arson incident with a corresponding date. She has refused the requests of numerous historians to see this document. However, Kate, who read Wyatt's story in Lake's book, had the opportunity to correct or refute it. She chose not to, possibly giving the story credibility.

45. Lake erroneously placed the time of Doc and Kate's departure as being prior to January 20, 1878, when he claimed that Wyatt returned to Fort Griffin. Wyatt was still in Fort Worth on January 25 when he was involved in a fight with a Mr. Russell at the Cattle Exchange Saloon where his brother James was tending bar. "Mr. Russell was the recipient of a first class pounding"; *Fort Worth Democrat*, January 26, 1878. Doc and Kate's departure was later than Lake claimed. It does appear that they arrived at Dodge City before Wyatt returned there in May; *Ford County Globe*, May 14, 1878.

46. Rister, *Fort Griffin on the Texas Frontier*, pp. 172–73. In the fall of 1876 Charles Rath, in partnership with Dodge City sutler Robert M. Wright, had pioneered this trail. Rath led a wagon train of supplies south from Dodge City across the Salt Fork and the Red River and up the Double Mountain Fork of the Brazos south of the Double Mountains, where he established a trading post— Camp Reynolds (or Rath City)—about fourteen miles southwest of what is now Hamlin, Texas.

47. Recollections of Catherine Holliday Neuhoff (niece of Martha Anne Holliday), Carolyn Holliday Manley, Decatur, Georgia, September 27, 1995, to the author, Fallbrook, California.

Chapter 9. Following the Circuit

1. *The Handbook of Texas*, vol. 2, ed. Walter Prescott Webb (Austin: Texas State Historical Society, 1952), p. 886.

2. *San Francisco Examiner*, August 2, 1896.

3. Richard A. Van Orman, *A Room for the Night: Hotels of the Old West*, p. 50.

4. Odie B. Faulk, *Dodge City: The Most Western Town of All*, p. 76.

5. Ibid., p. 125.

6. Thomas L. McCarty, M.D., received his medical education at Rush Medical College, Philadelphia (ibid., p. 124).

7. Fredric R. Young, *Dodge City: Up through a Century in Story and Pictures*, p. 160.

8. *Ford County Globe*, April 16, 1878.

9. Andy Adams, *The Log of a Cowboy: A Narrative of the Old Trail Days*, pp. 191–92.

10. *Dodge City Times*, June 28, 1878.

11. In the late 1890s Tilghman purchased Chant, winner of the 1894 Kentucky Derby.

12. Young, *Dodge City*, p. 65. Chalkley M. Beeson and Harris purchased the Long Branch Saloon in 1878 after they sold the Saratoga. Bill Harris was in charge of the liquor and gambling, while Beeson made the saloon famous for its orchestral concerts. He was an accomplished violinist.

13. *Dodge City Times*, July 27, 1878.

14. Eddie Foy and Alvin F. Harlow, *Clowning through Life*, p. 113.

15. District Court of the First Judicial District, County of Cochise, Document 48, and the Wells Spicer

Hearing (October 31, 1881–November 29, 1881), Document 94, as edited by Alford E. Turner, *The O.K. Corral Inquest*, p. 158.

16. *San Francisco Examiner*, August 2, 1896.

17. In 1926 John H. Flood, Jr., ghost–wrote a melodramatic autobiography for Wyatt, stating that in August 1878 an entourage of twenty Texas cowboys stalked the streets of Dodge City searching for Marshal Wyatt Earp. When they drew on him, Doc Holliday suddenly shouted, "'Throw 'em up!' as he backed against Earp and leveled his guns. And poor Bat Masterson, and the world, wondered long, long years at the loyalty of Wyatt Earp for the stranger who proved his friend" (Wyatt S. Earp, *Wyatt Earp*, pp. 57–62). Stuart Lake further enhanced the story. He added more cowboys led by Texas cattlemen Tobe Driskill and Ed Morrison and claimed that Doc's surprise appearance so shocked the cowboys, who already had their guns drawn, that Wyatt had time to draw his gun and Doc and Wyatt subdued the crowd together. A single shot from Doc's gun quelled the lone dissenter, who was hit in the shoulder and issued a howl of pain (Lake, *Wyatt Earp*, pp. 210–15). No newspaper of the time carried any version of this story and no arrests were recorded.

18. Cummings, "The O.K. Corral Fight at Tombstone," p. 76. Bat Masterson wrote that Doc shot and wounded a young gambler named Kid McCoy over a trivial disagreement, after having been in Trinidad less than a week ("'Doc' Holliday," p. 37). No documentation of this exists.

19. Cummings, "The O.K. Corral Fight at Tombstone," p. 79. Myers credits Doc with yet another undocumented killing during this trip—this time an un-named gunman allegedly faced Doc's guns with fatal results in Otero, New Mexico Territory (*Doc Holliday*, p. 112).

20. San Miguel County, New Mexico Territory, Deed Book 12, p. 184. The deed makes it evident that Doc and Kate were recognized as husband and wife in Las Vegas.

21. In 1846 an army hospital was established at the springs. It was abandoned by the government in 1862. In 1864 Dr. O. H. Bloodworth established a private hot springs there. The property next came into the possession of W. Scott Moore, who improved it and renamed the former army hospital the "Old Adobe House." In 1879, during John Henry's tenure in Las Vegas, the springs were sold to eastern promoters who later built a $75,000 three-story stone hotel on the property that came to be known as the Las Vegas Hot Springs Hotel. A stone bath house was then built near the center of the hot springs (Milton W. Callon, *Las Vegas, New Mexico: The Town That Wouldn't Gamble*, pp. 126–31).

22. Miguel Antonio Otero, *My Life on the Frontier: 1864–1882*, pp. 171–72.

23. Leonard left Las Vegas about July 1, 1879, and briefly settled in Las Cruces. Several weeks later he moved his business to Mesilla and eventually moved to Tombstone in the Arizona Territory; *Las Cruces Thirty-four* (a weekly newspaper), July 23, 1879. The friendship that developed between the two would later come to haunt Doc in Tombstone, when Leonard was involved in a stage robbery and Doc became a suspect, mainly because of this friendship.

24. *Las Cruces Thirty-four*, January 15 and 22, 1879.

25. Otero, *My Life on the Frontier*, p. 158.

26. San Miguel County, New Mexico Territory, Criminal Record Book (1876–79), pp. 391 and 401–2.

27. *Ford County Globe*, March 25, 1879.

28. Several Colorado papers place Thompson in command of the Santa Fe's force; *Colorado Springs*

Weekly Gazette, June 14, 1879; and *Pueblo (Colorado) Chieftain*, June 10, 1879.

29. Foy and Harlow, *Clowning through Life*, p. 103.

30. Robert K. DeArment, *Bat Masterson: The Man and the Legend*, pp. 148–51. Full details of the Santa Fe's struggle with the Denver and Rio Grande may be found in Robert G. Athearn's *Rebel of the Rockies: A History of the Denver and Rio Grande Western Railroad*, pp. 49–90.

31. Callon, *Las Vegas, New Mexico*, p. 84.

32. Otero, *My Life on the Frontier*, pp. 152–53.

33. F. Stanley, *Dave Rudabaugh: Border Ruffian*, p. 87.

34. *Las Cruces Thirty-four*, July 30, 1879.

35. *Las Vegas Gazette* (a weekly newspaper), July 26, 1879; reprinted in the *Santa Fe Weekly New Mexican*, August 2, 1879.

36. Two years to the day later, the *Las Vegas Daily Optic* ran an attempt by pro-cowboy publisher Russell A. Kistler to discredit the Holliday/Earp faction for their Tombstone activities: "Doc Holliday was at one time the keeper of a gin mill on Center Street near the present site of the Center Street bakery. He is the identical individual who killed poor, inoffensive Mike Gordon" (*Las Vegas Daily Optic*, July 20, 1881).

Significantly, the *Daily Optic* had not been founded at the time of Gordon's death and Kistler, then one hundred miles away in Otero, New Mexico, had no firsthand information. He would later also maintain that the corpse of Henry McCarty, alias "Billy the Kid," was brought to Las Vegas and that the skull was "boiled and scraped," while the body was buried until decomposition would allow for the skeleton to be "hung together by wires and shellac to make it presentable" (*Daily Optic*, September 10, 1881). Publisher Kistler was prone to fabrication and gross exaggeration to compete with Las Vegas's other two newspapers, the *Gazette* and the *Herald*. Masterson later further exaggerated the story when he claimed that the day after Doc shot Gordon Doc also shot Gordon's friend, a Mexican gambler, and was forced to leave Las Vegas; *Arizona Weekly Citizen* (Tucson), August 14, 1886. This was not true. Doc did not leave Las Vegas until the end of October 1879.

37. San Miguel County, New Mexico Territory, Deed Book 11, pp. 340–43.

38. Ibid., pp. 449–50. The site is presently located at 605 East Lincoln Street. The contract lien was paid and satisfied in full when Doc returned on April 24, 1880.

39. San Miguel County, New Mexico Territory, Deed Book 12, pp. 182–85. The deed acknowledged that this purchase was made "independent, apart from, voluntarily and without compulsion or illicit influence of his wife."

40. San Miguel County, New Mexico Territory, Criminal Record Book (1876–82), pp. 527–28.

41. Ibid., p. 539; dismissed March 12, 1880; Civil Record Book A of the District Court, San Miguel County, New Mexico Territory (1880–81), p. 94.

42. It is not known who managed the Holliday Saloon for Doc. On August 30, 1879, the stage running south between Las Vegas and Tecolote was robbed. On the evening of September 11, while dealing keno in the Holliday Saloon, Jordan Webb was arrested on suspicion of being one of the robbers and was charged with robbery of the United States mail. He was taken to Santa Fe for trial. Webb was tried in Santa Fe on February 28, 1880; when the jury failed to arrive at a verdict he was tried again on August 7. Again the jury failed to reach a verdict. Webb went on trial a third

time in the United States District Court in Santa Fe on February 11, 1881. The defense put Dave Rudabaugh (already behind bars) on the stand. Rudabaugh testified that he was the leader of the robbers and that Webb was not a participant in any of the robberies. Webb was promptly acquitted. A petition was soon circulated asking that Jordan J. Webb be appointed a policeman in East Las Vegas; *Las Vegas Gazette*, August 30 and September 11, 1879; *Daily Optic*, February 14 and 28, 1881.

43. Cummings, "The O.K. Corral Fight at Tombstone," p. 76. Kate further stated that they arrived in November 1877—an obvious error. It was in 1879.

44. Waters, *The Earp Brothers of Tombstone*, p. 75.

Chapter 10. Arrival in the Arizona Territory

1. Mary Katherine Cummings to Lillian Raffert, March 18, 1940, Prescott, Arizona. "We arrived in Prescott in November. Doc & I went to a hotel. Vegil [*sic*] Earp the oldest [older] Brother was already in Prescott. Was there two years ahead of us."

2. The imminent departure of the Earps was noted on November 14, 1879, by the *Arizona Weekly Journal Miner* (Prescott). The Earp party reached Tombstone on December 1 (Lake, *Wyatt Earp*, p. 232).

3. *Arizona Weekly Journal Miner* (Prescott), March 12, 1880.

4. Ibid., April 2, 1880.

5. San Miguel County, New Mexico Territory. Criminal Docket Book (August Term 1876 through March Term 1882), pp. 79–80; Criminal Record Book of the District Court, San Miguel County (1876–79), pp. 527–528,

539; Civil Record Book A of the District Court of San Miguel County, p. 121.

6. San Miguel County, New Mexico Territory, Deed Book 11, p. 449.

7. Otero, *My Life on the Frontier*, pp. 216–18.

8. This story has no documentation in the court records of San Miguel County or in surviving area newspapers. Otero maintained that no charges were brought against either party.

9. Otero, *My Life on the Frontier*, p. 218.

10. United States Government, 1880 Census Enumeration, Prescott, Yavapai Co., Arizona Territory, Enumeration District 26, Household 52, p. 4.

Holladay [*sic*], J H; W, M, 29; Single; Dentist; born Georgia; Father and Mother born South Carolina.

Richard E. Elliot; W, M, 45; Single; Miner; born Maine.

John J. Gosper; W, M, 39; Divorced; Miner and stock raiser; born Ohio.

11. *Arizona Weekly Journal Miner* (Prescott), April 1, 1871, June 15, 1877, and December 26, 1879.

12. Gosper died on May 14, 1913, in Los Angeles; Sharlot Hall Museum, Obituary Book, p. 191.

13. Cummings, "The O.K. Corral Fight at Tombstone," p. 77. Mrs. Cummings stated that they arrived in Tombstone long after the Earps (Mary Katherine Cummings, Prescott, Arizona, to Lillian Raffert, March 18, 1940). Photocopy of original provided by Craig Fouts, San Diego, California; photocopy of typewritten text supplied by Glenn G. Boyer.

14. In 1880 Globe was located in Pinal County, Arizona Territory. Subsequently Globe became the county seat for the new county of Gila. No deed was recorded for such a purchase in either county.

15. Cummings to Raffert, March 18, 1940. She claimed to have made a down payment of $500 and secured a mortgage. No mortgage was recorded in either Pinal or Gila County.

16. September 27, 1880, *The Great Register for Pima County*: "Number, 1483; name, Holliday, J. H.; age, 24 [*sic*]; local residence, Precinct No. 17."

17. When passing through Tucson, Virgil had his commission, issued in Yavapai County, altered by the deputy United States marshal there to cover Pima County.

18. John D. Gilchriese, note 25 in John P. Clum, *It All Happened in Tombstone*, p. 7.

19. On December 6, 1879, Virgil W. Earp, Wyatt S. Earp, James C. Earp, and Robert Winders filed a claim named 1st North ext. Mtn Maid, Book 1, Cochise County, Recorder's Office, Bisbee, Arizona.

20. Morgan resigned his position in Butte on March 10, 1880; Don Chaput, *The Earp Papers: In a Brother's Image*, p. 37.

21. Affidavit of Five Hundred Dollars Improvements, Pima County, Territory of Arizona, November 16, 1880, in Traywick, *John Henry: The "Doc" Holliday Story*, p. 93.

22. Holliday, Clark, and Wyatt Earp Water Rights, filed February 3, 1881, Millsites, Book 1, Cochise County, Recorder's Office, Bisbee, Arizona.

23. The building was owned by the Vizini and Cook partnership and was leased to Joyce.

24. *Tombstone Epitaph*, July 22, 1880; reprinted in Douglas D. Martin, *Tombstone's Epitaph*, pp. 53–54. Eleven months later, on June 22, 1881, the Oriental burned to the ground when a keg of whiskey blew up at the Arcade Saloon, three doors from the Oriental. The fire destroyed sixty-six stores, saloons, and restaurants (ibid., pp. 125–28). The Oriental was rebuilt.

25. Of the four men, only Dick Clark would remain in Tombstone, and he was the premier gambler of the community. He eventually purchased the Alhambra Saloon and, like John Henry Holliday, was ultimately a victim of tuberculosis. He visited Chicago in 1893 and died aboard the return train at Albuquerque. His body was brought to Tombstone for burial (C. L. Sonnichsen, *Billy King's Tombstone: The Private Life of an Arizona Boomtown*, pp. 117–41).

26. William Harris had also been a founder of the Bank of Dodge City.

27. Lake, *Wyatt Earp*, pp. 252–53; Waters, *The Earp Brothers of Tombstone*, p. 103.

28. Tyler would eventually cause trouble for Doc in Leadville, Colorado, two years later.

29. *Tombstone Epitaph* and *Tombstone Daily Nugget*, October 12, 1880.

30. *Tombstone Daily Nugget*, October 12, 1880. Stuart N. Lake, Wyatt's biographer, believed that the difficulties between Doc and Joyce could be traced to an interest in the same woman; Notes, Stuart Lake Collection, Letter Box 11, Huntington Library, San Marino, California.

31. Joyce, John H. Behan, [Harry?] Woods, and [Wesley?] Fuller were the four subpoenaed.

32. Justice Court Case No 25. Records provided by Ben T. Traywick, Tombstone, Arizona.

33. Indeed, at one time amputation was believed necessary in order to save Joyce's life; *Tombstone Epitaph*, October 23, 1880.

34. Traywick, *John Henry*, p. 91. When the lease of Rickabaugh, Clark, and Harris expired in 1881, Joyce would not renew it, leasing the gambling concession instead to John H. Behan.

35. Wyatt Earp, Vidal, California, to Walter Noble Burns, Chicago, Illinois, March 15, 1927, Walter Noble Burns Collection, AZ/291, University of Arizona, Tucson.

36. George W. Parsons, *The Private Journal of George W. Parsons*, p. 133.

37. Wyatt Earp to Walter Noble Burns, March 15, 1927.

38. Woodworth Clum, *Apache Agent: The Story of John P. Clum*, pp. 260–61.

39. Fred Dodge, *Under Cover for Wells Fargo: The Unvarnished Recollection of Fred Dodge*, p. 23.

40. DeArment, *Bat Masterson: The Man and the Legend*, p. 198.

41. A variation indicates that Wyatt told King that should he "continue to run with that crowd, you are going to get into serious trouble. My advice is to make a clean breast of this affair and I'll see that you are treated right" (Wyatt S. Earp, *Wyatt Earp*, p. 201). Still another variation stated that Wyatt told King that he knew that three men had committed the robbery, while the fourth held the horses. "I don't know which one he was, but, whoever he was, he's lucky. The other three will swing for this job." King promptly confessed to holding the horses (Lake, *Wyatt Earp*, p. 258).

42. Tombstone diarist George W. Parsons, who was made aware of the capture of King and the implica-

tion of Leonard, called him "a hard case," on Sunday, March 20 (*Private Journal*, p. 134).

43. Luther King is thought to be Luther Woods, a brother of *Nugget* editor Harry Woods. Following his escape, King traveled to Lake City, Colorado. Harry Woods moved there shortly thereafter and edited the local newspaper in 1883; Roy B. Young, *Cochise County Cowboy War: "A Cast of Characters,"* p. 75; Glenn G. Boyer to author, February 26, 1996.

44. *Tombstone Daily Nugget*, March 19, 1881.

45. Parsons, *Private Journal*, p. 136. This entry occurs under the heading "Monday, March 28th/81." It is apparent that Parsons did not routinely write in his diary each day, but periodically made entries for a number of days. One can only surmise that he confused entries in this instance and inadvertently labeled this entry improperly.

46. As cited in William M. Breakenridge, *Helldorado: Bringing the Law to the Mesquite*, pp. 212–13.

47. John P. Clum, "Autobiography," TMs, AZ/3, Box 1, University of Arizona, Tucson, Arizona, chapter 16, p. 13.

48. Testimony, John H. Behan, November 13, 1881; Turner, *The O.K. Corral Inquest*, pp. 142–43: "I went to Mr. Earp and told him I knew I would get the appointment of Sheriff, and that I would like to have him in the office with me. Something afterwards transpired that I did not take him into the office." Turner postulated that Behan reneged because of Josie's growing infatuation with Wyatt.

49. In 1931 Stuart Lake stated that the un-named "object of Johnny Behan's most ardent affections had given Johnny mitten and was publicly exhibiting a decided preference for the marshal's [Earp's] company" (*Wyatt Earp*, p. 276). In 1960 Frank Waters provided the object's name—

Sadie (aka Josie; *The Earp Brothers of Tombstone*, pp. 110ff.). In 1964 Ed Bartholomew wrote, "A young Jewish actress accompanying this traveling troupe was following John Behan from Tucson to Tombstone. This same lady, Josie, or Sadie, was later to become Mrs. Wyatt Earp!" (*Wyatt Earp: The Man and The Myth*, p. 55). In 1967 Glenn G. Boyer revealed the story of Wyatt's second wife, Celia Ann Blaylock, and Wyatt's rejection of her for Sadie or Josie—Josephine Sarah Marcus Earp (*Suppressed Murder of Wyatt Earp*).

50. Docket Book, Albert O. Wallace; *Arizona Weekly Star* (Tucson), March 31, 1881; both quoted in Bartholomew, *Wyatt Earp: The Man and The Myth*, p. 146.

51. Cochise County, *The Territory of Arizona v. J. H. Holliday*, Criminal Register of Actions, Case #23; records provided by Ben T. Traywick.

52. Cochise County, *The Territory of Arizona v. John H. Holliday*, Case #30; record provided by Glenn G. Boyer.

53. *Tombstone Daily Nugget*, July 7, 1881.

54. Ibid., July 10, 1881.

55. In 1882 Eureka's name was changed to Hachita.

56. *Arizona Weekly Star* (Tucson), June 23, 1881.

57. Ibid.; *New Southwest and Grant County Herald* (Silver City, New Mexico), June 25, 1881. The *Tombstone Epitaph* provided a varying account, indicating that the Hasletts were killed at Wes McFadden's Saloon, the lone killer being Jim Crane (June 22, 1881).

58. Wilcox to the Adjutant General of the Military Division of the Pacific, Presidio of San Francisco, June 9, 1881, United States National Archives, "Lawlessness and Cowboy Depredations in the Arizona Territory, 1881–1882," Film #2061.

59. Crawley Dake to Isaac W. MacVeagh, August 5, 1881, United States National Archives, "Lawlessness and Cowboy Depredations in the Arizona Territory, 1881–1882," Film #2061.

60. Turner, *The O.K. Corral Inquest*, p. 157.

61. Ibid. Wyatt Earp testified at the inquest: "I had an interview with them in the backyard of the Oriental Saloon. I told them I wanted the glory of capturing Leonard, Head and Crane and if I could do it, it would help me make the race for Sheriff at the next election. I told them if they would put me on the track of Leonard, Head and Crane, and tell me where those men were hid, I would give them all the reward and would never let anyone know where I got the information."

62. U.S. Marshal Crawley P. Dake's August 5 telegram to U.S. Attorney General MacVeagh specifically stated: "Have sent deputy and posse after cowboys." The Earps would have been the only posse Dake would have sent on such a mission; United States National Archives, "Lawlessness and Cowboy Depredations in the Arizona Territory, 1881–1882," Film #2061. Warren Baxter Earp, the youngest of the Earp brothers, had joined his brothers in Tombstone. He had arrived from Colton, California, prior to March 21, 1881, at which time he was arrested and fined twenty-five dollars "for discharging firearms within the city limits" (Richard Lapidus, "The Youngest Earp: The Troubled Life and Times of Warren Earp," *Journal* [Western Outlaw–Lawman History Association] 4 [Summer 1995]: 7).

63. *Tombstone Epitaph*, August 16, 1881; *Arizona Weekly Star* (Tucson), September 1, 1881.

64. No answer to the question "Who Killed Old Man Clanton?" will satisfy all. Initial reports had the cowboy party ambushed by Mexicans in retaliation for earlier depredations. However, from the outset the Earp posse was

suspected of having been involved. Milt Joyce postulated to William Ganzhorn, a bartender at the Occidental, that when Old Man Clanton and the Lang party were killed (presumably by Mexicans), Virgil, Wyatt, and Warren Earp, "with Doc Holliday, McMasters and others, were out of town supposedly hunting outlaws. Joice [*sic*] further alleged that aside from murdering Old Man Clanton and his crew, merely to make sure of killing Jim Crane, the Earps had acquired a nice bunch of cattle" (Jack Ganzhorn, *I've Killed Men: An Epic of Early Arizona*, p. 27). The Earp-led posse was known to be in the field; telegram from U.S. Marshal Dake to Attorney General McVeigh, August 5, 1881. Warren Earp disappeared from Tombstone. When he returned, he walked "lame from the effects of a gun-shot wound"; *Gunnison News Democrat*, June 4, 1882. At the 1995 Western Outlaw–Lawman History Association symposium, author Ben Traywick remarked that he had once viewed a letter in historian Alford Turner's collection written by Wyatt's sister Adelia. Paraphrased, it stated that Warren was not in Tombstone in October 1881 as he was recuperating at home from a bullet wound he had received in a fight with rustlers down on the border (*The Earp Controversies: The Range of Opinions*, produced by the Western Outlaw–Lawman History Association, 1995, videocassette). At the same symposium, author Michael Hickey stated that, in addition to the Earps and Holliday, Wells, Fargo and the Mexican Secret Service were involved in this affair, specifically that Captain Carrillo, Captain Jacobo Méndez, and Lieutenant Emilio Kosterlitzky were in the field with the Earps (the source of the view that Mexicans were involved?) (ibid.). Finally, if Mexican rustlers killed the party, are we to believe that they forgot to take the cattle with them? The cattle were left behind. In the author's judgment, the preponderance of evidence suggests that the cowboy party was attacked by the Earp posse, perhaps acting with support from Mexican authorities, resulting in the death of Old Man Clanton, Jim Crane, Dixie Gray, Bud Snow, and William Lang.

65. The story that John Henry took this occasion to return to Georgia to visit his family was the belief of Will McLaury, brother of Tom and Robert McLaury; Will McLaury, Tombstone, A. T., to D. D. Appelgate, Toledo, Iowa, November 9, 1881, copy in the Philip Rasch Papers, MS 677, Arizona Historical Society, Tucson, Arizona. Dr. T. H. Smith, Sr., a lifetime resident of Valdosta, stated that on one occasion Doc Holliday returned to the house on Savannah Street and remained for three or four days. "None saw him as he kept the shade drawn and the doors closed" (Vera D. Hagen, President, Lowndes County Historical Society, Valdosta, Georgia, to Dr. Philip Rasch, Jacksonville, North Carolina, January 15, 1972, Philip Rasch Papers, MS 677, Arizona Historical Society, Tucson, Arizona). There is no knowledge within the Holliday family that John Henry ever returned to Georgia after his departure in 1873.

66. Dodge, *Under Cover for Wells Fargo*, pp. 13–14.

67. Cochise County Criminal Docket, *The Territory of Arizona v. Stilwell and Spencer*, Quarter Ending September 30, 1881, No. 56.

68. This time bond was five thousand each, making a total of fourteen thousand that had been posted for Stilwell and Spencer by the cowboys (Bartholomew, *Wyatt Earp: The Man and the Myth*, pp. 208–12).

69. Cummings, "The O.K. Corral Fight at Tombstone," p. 79.

Chapter 11. Gunfight in Tombstone

1. Testimony of Ike Clanton, Turner, *The O.K. Corral Inquest*, p. 99. The name of present-day Sulphur

Springs Valley was singular during the 1880s; Lynn R. Bailey, *"We'll All Wear Silk Hats": The Erie and Chiricahua Cattle Companies and the Rise of Corporate Ranching in the Sulphur Spring Valley of Arizona, 1883–1909*, p. 8.

2. Turner, *The O.K. Corral Inquest*, p. 158.

3. Capt. William French, manager of the WS Ranch at Alma, New Mexico, described Clanton's voice: "It sounded rather like a rusty hinge and caused him to express himself in a high falsetto" (*Further Recollections of a Western Ranchman: New Mexico, 1883–1889*, pp. 286–89).

4. Turner, *The O.K. Corral Inquest*, p. 159.

5. Walsh's Can Can Lunch and Eating Counter, located in Building 6 of Block 18, should not be confused with Quong Kee's Can Can Restaurant, located in Building 1 of Block 17. Robert Mullins, "Map of Tombstone," Stuart N. Lake Papers, Huntington Library, San Marino, Calif,; Glenn G. Boyer, "C. 1880 Map of Tombstone and List of Buildings" (Tombstone, Ariz.: Red Marie's Bookstore, 1994).

6. Turner, *The O.K. Corral Inquest*, p. 97; "Doc's vocabulary of profanity and obscene language was monumental and he worked it proficiently in talking to Ike" (Dodge, *Under Cover for Wells Fargo*, p. 26).

7. Turner, *The O.K. Corral Inquest*, p. 97.

8. Virgil Earp had been appointed chief of police of Tombstone on June 6, 1881. He filled the vacancy left by the firing of Ben Sippy, who had been elected to replace the slain Fred White. He continued to hold his commission as deputy United States marshal.

9. Turner, *The O.K. Corral Inquest*, p. 191.

10. bid., pp. 98 and 109.

11. Ibid., p. 160.

12. To buffalo is to strike a victim alongside the ear with the barrel of a revolver. The Earps were experts at employing this approach to subduing adversaries.

13. Turner, *The O.K. Corral Inquest*, p. 161.

14. Ibid., pp. 123 and 126.

15. Cummings, "The O.K. Corral Fight at Tombstone," p. 79.

16. Cummings to Raffert, March 18, 1940.

17. Ibid.

18. Turner, *The O.K. Corral Inquest*, pp. 28–29.

19. Though the time is often disputed, this is the recollection of Reuben Franklin Coleman, an eyewitness; *Tombstone Epitaph*, October 27, 1881.

20. Ibid., pp. 40 and 65.

21. Clum, *It All Happened in Tombstone*, p. 11: "There has been much discussion as to who fired the first shot in the street battle. This question is utterly unimportant to me."

22. Both the *Daily Nugget* and Wyatt Earp—hardly co-conspirators—agreed that Wyatt fired the first shot.

23. This is suggested by the defense's cross-examination of Sheriff Behan: "Is it not a fact that the first shot fired by Holliday was from a shotgun; that he then threw the shotgun down and drew the nickel-plated pistol?" The question was not answered (Turner, *The O.K. Corral Inquest*, p. 146).

24. Ibid., pp. 77 and 134.

25. Ibid., pp. 38 and 77.

26. Ibid., pp. 30 and 177; *Daily Nugget*, October 27, 1881.

27. Turner, *The O.K. Corral Inquest*, p. 30.

28. Ibid., p. 38. There was little time for much talk—certainly not as much as was subsequently reported.

29. Ibid., p. 134; *Daily Nugget*, November 1, 1881.

30. Cummings, "The O.K. Corral Fight at Tombstone," p. 81.

31. Document 48, District Court of the First Judicial District, County of Cochise, filed December 1, 1881. Reprinted in Turner, *The O.K. Corral Inquest*, pp. 23–48.

32. Writ of Habeas Corpus; copy courtesy of Ben T. Traywick.

33. Turner, *The O.K. Corral Inquest*, pp. 217–26.

34. Acting Governor John J. Gosper, Prescott, A. T., to President Chester A. Arthur, Washington, D.C., December 12, 1881, United States National Archives, "Lawlessness and Cowboy Depredations in the Arizona Territory," Film #2061.

35. Clum, *It All Happened in Tombstone*, p. 18.

36. *Tombstone Epitaph*, December 15, 1881; Clum, *It All Happened in Tombstone*, pp. 19–28.

37. *Tombstone Epitaph*, December 29, 1881.

38. George W. Parsons indicated an apparent consensus that "Ike Clanton, 'Curly Bill' [Brocius] and [Will] McLowry [sic] did the shooting" (Parsons, *Private Journal*, p. 203).

39. Ibid., p. 206.

40. George W. Parsons, Los Angeles, California, to Stuart N. Lake, San Diego, California, October 25, 1928, Stuart N. Lake Collection, Letter Box 10, Huntington Library, San Marino, California.

41. *Tucson Weekly Citizen*, January 22, 1882; *Tombstone Epitaph*, January 18, 1882.

42. *Tombstone Epitaph*, January 18, 1882.

43. Turner, *The O.K. Corral Inquest*, appendix 2, pp. 230–46.

44. *Tombstone Epitaph*, March 20, 1882.

45. Parsons, *Private Journal*, p. 220.

46. *Gunnison (Colorado) Democrat*, June 4, 1882. Several variations exist of Morgan Earp's last words: "all [words] that were heard, except those whispered into the ears of his brother [Wyatt] and known only to him were, 'Don't, I can't stand it. This is the last game of pool I'll ever play'" (*Tombstone Epitaph*, March 20, 1882). What were those last whispered words? "I [Wyatt] promised my brother [Morgan] I'd get even" (*Gunnison [Colorado] Democrat*, June 4, 1882). Apparently there was some discussion of vengeance. John Flood later recorded Wyatt's version:

> "I'll get even Morg!"
> "Yes, but be careful."
> "If you had only taken my advice Morgan, This never would have happened."
> "Yes, Wyatt, you are right, you are always right." (*Wyatt Earp*, p. 274)

47. *Denver Republican*, May 22, 1881.

48. Marietta Spencer, the former Maria Duarte, had only recently married Pete Spencer on August 12, 1881; Cochise County, Arizona Territory, Marriage Records, Book 1, p. 9. She was a close friend of Josephine Marcus, the future Mrs. Wyatt Earp.

49. *Arizona Weekly Star* (Tucson), March 23, 1882.

50. Ibid. Behan's deputy, William Breakenridge, believed that Stilwell was at the Tucson train station to get a shot at Doc and the Earps when the train arrived (*Helldorado: Bringing the Law to the Mesquite*, p. 287).

51. *Tombstone Epitaph*, March 21, 1882; *San Francisco Alta California*, March 22, 1882. Both of

Stilwell's legs were shot through, a charge of buckshot had struck him in the right thigh, and another charge of buckshot had hit him in the chest—six buckshot holes within a radius of three inches, leaving powder burns on his coat.

52. *Arizona Weekly Star* (Tucson), March 23, 1882.

53. Ibid.

54. *Tombstone Epitaph*, January 24, 1882.

55. Ibid.

56. *Valdosta Times*, June 24, 1882.

57. *Atlanta Constitution*, October 28, 1881.

58. *Tombstone Epitaph*, March 23, 1882.

59. Ibid.

60. Ibid., March 25, 1882.

61. *San Francisco Alta California*, March 27, 1882.

62. Martin, *Tombstone's Epitaph*, pp. 230–31.

63. *Tombstone Epitaph*, April 14, 1882.

64. Martin, *Tombstone's Epitaph*, pp. 230–31.

65. *Epitaph* editor John Clum prefaced the publication of this letter with the statement: "It may be genuine and may not be; each reader may judge for himself." Wyatt's biographer Stuart Lake credited Wyatt with the letter's authorship, but the tone is completely uncharacteristic of the dour Earp (*Wyatt Earp*, p. 352). It is possible that New York–born editor Clum concocted the letter. However, it is my belief that the letter displays the trenchant style of Doc Holliday.

Chapter 12. Refuge in Colorado

1. The *New Southwest and Grant County Herald*, in Bartholomew, *Wyatt Earp: The Man and the Myth*, p. 324.

2. *Wyatt Earp*, pp. 326–27; Notes, Stuart N. Lake Collection, Letter Box 11, Huntington Library, San Marino, California. Frank McLane later returned to Dodge City and served as one of the so-called Dodge City Police Commissioners, formed to assist Luke Short in his 1883 saloon struggle with Mayor A. B. Webster.

3. The *Daily Trinidad News*, May 18, 1882, clearly implies that Doc headed on to Pueblo without the others. However, he maintained to a reporter that Wyatt and Dan Tipton were in Pueblo, leaving only one day prior to his own departure for Denver; *Denver Daily Times*, May 16, 1882.

4. Lake, *Wyatt Earp*, p. 356. Jack Johnson died in Salt Lake City in 1887. Sherman McMasters eventually joined the United States Army and served in the Spanish-American War. He died in the Philippines in 1898 (Wyatt S. Earp, *Wyatt Earp*, p. 336). Jack Vermillion settled in Big Stone Gap, Virginia, where he became a revivalist (Glenn G. Boyer to the author, April 30, 1996).

5. Lake, *Wyatt Earp*, p. 356.

6. *Pueblo Daily Chieftain*, May 17, 1882.

7. *Gunnison News-Champion*, July 17, 1930.

8. Doc identified the brother as Josh Stilwell; *Denver Republican*, May 22, 1882. He was probably referring to S. E. "Jack" Stilwell, a former army scout and Frank's older brother.

9. *Denver Republican*, May 22, 1882.

10. *Gunnison Daily New Democrat*, June 18, 1882; *Denver Daily Times*, May 16, 1882.

11. Owned by a British investment firm, the Denver Mansion Company, the hotel had been designed to resemble Windsor Castle. It opened on June 23, 1880 (Van Orman, *A Room for the Night*, p. 66).

12. *Denver Republican*, May 16, 1882.

13. *Denver Tribune*, May 16, 1882.

14. *Denver Republican*, May 22, 1882.

15. Ibid., May 19, 1882.

16. Pendleton and Thomas, *In Search of the Hollidays*, appendix, p. 20.

17. *Atlanta Constitution*, June 21, 1882 (interview with Lee Smith in which the reporter greatly advanced the cause of yellow journalism by sensationalizing the life of John H. Holliday and exaggerating his activities; Smith accurately reported the events with only minor errors).

18. *Atlanta-Post Appeal*, July 8, 1882.

19. Ibid.

20. *Leadville Daily Herald*, May 25, 1882.

21. *Denver Rocky Mountain News*, May 30, 1882.

22. Minutes of the District Court of Pueblo County, vol. 5, pp. 354–55, G.D. no. 1851: *The People v. J. H. Holliday [Larceny]*.

23. *Denver Rocky Mountain News*, May 22, 1882.

24. *Denver Republican*, June 2, 1882.

25. *Denver Rocky Mountain News*, June 14, 1882.

26. *Pueblo Daily Chieftain*, May 30 and 31, June 1 and 2, 1882.

27. *Gunnison News-Democrat,* June 4, 1882.

28. Ibid.

29. *Denver Rocky Mountain News,* June 14, 1882.

30. *Gunnison Daily-News Democrat,* June 18, 1882.

31. Ibid.

32. Wyatt and Warren Earp, heretofore cautious, low–key figures in and about Gunnison, Colorado, uncharacteristically gave an interview to a reporter in early June of 1882. Wyatt, unquestionably a vengeful man, told the journalist, "I promised my brother to get even and I have kept my word *so far* [author's emphasis]"; *Gunnison Daily-News Democrat,* June 4, 1882. There is little doubt that Wyatt wanted to take out Ringo.

33. *Leadville Daily Herald,* July 18, 1882.

34. *Salida Mountain Mail,* July 8, 1882.

35. Neither the author nor any one living today knows with absolute certainty the facts surrounding the death of John Ringo. Col. Henry Hooker's daughter-in-law, Forrestine C. Hooker, related about 1918 that Wyatt told her that he killed John Ringo (Forrestine C. Hooker, "An Arizona Vendetta: The Truth about Wyatt Earp—And Some Others" [ca. 1918], pp. 77–78). Earp stated to Frank Lockwood that he shot Ringo (Lockwood, *Pioneer Days in Arizona: From the Spanish Occupation to Statehood,* pp. 283 and 285). He also informed his biographer, John Flood, that he killed Ringo (*Wyatt Earp,* pp. 321–25). In each of these instances, Wyatt related that he shot Ringo prior to departing from Arizona for Colorado. This could not have been the case. Obviously, Wyatt knew that if he had been working under the long arm of the law he would have been protected by his deputy marshal's badge. If he admitted that

he returned from Colorado solely to kill Ringo, then the killing, for vengeance and bounty, was an act of homicide in the first degree, for which there was no statute of limitations. This opinion is based on the preponderance of the evidence that does survive. The combination of motive, opportunity, and confession, along with circumstantial evidence, invariably convicts in most courts of law, and there is no positive substantiation for any other theory.

36. This itinerary *could* have brought them back to Cochise County, Arizona, by the time of Ringo's death. They would have avoided the obvious route to Arizona via Pueblo, Trinidad, and Las Vegas on the Atchison, Topeka and Santa Fe, where Wyatt and particularly Doc were well known. They could have traveled approximately 525 miles by train—averaging better than twenty-one miles an hour. Twenty-one miles an hour was the rate of travel aboard the Denver and Rio Grande from Salt Lake City to Denver at that time (Athearn, *Rebel of the Rockies*, p. 122). The Atchison, Topeka and Santa Fe made the 146-mile run between Deming and Socorro at a rate of twenty-two and one-half miles per hour (C. M. Chase, *New Mexico and Colorado in 1881*, p. 129). They would have avoided San Simon, where the cowboy faction had lots of eyes and ears.

37. Minutes of the District Court of Pueblo County, Colorado, vol. 5, pp. 354–55, G.D. no. 1851, *The People v. J. H. Holliday [Larceny]*. The records of the District Court of Pueblo County state, "This day [July 11, 1882] came the said people, by Robert A. Quillian, Esq., District Attorney, and the said defendant [J. H. Holliday] in his own proper person as well as by his counsel, W. G. Hollins." Several attorneys have advised this author that "appearing in his own person" is common pro forma legal language that could be used even if the defendant were absent from the court. The author also appreciates that, as in almost every matter related to Ringo's

death, there is no uniform agreement on this legal issue. If Holliday did appear in court, he could not have been involved in the death of John Ringo, and the event is superfluous to his biography. However, whether Holliday was or was not present in court has no apparent bearing on the issue of whether Ringo met his death at the hand of Wyatt Earp.

38. *Tombstone Epitaph*, July 18, 1882.

39. Burns, *Tombstone*, pp. 262–63.

40. Wyatt S. Earp, *Wyatt Earp*, pp. 321–25. On June 15, 1929, five months after Wyatt's death, Fred Dodge, Wyatt's close friend and Wells, Fargo associate, emphatically responded to Stuart Lake that Wyatt did not kill Ringo and argued that Ringo was killed by Johnny-behind-the-Deuce (Dodge, *Under Cover for Wells Fargo*, p. 239). Wyatt probably related his killing of Ringo to Lake. Additionally, Lake had read John Flood's ghostwritten autobiography, which told of Wyatt's killing of Ringo. In my judgment, Dodge, unaware of Lake's prior knowledge, was protecting Wyatt's reputation.

41. District Court, First Judicial District, Cochise County, Arizona; filed November 3, 1882.

42. *Tombstone Epitaph*, July 18, 1882.

43. Robert M. Boller, one of the men who assisted in burying Ringo, described his pistol, with one empty shell, as having been caught in his watch chain ("Reminiscences of Robert M. Boller, 1926," typed MS, Arizona Historical Society, Tucson, Arizona, p. 3). While the caliber of Ringo's rifle was not specified, it could not have been the .45-.70 caliber model because that was not available until 1886.

44. District Court, First Judicial District, Cochise County, Arizona; filed July 14, 1882.

45. By the time of Ringo's death, John Clum had sold the *Epitaph* to Sam Purdy, a political supporter of

Johnny Behan. John Pleasant Gray, brother of Dixie Gray, who was slain in the shooting that took the life of Old Man Clanton, wrote in 1940: "It was never divulged who did this or caused it to be done [the killing of Ringo], but many of Ringo's friends felt they knew." Gray's aging memory, recalling an event fifty-eight years earlier, confused the sequence of a number of events. For example, he remembered the killing of Ringo to have taken place prior to the assassination of Morgan Earp. However, Gray clearly believed that Wyatt Earp somehow brought about the death of Ringo (John Pleasant Gray, "When All Roads Led to Tombstone" [1940], p. 36).

46. Ibid., p. 382; on November 25, 1882, the case was again continued.

47. *Pueblo Daily Chieftain*, July 19, 1882.

48. Lorenzo Walters says that Doc was in Deadwood in the summer of 1882, where he entered a saloon and encountered a large, coarse bartender threatening to shoot a miner unless he purchased a drink. Doc shot the bartender through the wrist. As a number of tough-looking citizens began to move toward Doc, he calmly announced, "Gentlemen, my name is Doc Holliday and I'm from Tombstone." The effect on the crowd was "electrical": the bartender apologized, and Doc dressed his wounded wrist while drinks were served on the house. Unfortunately this event, recorded by a man who attributed twenty-three killings to John Henry, is both undocumented and typically spurious (Lorenzo D. Walters, *Tombstone's Yesterday*, p. 88).

Chapter 13. The Final Years

1. Edward Blair, *Leadville: Colorado's Magic City*, p. 40.

2. Ibid.

3. Corbett and Ballenger, *Leadville City Directory* (1883), p. 153.

4. Corbett and Ballenger, *Leadville City Directory* (1884), p. 140.

5. Mary Billings-McVicar, Leadville, Colorado, interview with the author, March 3, 1996; Billing-McVicar to the author, March 18, 1996. The McVicars are the present owners of the Hyman building.

6. George F. Willison, *Here They Dug the Gold*, p. 206.

7. Ibid.

8. *Leadville Daily Chronicle*, December 7, 1882, in the *Leadville Herald Democrat*, December 23, 1966; copy courtesy of Ben T. Traywick.

9. Some sources spell the name Youngson.

10. Willison, *Here They Dug the Gold*, p. 206.

11. Ibid.

12. Sol Herman's clothing store had burned to the ground seven months earlier, in May 1882, when one of Leadville's worst fires occurred, leaving the entire block on East Chestnut, between Harrison and Oak, in ashes (Blair, *Leadville*, pp. 144–45; Rene L. Coquoz, *Tales of Early Leadville*, part two, p. 14).

13. *Leadville Daily Chronicle*, December 7, 1882, in the *Leadville Herald Democrat*, December 23, 1966.

14. Billings-McVicar to the author, March 18, 1996. Mrs. Billings-McVicar learned of Miller's dispensing of laudanum to Holliday from Miller's late grandson, John Miller, a pharmacist in Denver.

15. Clanton and Allen, along with C. H. Light, once posted $2,500 bail (each) for Frank Stilwell and Pete Spence.

16. Ibid.; Turner, *The O.K. Corral Inquest*, pp. 29, 61–64.

17. *Denver Tribune-Republican,* March 27, 1885.

18. *Leadville Daily Democrat,* July 24, 1884.

19. Ibid., August 20, 1884.

20. Ibid.

21. *Leadville Daily Herald,* August 26, 1885. It can be assumed that John Henry had other items of jewelry and a pocket watch in addition to his diamond stickpin available to pawn.

22. Ibid.

23. *Leadville Daily Democrat,* August 26, 1884. Another news account stated in error that Doc lived in the Star Block at the time. He resided there briefly upon his arrival in Leadville, then moved to Hyman's Saloon. The Star Block burned down in 1882; Mary Billings-McVicar, Leadville, Colorado, interview with the author, March 3, 1995.

24. *Leadville Daily Democrat,* August 20, 1884. The revolver described would be a Colt's Model 1877 Thunderer. Another news account described the revolver as a short-barrel single-action Colt's .44.

25. Ibid. The *Leadville Daily Herald,* August 20, 1884, stated that Doc's first shot missed; Allen turned to run, fell, and was struck by Doc's second shot. Both accounts agreed that Allen fell after the first shot and that this bullet ultimately broke the glass over the folding doors.

26. Ibid.

27. *Leadville Daily Herald,* August 26, 1884.

28. *Leadville Daily Democrat,* August 26, 1884.

29. Ibid., September 7, 1884.

30. *The People of the State of Colorado v. John Holliday,* Lake County Superior Court, Case No. 258.

31. John Myers Myers cited the *Yuma (Arizona) Sentinel*, September 13, 1884, which carried a September 3, 1884, dispatch from the *Tombstone Record*, reporting the shooting of Leadville's Constable Kelly at the hands of Doc Holliday. This was clearly a recounting of the Allen shooting, and the *Record*'s informant confused the name. Myers enhanced the story and had the victim die. The entire list of Leadville lawmen who were killed during this era is as follows: Marshal George O'Conner, 1878; Officer John Carville, 1880; Sgt. Lauriston Stewart, 1880; Officer Samuel Townsend, 1882; Ex-Marshal Martin Duggan, 1884. No one named Kelly was on the list.

32. "That night was the last time that Wyatt Earp or Doc Holliday were seen by me as they were both in the place at the time of the shootings. I am writing the facts as they occurred, as I was an eye witness to both affairs" (Frank D. Scotten, Jr., tax assessor, El Paso, Texas, to Stuart N. Lake, San Diego, California, October 10, 1928, Stuart Lake Collection, Box 10, Huntington Library, San Marino, California).

33. Wyatt Earp, Los Angeles, California, to Stuart Lake, San Diego, California, November 19, 1928, Stuart N. Lake Collection, Letter Box 6, Huntington Library, San Marino, California.

34. *Aspen Daily Times*, June 12, 1885.

35. The altitude of Leadville is 10,400 feet while Denver's is 5,280 feet.

36. Eugene Parsons, Denver, Colorado, to Stuart N. Lake, San Diego, California, June 30, 1930, Stuart N. Lake Collection, Letter Box 10, Huntington Library, San Marino, California.

37. Ibid., July 17, 1930.

38. Thomas J. Noel, *The City and the Saloon: Denver, 1858–1916*, p. 110.

39. "We wrote him in Denver in February of 1886 after our son Robert was born. As was so characteristic of him, when he replied he told us nothing of himself nor did he evidence interest in what we wrote to him, save for congratulating us on Robert's birth and his interest in Hub's [Robert A. Holliday's] efforts to establish the dental college. Yet his letter was not perfunctory. Rather it was quite long. Specifically I recall his disappointment in the failure of President Cleveland's administration to increase the government's purchasing of silver" ("Recollections, M. F. Holliday").

40. *Daily Denver Times*, June 15, 1886; *Valdosta South Georgian Times*, June 19, 1886.

41. *Daily Denver Times*, June 15, 1886.

42. Corbett and Ballenger, *Denver City Directory* (1887), p. 386.

43. Some newspaper reports referred to Blythe, not Smythe.

44. Denver Police Magistrate's Docket No. 1, April 1885<n>February 1889.

45. *Denver Tribune-Republican*, August 4, 1886.

46. *Denver Republican*, December 25, 1887.

47. Mary Billings-McVicar, Leadville, Colorado, to the author, April 6, 1996.

48. *Glenwood Springs Ute Chief*, November 12, 1887. A wire had been sent to Perry Malaby in Glenwood Springs from Leadville stating that Holliday was on his way, according to the *Denver Republican*, November 10, 1887, shortly after Holliday's death.

49. Nellie Duffy, "Doc Buried Here?" *Glenwood Post*, 1977, Holliday Files, Frontier Historical Society, Glenwood Springs, Colorado.

50. *Gunnison News-Champion*, July 17, 1930.

51. Information provided to author by Horony family members (Horony Family Reunion, San Antonio, Tex., July 1997); Hattie Harony Maddox and Albert Harony to Glenn G. Boyer. Their father, Alexander H. Harony, born in Pest, Hungary, in 1853, had settled in Colorado when he married Eva Bruchmann at Scoffield, Gunnison County, on May 27, 1886. Alexander Harony died in August 1916.

52. *Glenwood Springs Ute Chief,* November 12, 1887.

53. Lena M. Urquhart, *Glenwood Springs: Spa in the Mountains,* p. 48. The Hotel Glenwood burned to the ground in 1945, killing five people.

54. Eugene Parsons, Denver, Colorado, to Stuart N. Lake, San Diego, California, July 25, 1930, Stuart N. Lake Collection, Letter Box 10, Huntington Library, San Marino, California.

55. Ibid., June 30, 1930.

56. *Glenwood Springs Ute Chief,* November 12, 1887.

57. *Glenwood Post,* Centennial—Past Section, August 23, 1887.

58. *Aspen Daily Times,* November 9, 1887.

59. *Glenwood Springs Ute Chief,* November 12, 1887.

60. The *Glenwood Springs Ute Chief* of November 12, 1887, in its obituary of Holliday, stated that he had been baptized in the Catholic Church. This assertion was based on information the newspaper received about the correspondence found in his belongings from his cousin, Sister Mary Melanie. No evidence of a conversion exists among the papers of the Reverend Edward Downey, the records of St. Stephen's Catholic Church of Glenwood Springs, or the records of the Annunciation Catholic Church in Leadville; Charles

Hanlen, "Shepherd of the Snow: The Life and Times of Father Edward T. Downey," typed MS (1995). The family has no knowledge of a conversion to Catholicism by John Henry.

61. The gold stickpin, originally given to John Henry by his uncle, Dr. Holliday, in 1873, was returned to Georgia without its diamond. Sister Melanie requested that the stickpin be given to her brother James Robert Holliday (1864–1943), later the international advertising director of the *Atlanta Constitution.* He passed it on to his son, Edward R. Holliday, who had a new diamond set in the pin. Presently, it is in the possession of Edward Holliday's daughter and son-in-law, Frank and Carolyn Holliday Manley of Decatur, Georgia (Carolyn Holliday Manley, interview with the author, September 7, 1995). The small knife and gambling articles passed to Robert A. Holliday, D.D.S., and were subsequently given by his widow, Mrs. Robert A. Holliday (née Fulton), to her grandson-in-law, Carl B. Olson (husband of Mary Holliday Olson, mother of the author), in 1938. These items are presently in the possession of the author.

62. "Recollections, M. F. Holliday."

Epilogue

1. *Glenwood Springs Ute Chief,* November 12, 1887.

2. Pitkin County, Colorado, Marriage Record, March 2, 1890.

3. Coroner's Jury Report, No. 13, Cochise County, Arizona, July 7, 1915; copy provided by Glenn G. Boyer. In early July 1915 at Courtland, Arizona, George Cummings committed suicide by shooting himself in the head. It was determined that he was suffering from incurable cancer of the head.

4. Mary Catherine Cummings, Prescott, Arizona, to J. M. Sparks, Board of Directors of State Institutions, Phoenix, Arizona, November 4, 1940; copy provided by Glenn G. Boyer.

5. Cummings, "The O.K. Corral Fight at Tombstone," p. 72.

6. Ibid., pp. 83–84.

7. Ibid., p. 75.

8. *Atlanta Constitution,* February 26, 1893.

9. "Recollections, M. F. Holliday."

10. *Atlanta Historical Bulletin* 9 (April 1955): 69.

11. *Atlanta Journal,* January 2, 1894.

12. *Atlanta Constitution,* April 28, 1897; *Atlanta Journal,* April 27, 1897.

13. Robert did not take on a partner until 1890, three years after John Henry's death, when Herbert H. Johnson joined his practice. Robert later practiced briefly with Lewis B. Brooks ("Recollections, M. F. Holliday").

14. Georgia Dental Association, *History of Dentistry in Georgia* (Macon: Southern Press, 1962), p. 50.

15. The new Southern Dental College opened as the dental department of the Southern Medical College, with the cooperation of Thomas S. Powell, president of the school's Board of Trustees. It became an independent school in 1915. In 1917 it merged with the Atlanta Dental College, forming the Atlanta Southern Dental College. It became part of Emory University in 1944.

16. *Atlanta Journal,* November 10, 1906.

17. Holliday, "Love's Lament."

18. Four children were born to Dr. Robert Alexander and Mary Cowperthwaite Fulton Holliday: Robert Fulton Holliday, born January 26, 1886, died June 3, 1888; Lewis Ware Holliday, born August 21, 1887, died November

14, 1919; Clarence Fulton Holliday, born October 24, 1888, died September 23, 1912; Mary Adele Holliday, born December 2, 1890, died April 30, 1919.

           19. Holliday, "Love's Lament."

           20. Lake, *Wyatt Earp*, p. 198.

Appendix

           1. Col. E. Clarke, Statement of Service of William Holliday, Sr.; Discharge, William Holliday [Jr.]; Record Group 3-3-60, Georgia Surveyor General, Headright and Bounty Grant Warrants, Georgia Department of Archives and History, Atlanta, Georgia.

           2. His will, dated July 7, 1786, was proved in Wilkes County later that year. The first of his ten children listed in the will was William [Jr.], presumably his eldest son; Wilkes County, Georgia, Will Book D D, p. 73.

           3. Laurens County, South Carolina, Will Book F, p. 53.

           4. Henry Burroughs Holliday, Valdosta, Georgia, to Robert Alexander Holliday, D.D.S., Atlanta, Georgia, May 7, 1884, author's collection.

           5. Cary, *The History of Fayette County*, p. 16.

           6. Margaret Mitchell, *Gone with the Wind*, p. 7.

           7. Fayette County, Georgia, Deed Book B, p. 571.

           8. Ibid., Deed Book C, p. 82.

           9. United States Government, 1850 Census, Twenty-ninth District of Fayette County, Georgia, p. 20.

           10. Robert Alexander Holliday Family Bible, collection of Mrs. Constance McKellar, Atlanta, Georgia.

11. United States National Archives, Cherokee Indian War Pension WC-2762, Georgia, commencing February 23, 1893, Henry B. Holliday, SC-1908; Special Orders No. 86, Mexican War Pension, February 9, 1887, W-3780.

12. Henry Burroughs Holliday Family Bible (Troy, N.Y.: Merriam, Moore and Co., 1848), Collection of the Christian Broadcasting Network, Inc., Virginia Beach, Virginia. Photocopy supplied by Susan McKey Thomas.

13. Ibid.; Pendleton and Thomas, *In Search of the Hollidays*, p. 13.

14. Spalding County, Georgia, Deed Book A, p. 57.

15. Robert Alexander Holliday Family Bible, collection of Mrs. Constance McKellar, Atlanta, Georgia.

16. Fayette County, Georgia, Marriage Book B, p. 228.

17. George Washington Ware (1802–49) was the son of James Ware, Jr. (1779–1843), and his first cousin Letitia Ware (1781–1851). Letitia's sister, Elizabeth Ware (1789–1857), married Capt. James Long and was the mother of Crawford Williamson Long, M.D. (1815–78).

18. Fayette County, Georgia, Deed Book E, p. 362.

19. John Stiles Holliday Family Bible, collection of Mrs. Constance McKellar, Atlanta, Georgia.

20. Ibid.; Mary C. F. Holliday, *Treasury of Devotion*, author's collection.

21. Robert Alexander Holliday Family Bible, collection of Mrs. Constance McKellar, Atlanta, Georgia.

22. Ibid.; the Catholic marriage took place in Fayetteville, which was then within the parish of the Immaculate Conception Church of Atlanta (Stephens Mitchell, *Atlanta Historical Bulletin* 1 [September 1927]: 31).

23. Robert Alexander Holliday Family Bible, collection of Mrs. Constance McKellar, Atlanta, Georgia.

24. Ibid.; Fayette County, Georgia, Marriage Book B, p. 151.

25. Robert Alexander Holliday Family Bible, collection of Mrs. Constance McKellar, Atlanta, Georgia.

Bibliography

Holliday Family Records

Holliday, Henry Burroughs. Family Bible. Collection of the Christian Broadcasting Network, Virginia Beach, Virginia.

———. Valdosta, Georgia, to Robert Alexander Holliday, D.D.S., Atlanta, Georgia, May 7, 1884. Collection of Karen Holliday Tanner, Fallbrook, California.

Holliday, John Stiles. Family Bible. Collection of Constance McKellar, Atlanta, Georgia.

Holliday, Martha Anne. Deposition, Emancipated Slaves of Robert K. Holliday, September 9, 1926. Collection of Carolyn Holliday Manley, Decatur, Georgia.

Holliday, Mary Cowperthwaite Fulton. Book of Common Prayer. Collection of Karen Holliday Tanner, Fallbrook, California.

———. "Love's Lament, 1933." Typed MS (photocopy). Original in the collection of Morgan DeLancey Magee, Orange Park, Florida.

———. "Recollections of Mary Cowperthwaite Fulton Holliday, 1935–1940, as told to Carl Birger Olson." Typed MS, signed. Collection of Karen Holliday Tanner, Fallbrook, California.

Holliday, Robert Alexander. Family Bible. Collection of Constance McKellar, Atlanta, Georgia.

Holliday, Robert Kennedy. Commission, War Department, Confederate States of America. Collection of Carolyn Holliday Manley, Decatur, Georgia.

Holliday, Robert Lee. "Memoirs of Robert Lee Holliday, Sr.; May 19, 1915 to Only God Knows, part 1 (1915–1973)." Typed MS, 1995 (photocopy). Original in possession of Robert Lee Holliday, Sr., New Orleans, Louisiana.

Holliday, William. Family Bible. Collection of Constance McKellar, Atlanta, Georgia.

Murphy, Sophie Walton. "Recollections of Sophie Walton; 1930–1932, as told to Carl Birger Olson." Typed MS, signed. Collection of Karen Holliday Tanner, Fallbrook, California.

Olson, Carl Birger. "Sheriff John Holliday; Too Perfect an Alibi, 1934." MS, signed. Collection of Karen Holliday Tanner, Fallbrook, California.

Manuscript Collections

Boller, Robert. "Reminiscences of Robert M. Boller, 1926." Typed MS. Arizona Historical Society, Tucson, Arizona.

Burns, Walter Noble. Papers. Collection AZ/29, University of Arizona, Tucson, Arizona.

Clum, John P. Papers. Collection AZ/3, University of Arizona, Tucson, Arizona.

Bibliography

Earp, James C. Affidavit. MS 237, Arizona Historical Society, Tucson, Arizona.

Goodfellow, Dr. George E. Papers. MS 296, Arizona Historical Society, Tucson, Arizona.

Gray, John Pleasant. "When All Roads Led to Tombstone" (1940). MS 312, Arizona Historical Society, Tucson, Arizona.

Hancock, James C. Papers. MS 325, Arizona Historical Society, Tucson, Arizona.

Hooker, Forrestine C. "An Arizona Vendetta: The Truth about Wyatt Earp—And Some Others" (ca. 1918). Typed MS, Braun Research Library, Southwest Museum, Los Angeles, California.

Jones, Melvin W. Papers (1932). MS 392, Arizona Historical Society, Tucson, Arizona.

Lake, Stuart N. Papers. Huntington Library, San Marino, California.

Rasch, Philip. Papers. MS 677, Arizona Historical Society, Tucson, Arizona.

Court Records

Arapahoe County (Colorado) District Court Index. 1875–77 and 1882–87.

Cochise County (Arizona Territory). Coroner's Inquest—Johnny Ringo, District Court of the First Judicial District, Cochise County, Arizona. Filed November 3, 1882.

———. Criminal Docket, *Territory of Arizona v. John H. Holliday* (Murder). Quarter Ending September 30, 1881, No. 30.

———. Criminal Docket, *Territory of Arizona v. Stilwell and Spencer*. Quarter Ending September 30, 1881, No. 56.

————. Document 48, District Court of the First Judicial District, filed December 1, 1881. Reprinted in Alford Turner, ed., *The O.K. Corral Inquest,* pp. 23–48.

Cochise County (Arizona). Coroners Jury Report, No. 13, George M. Cummings. Filed July 7, 1915.

————. Probate, John J. Howard. Probate Orders, Book 6, p. 199.

Dallas County (Texas). Court Minutes, 1874–78. Case 2236, *State of Texas v. J. H. Holliday,* April 13, 1875.

————. Case 2643, *State of Texas v. J. H. Holliday,* January 18, 1875.

Denver, Colorado. Police Magistrates Court Docket No. 1. April 1885–February 1889.

Lake County (Colorado). Minutes of the Superior Court. Case No. 258, *The People of the State of Colorado v. John Holliday,* March 28, 1885.

Pueblo County (Colorado). Minutes of the District Court, *The People v. J. H. Holliday* (Larceny), vol. 5, pp. 354–55, G.D. No. 1851.

San Miguel County (New Mexico Territory). Civil Record Book A of the District Court, San Miguel County (1880–81).

————. Criminal Record Book of the District Court, San Miguel County (1876–79).

————. San Miguel County District Court Dockets, August Term 1876 through March Term 1882; Causes No. 937, 990, 996, *The Territory of New Mexico v. John Holliday.*

Shackelford County (Texas). Minutes of the District Court, vol. A, 6–7 [18]75 to 3-1-[18]84, Case #34, *State of Texas v. Dock* [sic] *Holliday,* June 12, 1875, pp. 16 and 49.

Yavapai County (Arizona Territory). District Court Criminal Cases 1878-80. Unnumbered, Alpha by year.

Public Records

Colorado, State of. Colorado Executive Record, vol. 4 (1881–85). Papers of Governor Frederick W. Pitkin. Colorado State Archives.

———. Governor Frederick W. Pitkin Papers. Colorado State Archives, #3 61-399.

Dallas County (Texas). Assessment Roll of Precinct No. 1, 1874.

Lowndes County (Georgia). Deed Books.

Pima County (Arizona). Pima County Recorder, The Great Register, 1880.

San Miguel County (New Mexico). Deed Books.

Spalding County (Georgia). Deed Books.

United States National Archives. "Lawlessness and Cowboy Depredations in the Arizona Territory, 1881–1882." #2061.

Yavapai County, Arizona. Deed Books.

Newspapers

Arizona Territory

Arizona Weekly Citizen (Tucson).
Arizona Weekly Journal Miner (Prescott).
Arizona Weekly Star (Tucson).
Tombstone Daily Nugget.
Tombstone Epitaph.

California

San Diego Union.
San Francisco Alta California.
San Francisco Examiner.

Bibliography

Colorado

Aspen Daily Times.
Daily Chieftain (Pueblo).
Daily-News Democrat (Gunnison).
Denver Daily Times.
Denver Republican.
Denver Tribune.
Leadville Daily Democrat.
Leadville Daily Herald.
Rocky Mountain News (Denver).
Salida Mountain Mail.
Trinidad Daily News.
Ute Chief (Glenwood Springs).

Dakota Territory

Black Hills Daily Pioneer (Deadwood).
Black Hills Pioneer (Deadwood).

Georgia

Atlanta Constitution.
Atlanta Journal.
South Georgia Times (Valdosta).
Valdosta Times.

Kansas

Ford County Globe.
Times (Dodge City).

New Mexico Territory

Albuquerque Review.

Daily Optic (Las Vegas).
Gazette (Las Vegas).
Thirty-four (Las Cruces).
Weekly New Mexican (Santa Fe).

Texas

Albany Echo.
Albany Star.
Daily Dallas Herald.
Dallas Daily Commercial.
Democrat (Fort Worth).
Denison Daily Cresset.
Fort Griffin Echo.
Frontier Echo (Jacksboro).
Weekly Herald (Dallas).

Wyoming

Daily Leader (Cheyenne).
Daily Sun (Cheyenne).
Wyoming Weekly Leader (Cheyenne).

Books and Articles

Adams, Andy. *The Log of a Cowboy: A Narrative of the Old Trail Days.* Lincoln: University of Nebraska Press, 1964.

Athearn, Robert G. *Rebel of the Rockies: A History of the Denver and Rio Grande Western Railroad.* New Haven: Yale University Press, 1962.

Bailey, Lynn R. *"We'll All Wear Silk Hats": The Erie and Chiricahua Cattle Companies and the Rise of Corporate Ranching in the Sulphur Spring Valley of*

Arizona, 1883–1909. Tucson: Westernlore Press, 1994.

Barnes, Will. *Apaches & Longhorns: The Reminiscences of Will C. Barnes.* Los Angeles: Ward Ritchie Press, 1941.

Bartholomew, Ed. *Wyatt Earp: The Man and the Myth.* Toyahvale, Tex.: Frontier Book Co., 1964.

——. *Wyatt Earp: The Untold Story.* Toyahvale, Tex.: Frontier Book Co., 1963.

Bennett, Estelline. *Old Deadwood Days.* New York: J. H. Sears, 1928.

Biggers, Don H. *Shackelford County Sketches.* Albany, Tex.: Albany News Office, 1908; reprint, Joan Farmer, ed., Albany and Fort Griffin, Tex.: Clearfork Press, 1974.

Blair, Edward. *Leadville: Colorado's Magic City.* Boulder, Colo.: Pruett Publishing Co., 1980.

Boyer, Glenn G. "Big Nosed Kate." *Westward* 6 (September 21, 1979): 3–4.

——. *The Illustrated Life of Doc Holliday.* Glenwood Springs, Colo.: Reminder Publishing Co., 1966.

——. "On the Trail of Big Nosed Kate." *Real West* 24 (March 1981): 14–20, 50.

——. *Suppressed Murder of Wyatt Earp.* San Antonio, Tex.: Naylor Co., 1967.

Breakenridge, William M. *Helldorado: Bringing the Law to the Mesquite.* Lincoln: University of Nebraska Press, 1992.

Brown, Robert L. *Saloons of the American West.* Silverton, Colo.: Sundance Publications, 1978.

Burns, Walter Noble. *Tombstone: An Iliad of the Southwest.* Garden City, N.Y.: Doubleday, Page, and Co., 1927.

Burrows, Jack. *John Ringo: The Gunfighter Who Never Was.* Tucson: University of Arizona Press, 1987.

Callon, Milton W. *Las Vegas, New Mexico: The Town That Wouldn't Gamble*. Las Vegas, N. Mex.: Las Vegas *Daily Optic*, 1962.

Cary, Carolyn C., ed. *The History of Fayette County: 1821–1971*. Fayetteville, Ga.: Fayette County Historical Society, 1977.

Cashion, Ty. "(Gun)Smoke Gets in Your Eyes: A Revisionist Look at 'Violent' Fort Griffin." *Southwestern Historical Quarterly* (July 1995): 81–94.

———. "Rewriting the Wild West for a New History." *Journal of the West* 34 (October 1995): 54–60.

Chaput, Don. *The Earp Papers: In a Brother's Image*. Encampment, Wyo.: Affiliated Writers of America, 1994.

———. *Virgil Earp: Western Peace Officer*. Encampment, Wyo.: Affiliated Writers of America, 1994.

Chase, C. M. *New Mexico and Colorado in 1881*. Fort Davis, Tex.: Frontier Book Co., 1968.

Clum, John P. *It All Happened in Tombstone*. Flagstaff, Ariz.: Northland Press, 1965.

Clum, Woodworth. *Apache Agent: The Story of John P. Clum*. Boston: Houghton Mifflin, 1936.

Cook, John R. *The Border and the Buffalo: An Untold Story of the Southwest Plains*. New York: Citadel Press, 1967.

Coquoz, Rene L. *Tales of Early Leadville*. Part Two. Boulder, Colo.: Johnson Publishing Co., 1964.

Corbett and Ballenger. *Denver City Directory*. Denver: Corbett and Ballenger, 1887.

———. *Leadville City Directory*. Leadville, Colo.: Corbett and Ballenger, 1883 and 1884.

Corbett, Hoye, and Co. *City Directory, Denver*. Denver: Corbett, Hoye, and Co., 1875, 1876, 1882.

Cox, William R. *Luke Short and His Era*. Garden City, N.Y.: Doubleday and Co., 1961.

Cummings, Mary Katherine [Kate Elder]. "The O.K. Corral Fight at Tombstone: A Footnote by Kate Elder." Ed. A. W. Bork and Glenn G. Boyer. *Arizona and the West* 19 (Spring 1977): 65–84.

Cunningham, Eugene. *Triggernometry: A Gallery of Western Gunfighters.* Caldwell, Idaho: Caxton Printers, 1947.

DeArment, Robert K. *Bat Masterson: The Man and the Legend.* Norman: University of Oklahoma Press, 1979.

———. *Knights of the Green Cloth: The Saga of the Frontier Gamblers.* Norman: University of Oklahoma, 1982.

DeMattos, Jack. *Mysterious Gunfighter: The Story of Dave Mather.* College Station, Tex.: Creative Publishing Co., 1992.

Dodge, Fred. *Under Cover for Wells Fargo: The Unvarnished Recollections of Fred Dodge.* Ed. Carolyn Lake. Boston: Houghton Mifflin Co., 1969.

Earp, Wyatt S. *Wyatt Earp.* Ed. John Flood; collected and introduced by Glenn G. Boyer. Sierra Vista, Ariz.: Yoma V. Bissette, copyright Glenn G. Boyer, 1981.

———, et al. *The Earps Talk.* Ed. Alford E. Turner. College Station, Tex.: Creative Publishing Co., 1980.

Faulk, Odie B. *Dodge City: The Most Western Town of All.* New York: Oxford University Press, 1977.

———. *The Geronimo Campaign.* New York: Oxford University Press, 1969.

———. *Tombstone: Myth and Reality.* New York: Oxford University Press, 1972.

Fisher, Truman Rex. "Biographer John Henry Flood, Jr.: The Lion of Tombstone's Ghost." *Old West* 31 (Spring 1995): 50–58.

Foy, Eddie, and Alvin F. Harlow. *Clowning through Life.* New York: E. P. Dutton and Co., 1928.

French, Capt. William. *Further Recollections of a Western Ranchman: New Mexico, 1883–1889.* New York: Argosy-Antiquarian Ltd., 1965.

———. *Some Recollections of a Western Ranchman: New Mexico, 1883–1889.* New York: Argosy-Antiquarian Ltd., 1965.

Galbreath, Lester W. *Fort Griffin and the Clear Fork Country.* Albany, Tex.: n.p., 1995.

Ganzhorn, Jack. *I've Killed Men: An Epic of Early Arizona.* New York: Devin-Adair Co., 1959.

Gatto, Steve. *John Ringo: The Reputation of a Deadly Gunman.* Tucson, Ariz.: San Simon Publishing Co., 1995.

Griswold, Don L., and Jean Harvey Griswold. *The Carbonate Camp Called Leadville.* Denver: University of Denver Press, 1951.

Holden, Frances Mayhugh. *Lambshead before Interwoven: A Texas Range Chronicle, 1848–1878.* College Station: Texas A & M University Press, 1982.

Hunter, J. Marvin. *The Story of Lottie Deno: Her Life and Times.* Bandera, Tex.: 4 Hunters, 1959.

Jahns, Pat. *The Frontier World of Doc Holliday, Faro Dealer from Dallas to Deadwood.* Lincoln: University of Nebraska Press, 1957.

Johnson, H. Herbert, ed. *Biographies of Past Presidents of the Georgia State Dental Society.* N.p.: Published by the Georgia State Dental Society, 1927.

Lake, Stuart N. *Wyatt Earp: Frontier Marshal.* New York: Houghton Mifflin, 1931.

Lapidus, Richard. "The Youngest Earp: The Troubled Life and Times of Warren Earp." *Journal* (Western Outlaw-Lawman History Association) 4 (Summer 1995): 6–10.

Lawson and Edmondson. *Dallas City Directory.* Springfield, Mo.: Missouri Patriot Book Co., 1873.

Lewis, Alfred Henry (Dan Quin). *Wolfville Nights.* New York: Grosset and Dunlap, 1902.

Lockwood, Frank. *Pioneer Days in Arizona: From the Spanish Occupation to Statehood.* New York: Macmillan Co., 1932.

Lynch, Sylvia D. *Aristocracy's Outlaw: The Doc Holliday Story.* New Tazewell, Tenn.: Iris Press, 1994.

Martin, Douglas D. *Silver, Sex and Six Guns: Tombstone Saga of Buckskin Frank Leslie.* Tombstone, Ariz.: Tombstone Epitaph, 1962.

————. *Tombstone's Epitaph.* Albuquerque: University of New Mexico Press, 1951.

Masterson, W. B. ("Bat"). *Famous Gun Fighters of the Western Frontier.* Monroe, Wash.: Weatherford Press, 1982.

Mathews, Sallie Reynolds. *Interwoven: A Pioneer Chronicle.* College Station: Texas A & M University Press, 1982.

McIntyre, Jim. *Early Days in Texas: A Trip to Hell and Heaven.* Ed. Robert K. DeArment. Norman: University of Oklahoma Press, 1992.

Metz, Leon C. *John Selman, Gunfighter.* Norman: University of Oklahoma Press, 1992.

Mitchell, Margaret. *Gone with the Wind.* New York: Macmillan Co., 1936.

Myers, John Myers. *Doc Holliday.* Boston: Little, Brown and Co., 1955.

Myrick, David F. *New Mexico's Railroads.* Albuquerque: University of New Mexico Press, 1990.

Nineteenth Annual Announcement of the Pennsylvania College of Dental Surgery. Philadelphia: W. B. Selheimer, 1874.

Noel, Thomas J. *The City and the Saloon: Denver, 1858–1916.* Lincoln: University of Nebraska Press, 1982.

Olsson, Jan Olaf. *Welcome to Tombstone.* Tr. Maurice Michael. London: Elek Books, 1956.

Otero, Miguel Antonio. *My Life on the Frontier: 1864–1882.* New York: Press of the Pioneers, 1935.

Parsons, George W. *The Private Journal of George W. Parsons.* Tombstone, Ariz.: *Tombstone Epitaph,* 1972.

Pendleton, Albert S., Jr., and Susan McKey Thomas. "Doc Holliday's Georgia Background." *Journal of Arizona History* 14 (Autumn 1973): 185–204.

———. *In Search of the Hollidays: The Story of Doc Holliday and His Holliday and McKey Families.* Valdosta, Ga.: Little River Press, 1973.

———. "Valdosta's John Henry (Doc) Holliday." In *A Pictorial History of Lowndes County, Georgia: 1825–1975.* N.p., n.d.

Rister, Carl Coke. *Fort Griffin on the Texas Frontier.* Norman: University of Oklahoma Press, 1986.

Robinson, Charles, III. *The Frontier World of Fort Griffin.* Seattle: Arthur H. Clarke Co., 1992.

Rose, Cynthia. *Lottie Deno: Gambling Queen of Hearts.* Santa Fe: Clear Light Publishers, 1994.

Ruffner, Melissa. *Prescott: A Pictorial History.* Prescott, Ariz.: Primrose Press, 1981.

Rye, Edgar. *The Quirt and the Spur: Vanishing Shadows of the Texas Frontier.* Chicago: W. B. Conkey Co., 1909 (facsimile reprint, Austin, Tex.: Steck-Vaughn Co., 1967).

St. Louis City Directory. St. Louis: Edward's, 1870.

St. Louis City Directory. St. Louis: Gould, 1876.

Seventeenth Annual Announcement of the Pennsylvania College of Dental Surgery. Philadelphia: W. B. Selheimer, 1872.

Sonnichsen, C. L. *Billy King's Tombstone: The Private Life of an Arizona Boomtown.* Caldwell, Idaho: Caxton Printers, 1951.

———. *I'll Die Before I'll Run: The Story of the Great Feuds of Texas.* Lincoln: University of Nebraska Press, 1988.

319

Spring, Agnes Wright. *The Cheyenne and Black Hills Stage and Express Routes.* Lincoln: University of Nebraska Press, 1967.

Stanley, F. (Father Stanley Francis Louis Crocchiola). *Dave Rudabaugh: Border Ruffian.* Denver: World Press, 1961.

———. *Desperadoes of New Mexico.* Denver: World Press, 1953.

———. *The Las Vegas, New Mexico, Story.* Denver: World Press, 1951.

———. *The Otero, New Mexico, Story.* Denver: World Press, 1962.

———. *Raton Chronicle.* Denver: World Press, 1948.

Stokes, George W., and Howard R. Driggs. *Deadwood Gold: A Story of the Black Hills.* Chicago: World Book Co., 1926.

Traywick, Ben T. *John Henry: The "Doc" Holliday Story.* Tombstone, Ariz.: Red Marie's, 1996.

Turner, Alford E., ed. *The O.K. Corral Inquest.* College Station, Tex.: Early West, 1981.

Urquhart, Lena M. *Glenwood Springs: Spa in the Mountains.* Glenwood Springs, Colo.: Taylor Publishing Co., 1970.

Van Orman, Richard A. *A Room for the Night: Hotels of the Old West.* Bloomington: Indiana University Press, 1966.

Walling, Emma. *John "Doc" Holliday: Colorado, Trials and Triumphs.* Snowmass, Colo.: By the author, 1994.

Walters, Lorenzo D. *Tombstone's Yesterday.* Tucson: Acme Printing Co., 1928.

Waters, Frank. *The Earp Brothers of Tombstone: The Story of Mrs. Virgil Earp.* New York: Bramhall House, 1960.

Willison, George F. *Here They Dug the Gold.* New York: Reynal and Hitchcock, 1946.

Wright, Robert M. *Dodge City: The Cowboy Capital and the Great Southwest.* Wichita, Kans.: Wichita Eagle Press, 1913.

Young, Fredric R. *Dodge City: Up through a Century in Story and Pictures.* Dodge City, Kans.: Boot Hill Museum, 1972.

Young, Roy B. *Cochise County Cowboy War: "A Cast of Characters."* Apache, Okla.: Young and Sons Enterprises, 1999.

Index

Index

Index

Index

333